AF608240

THE CATHOLIC UNIVERSITY OF AMERICA
CANON LAW STUDIES
No. 185

THE BLESSING OF CEMETERIES

AN HISTORICAL SYNOPSIS AND COMMENTARY

BY

Rev. Cornelius Michael Power, J.C.L.
Priest of the Diocese of Seattle

A DISSERTATION

Submitted to the Faculty of the School of Canon Law of the Catholic University of America in Partial Fulfillment of the Requirements for the Degree of Doctor of Canon Law

THE CATHOLIC UNIVERSITY OF AMERICA PRESS
WASHINGTON, D. C.
1943

Nihil Obstat:

EDUARDUS G. ROELKER, S.T.D., J.C.D.,
Censor Deputatus.

Washingtonii, D. C., die 24 maii, 1943.

Imprimatur:

✠ GERALDUS SHAUGHNESSY, S.M., S.T.D.,
Episcopus Seattlensis.

Seattli, Wash., die 24 maii, 1943.

Printed by
THE PAULIST PRESS
New York 19, N. Y.

51

To

The Cherished Memory

of

My Mother

TABLE OF CONTENTS

PAGE

CHAPTER X

CHAPTER XI

CHAPTER XII

FOREWORD

Although it is impossible to say at what exact time the cemeteries of the Church were first blessed, it is entirely reasonable to hold that the blessing of cemeteries goes back to very early times. The first five centuries give very little direct evidence on cemetery blessing, but from the sixth century on there is sufficient though not abundant testimony of the blessing of cemeteries. In the period from the first to the sixth century can be considered as the first phase of the legal aspect of the blessing of cemeteries, there are, to speak in a general way, two other phases. The second phase includes that long period in the history of cemeteries from the sixth to the twentieth century, i. e., up to the time of the present Code, when the field of cemeteries had very little legislation of its own. During this period cemeteries and churches were included by the legislator in one and the same category with regard to consecration, blessing, immunity, violation and reconciliation. At times both were mentioned side by side; but more often the legislator mentioned only churches, now and then explaining that the same applied to cemeteries also. The historical treatment of the blessing of cemeteries could have embraced greater detail; but since the legislator and the numerous commentators on the law, official and non-official, have given their attention primarily to churches and disposed of cemeteries with just a word or two by referring to what had been said of churches, it has been thought wise to avoid detail which may better be treated with reference to churches, and preclude thereby unnecessary duplication. It is impossible, however, to take up the subject of the blessing of cemeteries which, especially from the historical standpoint, runs parallel to the consecration and blessing of churches and is so intimately associated with the legislation on churches, without frequent reference to the latter.

The Code of Canon Law in 1918 opened the third phase of cemetery legislation when it took up the matter of cemeteries in a section all its own. This does not mean that the legislation on cemeteries is now entirely divorced from the legislation on churches. In very many instances, as before the Code, cemetery law is based on or is enacted on principles parallel to those of the law for churches; the difference between present and previous legislation is that the Code in its special section specifies that cemeteries are in this or that aspect to be governed by the parallel law on churches, e. g., with regard to interdict, violation and reconciliation (c. 1207).

The first two historical phases of the subject are comprised in the historical synopsis, which forms the first part of this work. The third phase is treated in the canonical commentary, which embraces the second part of this dissertation. In these sections will be found treatment not only of the blessing of cemeteries and the necessity of blessing, but also of those topics which directly affect blessed cemeteries, such as ecclesiastical immunity, violation, reconciliation and interdict. These latter topics, both before and since the Code of Canon Law, have received their fullest treatment in reference to churches, but since they can be dealt with briefly in their relation to cemeteries, they have been included in this work on the blessing of cemeteries where they also quite naturally belong.

In the canonical commentary more will be said on the subject of terminology, but it is advisable to point out that the word "consecration" when used of cemeteries is not an altogether exact term, the more correct term being "solemn blessing," if these terms are to be used as they are understood today. But since in the pre-Code terminology cemeteries were more often than not referred to as being either consecrated or blessed, when today they would be said to be solemnly or simply blessed, the term "consecration" has been retained as a synonym for solemn blessing especially in the historical part.

The writer wishes to make grateful acknowledgment to all who had a part in making this work possible: to His Excellency, the Most Reverend Gerald Shaughnessy, S.M., S.T.D., for the opportunity of pursuing the study of Canon Law at the Catholic University of America, and for his inspiring interest in his work; to the individual members of the Faculty of the School of Canon Law for their expert and generous guidance and assistance; and to all others unnamed who have given of their time and talents toward the completion of this study.

PART ONE

HISTORICAL SYNOPSIS

CHAPTER I

THE BLESSING OF CEMETERIES DURING THE FIRST SIX CENTURIES

A SACRED place *(locus sacer)* is one which by consecration or by blessing is set aside for divine worship or for the burial of the faithful.[1] By definition,[2] therefore, Christian cemeteries are sacred places, since they are destined by special blessing, whether solemn or simple, to serve as the final resting place for the bodies of the faithful departed.[3]

The Church has made it one of her laws that the remains of her deceased be interred in blessed cemeteries which she provides for this purpose.[4] A cemetery is solemnly blessed by a rite in which five wooden crosses, set up in determined parts of the cemetery, are blessed by the bishop according to the manner established by the *Pontificale Romanum.*[5] On the other hand, a cemetery is simply blessed when a priest delegated by the bishop, in accordance with the rite found in the *Rituale Romanum,*[6] performs the prescribed ceremonies, the chief of which is the blessing of a wooden cross placed in the middle of the cemetery.[7]

[1] C. 1154.

[2] C. 1205, § 1.

[3] Wernz, *Ius Decretalium* (6 vols., Romae, 1898-1905), III, n. 471; Bargilliat, *Praelectiones Iuris Canonici* (2 vols., 2. ed., Parisiis, 1895), n. 1328.

[4] C. 1205, § 1.

[5] *Pontificale Romanum Summorum Pontificum iussu editum a Benedicto XIV et Leone XIII Pontificibus Maximis recognitum et castigatum* (Mechliniae, 1895), hereafter cited as *Pontificale Romanum,* tit. *De Coemeterii Benedictione.*

[6] *Rituale Romanum Pauli V Pontificis Maximi iussu editum aliorumque Pontificum cura recognitum atque auctoritate Sanctissimi D. N. Pii Papae XI ad normam Codicis Iuris Canonici accomodatum* (6. ed. post typicum, Turonibus: Mame, 1936), tit. VIII, c. 29 (hereafter cited as *Rituale Romanum*).

[7] Coronata, *Institutiones Iuris Canonici* (5 vols., Taurini: Marietti, 1933-1939. Vols. I-II, 2. ed., 1939; Vol. III, 1933; Vol. IV, 1935; Vol. V, 1936), n. 795. Hereafter this work will be cited as *Institutiones.* Wernz-Vidal, *Ius Canonicum ad Codicis Normam Exactum* (7 vols. in 8, Romae: apud Aedes Universitatis Gregorianiae, 1927-1938. Vol. IV, pars I, 1934), IV, n. 670 (hereafter to be cited as *Ius Canonicum*).

Article I. Immortality and the Blessing of Cemeteries

From the very beginning the Church strove to have her own cemeteries. She had her difficulties as everyone who is acquainted with the history of the catacombs knows, but even in the face of such great opposition she found a way to care for her dead. Because of her great concern that the bodies of the deceased should have undisturbed peace and rest while awaiting the trumpet-call of Christ,[8] the Church from the earliest times not only possessed her own cemeteries, but took steps to make holy places of the sepulchers and cemeteries of her dead. Her burial places were sacred not in just a metaphorical sense, but in a very real sense, for it was by a special liturgical blessing that they were made holy.

The reason for the Church's particular interest in the burial of her dead arose quite naturally from her belief concerning a future life after death.[9] For example, very early the Church began to call the burial grounds of her deceased by the name "cemetery," the first time the word was ever used with such a meaning.[10] The term, therefore, is a truly Christian one: Christian in origin, Christian in meaning, Christian in significance.[11] The word itself, coming from

[8] I Cor. xv, 52.

[9] The numerous prayers said by the bishop or priest in the ceremony of the blessing of cemeteries are full of the happiness and hopefulness that comes from the thought of immortality. Cf. *Pontificale Romanum,* tit. *De Coemeterii Benedictione*; *Rituale Romanum,* tit. VIII, c. 29.

[10] Tertullian (ca. 160-ca. 240) was most certainly not the first to use the term "cemetery" to refer to the Christian places of burial, but it is in his work *De Anima* (c. 51) that one first comes across the word.—Migne, *Patrologiae Cursus Completus, Series Latina* [*MPL*] (221 vols., Parisiis, 1844-1864), II, 738. Cf. Prümmer, *Manuale Iuris Canonici* (3. ed., Friburgi Brisgoviae: Herder, 1922), n. 373; Herbert Thurston, "Cemetery," *The Catholic Encyclopedia* (15 vols., New York, 1907-1912), III, 504; Spence-Jones, *The Early Christians in Rome* (New York, 1911), pp. 154-155.

[11] By the third century the Christians had numerous places of burial, to which they, as well as the imperial government, referred as cemeteries. This usage was exclusively reserved for Christian burial grounds.—H. Leclercq, "Cimetière," *Dictionnaire d'Archéologie Chrétienne et de Liturgie* [*DACL*] (14 vols., Paris, 1924—), III, 1630. Cf. also: Jalabert, "Epigraphie," *Dictionnaire Apologétique de la Foi Catholique* (4 vols., Paris, 1911), I, 1454; Northcote-Brownlow, *Roma Sotterranea* (London, 1869), p. 29; Edmund Venables,

the Greek κοιμητήριον, signifies a sleeping place, or more particularly a place for those who are sleeping the sleep of death.[12] The Christians were not the first to look upon death as a sleep. The pre-Christian Jews [13] and pagans had often referred to death as a sleep, but they were not always so sure that it would not be an eternal sleep, a sleep from which there would be no rising, especially for the body.[14]

The gloomy, almost hopeless outlook on death which was so characteristic of pagan peoples [15] had its effect on the treatment of the deceased, as well as on the ceremonies and circumstances of burial.[16] It is true that from time to time, and with certain peoples, a happier outlook on death was prevalent.[17] But for the most part in pre-Christian times knowledge concerning life after death was very uncertain, and its details very confused. Thus it is easy to understand the pessimistic outlook on death and the attitude on burial which was so filled with gloom and melancholy.

"Cemetery," in Smith-Cheetham, *Dictionary of Christian Antiquity* (2 vols., Hartford, 1880), I, 329.

[12] Moulart, *De Sepultura et Coemeteriis* (Louvanii, 1862), p. 8, esp. note 1; Hornstein, *Les Sepultures* (Paris, 1868), p. v.

[13] E. g., I Kings i, 21; Deut. xxxi, 16; Psalms xiii, 3; Dan. xii, 2.

[14] Cf. Orellius, *Inscriptionum Latinarum Selectarum Amplissima Collectio* (3 vols., Turici, 1828-1856; Vol. III edited by G. Henzen), II, n. 4796.

[15] Speaking of the pagan viewpoint on death Rush has this to say: "It is in the funeral inscriptions that the popular outlook on death and the future life appear, for here the people manifest what they really feel and believe concerning the inevitable reality of death. From a study of pagan inscriptions, the conclusion is unavoidable that their chief characteristic is a dreary outlook, an utter lack of prospect of anything beyond the grave; and once they venture to look beyond the grave, all is dark and gloomy."—*Death and Burial in Christian Antiquity,* The Catholic University of America Studies in Christian Antiquity, n. 1 (Washington, D. C.: The Catholic University of America Press, 1941), p. 8.

[16] Rush, *op. cit.*, pp. 239-241.

[17] After 2500 B.C. the Egyptians believed in some sort of after-life. Cf. Breasted, *Development of Religion and Thought in Ancient Egypt* (New York, 1912), pp. 51-62. The Greeks, too, had a brighter view of death when they came to strengthen their belief in immortality. Cf. Rohde, *Psyche, the Cult of Souls and Belief in Immortality Among the Greeks* (translated from the 8. ed. by W. Hillis, London, 1925), pp. 19-21; 253. The Jews in contrast to the pagans did believe in life after death, as the Old Testament attests, but it was because of their unique intimate association with God.

The pagan idea of immortality, though some conceptions of it envisioned an after-life for the body as well as for the soul, seemed most often to leave the body out of consideration. So frequently in pagan writings immortality meant only immortality of the soul. The soul was spoken of as being liberated from the body at death, allowing the soul to wing its way to its predestined happiness with the deity,[18] much like the butterfly sheds the furry coat of the caterpiller which had held it imprisoned for so long a time to rise aloft to a higher and better life. The body, abandoned by the soul, had to be disposed of; and it was sometimes out of reverence for the soul of the deceased, and at other times mainly out of dread of contamination from the decaying body, that the survivors interred the remains.[19]

With the coming of Christ, however, the details in the concept of immortality were filled in. Not only the soul would live on, but the body of man was destined also for immortality.[20] It was true

[18] Rohde, *op. cit.*, pp. 56-64; 259.

[19] Bauwens, *Inhumation et Crémation* (2. ed., translated by A. De Mets from the original Flemish, Bruxelles, 1891), p. 4; Moulart, *De Sepultura et Coemeteriis*, p. 1.

[20] I Cor. xv, 42-44; 52. The first oration in the solemn blessing of a cemetery (tit. *De Coemeterii Benedictione—Pontificale Romanum*) expresses this immortality of the body so well: "Almighty God, who art the keeper of souls and their sure salvation and the object of faith of believers, look graciously upon the ministry of Thy servants, so that at our coming in, this cemetery may be purified, blessed, consecrated and hallowed, to the end that the bodies of those who rest here after the course of their life may, on the great day of judgment, together with their blessed souls, obtain the joys of eternal life." This same thought is again in a later oration so beautifully expressed in the words: "Holy Lord, Father Almighty, eternal God, who hallowest every place and betterest it, from whom and through whom all blessings come down from heaven to earth: deign to bless this site as a cemetery and a place of sweet rest and repose for the dead. May the souls whose bodies are buried or shall be buried here enjoy the sweetness of Thy delights; may they rejoice and be glad for a while in the Jerusalem that is above until on the great day of judgment the grave shall restore to them their own bodies, that so they may run forward to meet the Lord when He shall come to judge, carrying in their hands the fruits of their good works."—Translation of the Benedictine Monks of the Buckfast Abbey in the article entitled: "The Consecration of a Cemetery"—*The Homiletic and Pastoral Review* (New York, 1900—), XXX (1930), 981-982.

that the body of man would have to die, but somewhat as a seed dies.[21] It would lie "dormant," would sleep for a while,[22] and then it would rise again to partake of the immortality of the soul. A body that was destined to see God face to face [23] certainly deserved the most profound consideration. And therefore during the time when it would be awaiting its reunion with the soul, it should have all the care, and the deference and the protection that God and men could give it.[24] Add to the above reason the fact that this body during its life on earth was the living temple of the Holy Spirit,[25] and from time to time tabernacled the sacramental Presence of Christ,[26] and you have the three strongest and best reasons why the Catholic Church has always had such high regard for the bodies of the deceased and has had such great solicitude that they "rest in peace." [27]

Article II. The Sacredness of Burial Ground in Roman Law

Although the Church has always treated her cemeteries with the most profound reverence, it would be a mistake to create the impression that the Christians were the first to consider ground used for burial as different and to be set apart from other ground. The Jews, for example, as far back as their history goes, had the highest regard for the place of the burial of their deceased.[28]

[21] I Cor. xv, 36.

[22] St. Jerome, *Epistola LXXV*: "Neque enim mors, sed dormitio et somnus, appellatur."—*MPL,* XXII, 686. Cf. also Funk, *Didascalia et Constitutiones Apostolorum* (2 vols., Paderbornae, 1905), I, 376; Hornstein, *Les Sépultures,* p. v.

[23] I Cor. xiii, 12.

[24] St. Augustine, *De Civitate Dei,* lib. I, c. 13: "Verum istae auctoritates non hoc admonent, quod inest ullus cadaveribus sensus, sed ad Dei providentiam, cui placent etiam talia pietatis officia, corpora mortuorum pertinere significant propter fidem resurrectionis astruendam."—*Corpus Scriptorum Ecclesiasticorum Latinorum* [*CSEL*] (ed. consilio et impensis Academiae Litterarum Caesareae Vindobonensis, Vindobonae, 1866—), XL, 1, 25. Also cf. Origen, *Contra Celsum,* lib. VIII, n. 30—Migne, *Patrologiae Cursus Completus, Series Graeca* [*MPG*] (161 vols., Parisiis, 1857-1866), XI, 1562.

[25] I Cor. iii, 16, 17; vi, 19.

[26] John vi, 52, 57.

[27] *Rituale Romanum,* tit. VI, c. 1.

[28] Gen. xxiii; xxxv, 19-20; Ecclus. xxxviii, 16 ff.; Tob. ii, 9; xii, 12 ff.

The Romans had even a distinct ceremony for transforming burial plots into religious places.[29] Cicero (106-43 B. C.) stated in his *De Legibus* [30] that it was to the pagan priests that the Roman people confided the right to render to their dead the last honors; it was to the priests that they gave the right of throwing in the handful of earth (*"iniectio glebae"*) into the grave. It was the priests who by symbolic rites gave the place of sepulture all the rights, immunities and privileges of religious places. Religion was intimately bound up with the Roman burial and with the place of burial.[31] The civil law *(ius)*, not so exacting as the pagan pontifical law *(fas)*, required for ground to be considered *"religiosus"* the fulfillment of only one condition: that the place contain the remains of some one deceased.[32]

Under Roman law there was no provision for establishing a whole section of land *"religiosus,"* as for instance a whole cemetery.[33] Land devoted to burials would become *religiosus* little by little, one grave at a time.[34] Thus it was only when an area was completely taken up with tombs, and not before, that it would be considered religious.[35] There was a way, however, of getting around this law which restricted the religious character to the land actually occupied by the tomb or tombs. The entire plot, even before it was filled with sepulchers, could be consecrated to some god or goddess.[36] This

[29] Gaius asserted that things were "religiosae quae diis manibus relictae sunt."—(2, 4).

[30] II, 22.

[31] Cicero, *loc. cit.* Cf. also Bauwens, *Inhumation et Crémation,* pp. 5-6; Marucchi, *Éléments d'Archéologie Chrétienne* (3 vols., Paris, 1902-1905. Vol. I, 2. ed., 1905; Vol. II, 2. ed., 1903; Vol. III, 1902), I, 113-114.

[32] D (11, 7) 44; G (2, 6).

[33] The Romans used the word cemetery (*coemeterium*) in its literal sense, as denoting a sleeping place. As a term referring to places of burial, it was both unknown and hardly intelligible to them. Cf. *supra,* p. 2.

[34] D (11, 7) 2, 4. Also see: H. Leclercq, "Domaine Funeraire," *DACL,* IV, 1284.

[35] Orellius, *Inscriptionum Latinarum Selectarum Amplissima Collectio,* II, n. 4405.

[36] H. Leclercq, *loc. cit.*

consecration, by ceremonies which have not come down to us, made of the place a *"locus sacer."* [37]

The severe laws against the violation of sepulchers show that Roman law was in earnest about the sacredness of burial places. The Emperor Gordian (238-244), for example, decreed that places of burial were places *dedicated to religion,* and that violators of graves were to be prosecuted as criminals guilty of an injury done to religion.[38] Julian (361-363) ruled that it was *near sacrilege* to steal any ornaments from the tombs of the dead, since these graves were consecrated.[39] Justinian, in repeating in his Code (529) the law of Julian, called robbing the graves a sacrilegious crime and deserving of the punishment meted out to those guilty of sacrilege.[40]

After a human body had once been interred, that grave became *"religiosus,"* and it was under the direct supervision and jurisdiction of the pagan pontiffs.[41] Indeed, it was theirs to assign the place for burial, unless there was question of hereditary sepulchers. If one wished to exhume the remains of even one's own dead, from one's own land, permission had to come from the emperor or from the pontiffs.[42] And more than that, if one wished to erect a monument over a grave, the pontiffs had to be consulted.[43]

Thus Roman law looked upon the graves of the dead as religious

[37] G (2,4).

[38] "Res religioni destinatas, quin immo religionis effectas, scientes qui contigerint et emere et distrahere non dubitaverint, tametsi iure venditio non subsistat, laesae tamen religionis in crimen inciderunt."—C (9,19) 1.

[39] "Pergit audacia ad busta diem functorum et aggeres consecratos, cum et lapidem hinc movere et terram sollicitare et cespitem vellere *proximum sacrilegio* maiores semper habuerint: sed et ornamenta quaedam triclinis aut porticibus auferri de sepulchris. Quibus primis consulentes, ne in piaculum incidant contaminata religione bustorum, hoc fieri prohibemus poena sacrilegii cohibentes."—C. Th. (9,17) 5. However, the graves of enemies were not religious and therefore were not violated when such actions affected them.—D (47,12) 4.

[40] C (9,19) 5.

[41] Moulart, *De Sepultura et Coemeteriis,* p. 73; Marucchi, *Éléments d'Archéologie Chrétienne,* I, 113-114.

[42] "Ossa quae ab alio illata sunt vel corpus an liceat domino loci effodere vel eruere sine decreto pontificum seu iussu principis, quaestionis est: et ait Labeo expectandum vel permissum pontificale seu iussionem principis."—D (11,7), 8.

[43] D (11,8) 5, 1.

places, and as such they came under the jurisdiction of the pagan pontiffs. The law required no ceremony for a grave to become *"religiosus,"* although, according to Cicero,[44] there was a very definite sacerdotal ritual performed at the grave at the time of burial. There was no way in Roman law for a section of ground to become *"religiosus"* if it was not entirely occupied with the bodies of the deceased. Therefore, the only cemetery "blessing" in the Roman empire was a ceremony (which has not come down to our day) whereby the land was declared to be henceforth dedicated to a god or goddess. This latter rite rendered the ground sacred (*"sacer"*).

Article III. Evidence of Blessing During the First Three Centuries

And now, returning again to Christian graves and cemeteries, one should state frankly at the outset that there is absolutely no record of any rite of blessing of cemeteries until mention is made of it in the latter part of the sixth century by St. Gregory of Tours (538-594).[45] His mention of it,[46] however, does not leave us with the impression that the custom of blessing ground for the reception of the remains of the faithful was beginning only in his day. On the contrary, his casual reference to the rite leaves us to conclude that it must have been long in use and quite generally practiced in the Church by the sixth century.[47]

It must be remembered, however, that at least the first three

[44] *De Legibus,* II, 22.

[45] Duranti, *De Ritibus Ecclesiae Catholicae Libri Tres* (Lugduni, 1608), lib. I, c. 23, n. 9; Moulart, *De Sepultura et Coemeteriis,* p. 75; Bingham, *The Antiquities of the Christian Church* (2 vols., London, 1856), 1237; Many, *Praelectiones de Locis Sacris* (Parisiis, 1904), n. 139, hereafter to be cited as *De Locis Sacris*; Coronata, *De Locis et Temporibus Sacris* (Taurini: Marietti, 1922), n. 136.

[46] *De Gloria Confessorum,* c. 104—*Monumenta Germaniae Historica (MGH): Scriptores Rerum Merovingicarum* (Tom. I, Edd. W. Arndt et B. Krusch, Hannoverae, 1885), I, 815.

[47] Devoti, *Institutionum Canonicarum Libri IV* (4 vols. in 3, ed. prima Romana post quintam, Romae, 1825-1826), II, 364, note 2; Maringola, *Institutiones Liturgicae* (2 vols., Neapoli, 1864-1865), I, 132.

centuries were difficult ones for the Church. During these centuries not only did the Church have no formal recognition as a legal person in the law of the Roman Empire, but was even an illegal and illegitimate religious society.[48] The members of the infant Church were tracked down and murdered for the public crime of being Christians. The bodies of the martyrs had often to be furtively snatched at night from under the drowsy eyes of the executioners to give them Christian burial.[49] And though the other Christian dead were as a rule not discriminated against, and their burial was carried out in an orderly manner and without molestation, still there was little room for any elaborate blessing of either grave or cemetery.[50]

Moulart (1832-1904) [51] holds tenaciously to the opinion that cemeteries, or at least individual graves, received some sacerdotal blessing even in the times of the Apostles. And by sacerdotal blessing he does not mean something quite primitive and obscure. He means by it an act of religion by which a minister, legitimately deputed for it, through the prayers and merits of the Church, begs God to apply the effects of grace to persons or things according to the intention of the Church. He says that he cannot see how it can be denied that this rite of blessing was from the beginning of Christianity applied to the graves of the faithful.

There are two arguments upon which Moulart rests the weight of his proof. He says, in the first place, that the Romans, pagans as they were, had at the time of early Christianity a special ceremoney performed by their priests by which graves were to be con-

[48] Goodwine, *The Right of the Church to Acquire Temporal Goods,* The Catholic University of American Canon Law Studies, n. 131 (Washington, D. C.: The Catholic University of America Press, 1941), pp. 58, 99.

[49] Cf. Allard, *Ten Lectures on the Martyrs* (translated by Luigi Cappadelta, New York, 1907), pp. 316-319.

[50] "For the Christians during a considerable period after the foundation of their faith, anything but the simplest and least imposing ceremonies in connection with consecration [of churches and cemeteries] would have been both out of place and practically impossible."—David Phillips, "Consecration," *Encyclopedia of Religion and Ethics* (13 vols., New York: Scribner's Sons, 1908-1927), IV, 59.

[51] *De Sepultura et Coemeteriis,* pp. 75-78.

sidered religious.[52] If the Romans "blessed" their places of burial, he argues, then certainly the Christians blessed theirs, for can it be said that the pagans had more reverence for the dead than the Christians, or were more religious than the faithful! And furthermore, it was quite within the policy of the early Christian Church to substitute whenever possible, and therefore to supplant, pagan religious practices with Christian rites.

His second argument may be expressed something like this: when one first comes across a positive statement concerning the blessing of ground destined for the burial of the faithful (referring of course to that of St. Gregory of Tours),[53] one finds a practice that seems to have been at the time (590) generally observed throughout the Church. He then quotes St. Augustine (354-430) [54] to the effect that if one finds a general practice which he cannot trace to any written document, and which seems to be something handed down through many generations, there can be only one of two explanations. Either that practice must have been begun by the Apostles, or it must be one that was recommended or established by a plenary council. But, Moulart points out, this rite of the blessing of cemeteries cannot be found in the decrees of any plenary council. Therefore it remains that it has come down to us from the Apostles.

The conclusion of Moulart is quite possible and even probable. And yet it can hardly be given the factual certainty with which he expounds it. It is conceivable, and it would seem just as probable, that for a generation or longer after the beginning of Christianity there was no blessing by the priest or bishop of graves or cemeteries. The first Christians, it must be borne in mind, were recruited from amongst the Jewish people.[55] When their new Faith did not forbid

[52] Moulart (*op. cit.*, p. 76): "*Actus requirebatur sacerdotalis*, glebae nempe iniectio quae, solutis iustis, a *sacerdote publico* fieri super tumulum debebat: aeque accedente, ut ait Cicero (*De Legibus*, II, 22, 57), tum corpus humatum dicebatur, tum sepulcrum vocabatur, tum denique *religiosa complectebatur iura*."

[53] *De Gloria Confessorum*, c. 104—*MGH, Scriptores Rerum Merovingicarum*, I, 815.

[54] *Epistola ad Ianuarium*, LIV, c. 1—*CSEL*, XXXIV, 2, 159.

[55] The twelve Apostles were of the Jewish race: Acts ii, 7. The first converts were for the greater part Jewish: Acts ii, 5-6, 41.

it, and when it would not be compromised thereby, these early Christians retained at least for their generation many of the customs of their race.[56] Therefore they were very likely laid to rest with their forefathers outside the city walls in the family tomb.[57] It is not heretical to maintain that many of the practices, rites and ceremonies, which we consider so essential and so intimately bound up with our Faith today, were not given to us directly by Christ or the Apostles. It was within the plan of God that the Church, under the guidance of the Holy Spirit, would develop these institutions as the occasion or the need presented itself.

Sometime within the first century the Christians began to have cemeteries of their own.[58] One of the faithful, favored with a more generous share of this world's goods, possessing among other things a country home and family sepulcher outside the city walls [59] on one of the great highways leading from Rome [60] or from one of the other cities, would open up his villa to his fellow Christians and afford them burial there, so that they could be united not only in life but also

[56] For example, the custom of laying out the body before burial was a Jewish custom; the Christians retained it: Acts ix, 37. Cf. also Acts xv, 28-29, for the decrees of the First Council of Jerusalem commanding abstinence from blood and things strangled.

[57] This was the custom of the Jews. The tomb of Lazarus, for example, was some little distance from his house, presumably outside the city of Bethany: John xi, 38. The tomb of Joseph of Arimathea was outside the city walls: John xix, 41. At the Crucifixion of Christ, the tombs of the deceased were split asunder by the earthquake. The Sacred Text says that after the Resurrection of Christ many of the dead arose and went into the city of Jerusalem: Matt. xxvii, 52-53.

[58] Northcote-Brownlow, *Roma Sotterranea,* pp. 64-65.

[59] Roman law forbade burial within the city. This was first expressed in the Twelve Tables: "Hominem mortuum in urbe ne sepelito, neve urito"—Tab. 10, n. 1; and it was later reiterated by Emperors Hadrian (117-138)—D (47,12) 3, and Diocletian (284-305)—C (3,44) 12: "Mortuorum reliquias, ne sanctum municipiorum ius polluatur, intra civitatem condi iam pridem vetitum est."

[60] Northcote-Brownlow in their *Roma Sotterranea,* pp. xiv-xv, give a list of cemeteries mentioned in ancient historical records together with the road or "via" on which they are to be found.

in death.[61] In a short time this erstwhile family burial plot was no longer a place of repose for those bound together by human ties of blood, but for those united by the spiritual ties of the Blood of Jesus Christ.[62]

One after another of these private cemeteries were made accessible to the Christians.[63] Especially around Rome, every road leading out of the city had its Christian burial place. And since the cemeteries were generally underground catacombs,[64] there sprang into being during the course of a few centuries a maze of corridors, hundreds of miles of passage-ways, linking one catacomb with another.[65]

In the vestibule of one of the earliest of such cemeteries, that of Domitilla, there is a stone pillar on which the following inscription appears: *"Locus sacer sacrilege cave malu(m)."* This inscription is considered to be an early second century inscription.[66] As has been seen,[67] any sepulcher of Christian and pagan alike became by law a *locus religiosus.* A religious place did not become a *locus sacer* unless by a pagan rite it was dedicated to some god or goddess.[68] It goes without saying that the Christians could never have resorted to a dedication to pagan gods by pagan priests in order to have their

[61] The subterranean single-chamber crypt, meant originally for the use of a family, was enlarged, and long corridors extended in every direction opening into other crypts. This was the origin of the Christian catacombs. Cf. H. Leclercq, "Domaine Funeraire," *DACL,* IV, 1286; Northcote-Brownlow, *op. cit.,* pp. 61-62; Spence-Jones, *The Early Christians in Rome,* pp. 111-112.

[62] Edmund Venables, "Cemetery," in Smith-Cheetham, *Dictionary of Christian Antiquities,* I, 330; Scaglia, *Manuel d'Archéologie Chrétienne* (Turin, 1916), pp. 26-27.

[63] P. Allard, "Cimetière," *Dictionnaire Apologétique de la Foi Catholique,* I, 463.

[64] Hornstein, *Les Sépultures,* p. 109; Anton de Waal, "Catacombs," *The Catholic Encyclopedia,* III, 418; Edwin K. Mitchell, "Death and Disposal of the Dead," *Encyclopedia of Religion and Ethics,* IV, 457; also Giorgio Schneider, "Catacombs," *Encyclopedia of Religion and Ethics,* III, 248.

[65] Allard, *Ten Lectures on the Martyrs,* p. 66.

[66] De Rossi, *La Roma Sotterranea Cristiana* (3 vols., Romae, 1864-1877), III, 434.

[67] *Supra,* pp. 6, 7-8.

[68] *Supra,* pp. 6, 8.

cemeteries classified as sacred places in the meaning of the law of Rome.

The question arises, therefore, how could this engraved monument at the entrance of the cemetery of Domitilla call the cemetery a *locus sacer*? How could it become a *locus sacer*? Certainly it was not by any pagan rite, for at the time the inscription was made—and it is no less an authority than the eminent archeologist De Rossi (1822-1894) who states that it is a product of the second century [69]—this cemetery was in Christian hands. And if without some sort of formal rite a burial place was only *religiosus*, might we not be allowed the opinion, at least, that it was by some Christian rite that a *locus religiosus* became a *locus sacer?* It cannot be argued that the early Christian Church would not use the term *locus sacer*, because of the fact that it already had a pagan significance. During the first three centuries the Church actually did use the term; but by the fourth century the Church had practically abandoned the term *locus sacer*, for in the ambiguity of the first three centuries it could refer to places made sacred by pagan as well as by Christian dedication, and had adopted the unequivocal Christian term of *locus sanctus*.[70] On the other hand it is quite possible that the Church designedly applied the term of *locus sacer* to her cemeteries during the first three centuries, after having substituted for the pagan rite of dedication to the false gods a sacred rite of her own, so that she might gain for those cemeteries the public recognition and legal protection enjoyed by the pagan places of burial. Accordingly, although no final conclusion can be drawn, it is not altogether improbable that the evidence of this mute but eloquent inscription in the cemetery of Domitilla points to a liturgical rite of the blessing of cemeteries even as early as the second century.

With the official recognition of Christianity by Emperor Constantine in the Edict of Milan (313), and with imperial favor and funds for the first time at her disposal, the Church began the erection of large basilicas over the tombs of the martyrs.[71] These were strictly

[69] *Loc. cit.*

[70] H. Leclercq, "Cimetière," *DACL*, III, 1644-1645.

[71] De Rossi, *La Roma Sotterranea Cristiana*, III, 454, ff.; Allard, *Ten Lectures on the Martyrs*, pp. 333-334.

cemetery churches.[72] There is evidence of the dedication or the consecration of churches by this time [73] and it is very likely that, if cemeteries had up to this time no special blessing of their own, the consecration of the church must have included the consecration of the cemetery beneath and around that church.[74] The dedication of which Eusebius speaks (314) is not one of any set ritual, for in his day there was no hard and fast rite of consecration. Bishops from all the neighboring dioceses, as well as great numbers of the faithful, assembled at the church to be dedicated.[75] It seems that the consecration consisted principally in the solemn celebration of Mass for the first time in the new edifice. A dedicatory sermon was delivered on the occasion by some well-known orator and churchman, usually a bishop.[76]

[72] Edwin K. Mitchell, "Death and Disposal of the Dead," *Encyclopedia of Religion and Ethics,* IV, 457; Spence-Jones, *The Early Christians in Rome,* p. 272. Prior to the fourth century there were in most of the larger catacombs cemetery chapels where divine services and meetings were carried on. These chapels became no longer necessary for public worship after the Edict of Constantine, although some of them still served as memorial chapels. Cf. H. Leclercq, "Chapelle," *DACL,* II, 407-408; Edmund Venables, "Cemetery," in Smith-Cheetham, *Dictionary of Christian Antiquities,* I, 327-328; De Rossi, *La Roma Sotterranea Cristiana,* III, 478-487; Northcote, *Les Catacombes Romaines* (Rome, Paris, 1859), pp. 41-57.

[73] Eusebius, *Historiae Ecclesiasticae,* X, 3—*MPG,* XX, 846-847; Maringola, *Antiquitatum Christianarum Institutiones* (2 vols. in 1, Neapoli, 1857), I, p. 268; Wernz, *Ius Decretalium,* III, n. 436, note 32.

[74] Ferraris, *Prompta Bibliotheca, Canonica, Iuridica, Moralis, Theologica, necnon Ascetica, Polemica, Rubricistica, Historica* (9 vols., Romae, 1885-1899), v. "coemeterium," nn. 3, 4 (hereafter cited as *Bibliotheca*) ; Catalanus, *Pontificale Romanum in Tres Partes Distributum Clementis VIII ac Urbani VIII auctoritate recognitum* (nova. ed., 3 vols., Parisiis, 1850-1851), pars 2, tit. 6, n. 27, Vol. II, 298 (hereafter cited as *Pontificale Romanum*); Moulart, *De Sepulturis et Coemeteriis,* p. 101; Kerin, *The Privation of Christian Burial,* The Catholic University of America Canon Law Studies, n. 136 (Washington, D. C.: The Catholic University of America Press, 1941), p. 6.

[75] Eusebius, *De Vita Constantini,* lib. IV, c. XLIII—*MPG,* XX, 845-846; Sozomen, *Historia Ecclesiastica,* lib. II, c. XXVI—*MPG,* LXVII, 1007.

[76] Duchesne, *Christian Worship: Its Origin and Evolution* (translated from the 3. French ed. by M. J. McClure, London, 1903), p. 400; Devoti, *Institutionum Canonicarum Libri IV,* II, 326.

ARTICLE IV. THE TESTIMONY OF ST. GREGORY OF TOURS (538-594)

Some time between the fourth and fifth century when the catacombs ceased to function as burial places for the faithful,[77] because of the general disregard for the law of the Twelve Tables which forbade burial within the city walls,[78] it became the custom to bury the faithful inside the cities next to the urban churches.[79] During the first three centuries the faithful were not always buried in the underground passages of the catacombs, but now it became the practice for them to be buried in the churchyards in surface graves under the open sky (*sub divo*).[80]

Churchyard cemeteries did not prove adequate, and during this time there were constructed city cemeteries, belonging to some church, but nevertheless separated from it. Did these burial places go unblessed inasmuch as they could in no way be considered to border on or be a part of an adjacent church and thus partake of the consecration of the church, or did they receive some special cemetery blessing?

It is possible that the answer to this question is to be found in a passage of St. Gregory of Tours to which reference has already been made.[81] Gregory, upon receiving news of the death of Radegunde (+587), the saintly queen of the Franks, advised the Abbess of the monastery of Poitiers, of which Radegunde had been a member at the time of her death, to proceed with the arrangements for the burial. But the Abbess wrote: *"Et quid faciemus, si episcopus urbis non advenerit, quia locus ille quo sepeliri debet, non est sacerdotali*

[77] Northcote-Brownlow, *Roma Sotterranea*, pp. 95, 103.

[78] Cf. *supra*, p. 11. See also Vermeersch-Creusen, *Epitome Iuris Canonici* (3 vols., Vol. I, 6. ed., 1937; Vol. II, 5. ed., 1934; Vol. III, 5. ed., 1936, Mechliniae et Romae: Dessain), II, 301 (hereafter cited as *Epitome*); Wernz-Vidal, *Ius Canonicum*, IV, n. 672.

[79] Wernz, *Ius Decretalium*, III, n. 468.

[80] Edmund Venables, "Cemetery," in Smith-Cheetham, *Dictionary of Christian Antiquities*, I, 333; R. Naz, "Cimetière," *Dictionnaire de Droit Canonique* (ed. R. Naz, 3 vols., Paris: Letouzey et Ane, 1924—), III, 730; Leclercq, *Manuel d'Archéologie Chrétienne* (2 vols., Paris, 1907), I, 322-334.

[81] *De Gloria Confessorum*, c. 104—*MGH*, *Scriptores Rerum Merovingicarum*, I, 815; cf. *supra*, p. 8.

benedictione sacratus?" The citizens and civic authorities begged Gregory, Bishop of Tours, a neighboring diocese, to bless the ground, using as their argument that Maroveus, the Bishop of Poitiers, would not only not mind, but would consider that he had been done a great favor. Their entreaties prevailed, and Gregory tells how he went to Poitiers and blessed that place of burial.

Although the authors who touch on the subject point to St. Gregory of Tours for the first substantial statement on the blessing of cemeteries, it is only fair to point out that Gregory does not use the word "cemetery," but rather the very general term "place." Such a term as "locus" could refer to a single plot or to a whole cemetery. None of the authors, however, seem to raise any question as to its meaning. They take it to mean a cemetery, for they all refer to the above passage in St. Gregory of Tours as the first real evidence of a cemetery blessing. However, the "locus" in the text of Gregory may, and probably does refer only to the grave of Radegunde. No matter what the "locus" of Gregory means, the important point to be made is that it could not have been the ordinary procedure of that day to bless one grave at a time, and that at the time of burial. For if one were to hold that view and were to make it the general practice of those times, he is forced to accept a very inconvenient, and in fact, impossible conclusion. If blessed cemeteries were not provided for the burial of the faithful, then the ceremony of blessing would have had to take place probably as a rite which was a part of, or a ceremony immediately preceding the rite of burial. This would mean that the bishop of the place would have had to preside at the burial of every one of the faithful of his diocese, because, as will be seen later, it was the bishop and not a priest, who was the one to perform this rite of blessing. For a bishop to be present at all burials so as to bless the grave would have been a physically impossible task for him to accomplish. It must be remembered that those were days when the average person was buried within hours, not days, after death had set in; embalming was still within the reach of only a comparative few. Therefore the burial of the deceased could not have been postponed indefinitely. But if the faithful were not to be buried in anything but blessed ground, as the text of St. Gregory seems to take for granted, the bishop would have had to bless each single grave before any of the faithful could have been buried. This might have been necessary if the burial had to be made in separate plots; but from the very beginning Christians were buried close to one another in large cemeteries, not separately in private graves. Thus it is logical to conclude that the bishop blessed cemeteries for the use of the faithful, and not individual graves save by way of exception. And as for the grave of Radegunde, perhaps the little cemetery of the monastery was already completely occupied and no other blessed ground was at hand, making it necessary for the Abbess to call in St. Gregory for the blessing of the grave. It is also possible that because of the dignity of the deceased queen she was to have burial in a special place.

The account of St. Gregory of Tours leaves much to be desired. However, it gives some indication as to the practice of his day relative to the blessing of ground used for the burial of the faithful. His testimony makes the three following points clear:

First, it was evidently necessary that the ground be blessed. Did not the Abbess write to Gregory to tell him that it was impossible to bury Radegunde, since the ground where she was to be buried had not as yet been blessed? Had the burial plot or cemetery already been constituted as sacred ground there would have been no difficulty.

Secondly, the blessing was not one which was allowed to priests, but one which the ordinary himself performed. For certainly if a priest had been the ordinary minister of this rite, there would surely have been enough priests at hand in the city of Poitiers, where the monastery was situated, to make it possible for at least one of them to be free for this purpose. As it happened, since the local ordinary was not in the city, and was therefore unable to attend to the matter, it was necessary that Gregory, being a neighboring bishop, journey from Tours to Poitiers to perform this act of blessing.

Thirdly, it can be inferred from what has just been mentioned, that it must have been an accepted procedure for the bishop of a near-by diocese to presume, for a reasonable cause, the permission of the local ordinary, in order to bless, in the territory of the latter, the grave or the cemetery which the emergency made it his duty to do.

Of the rite which Gregory used in this blessing there is nothing said. One can assume, however, that there was no established rule as to the rite used in the blessing of burial ground, since in the consecration of a church there was not as yet any generally accepted ritual. In all likelihood, in view of the many rites of cemetery blessing to be found between the sixth and the fifteenth centuries,[82] there were many existing rites of the blessing of cemeteries in Gregory's time, some used in one locality, some in another.

The importance, therefore, of this text of St. Gregory of Tours lies in the fact that it reveals to us of a later century our first positive, unequivocal evidence that in the West cemeteries of the sixth century at least were blessed.[83] And the importance is further increased in that it gives undeniable proof that the blessing of ground for burial did not depend on any consecration or dedication of an adjacent church.

[82] Martène, *De Antiquis Ecclesiae Ritibus* (3 vols., Rotomagi, 1700-1702), lib. II, c. 20, Vol. III, 361-368.

[83] Migne, *Theologiae Cursus Completus* (28 vols., Parisiis, 1863-1866), XVI, 255; R. Naz, "Cimetière," *Dictionnaire de Droit Canonique*, III, 736; Devoti, *Institutionum Canonicarum Libri IV*, II, 364; Moulart, *De Sepultura et Coemeteriis*, p. 75.

CHAPTER II

THE BLESSING OF CEMETERIES FROM THE TIME OF ST. GREGORY OF TOURS TO THE THIRTEENTH CENTURY

In the first six centuries the cemeteries, which were before that time outside the walls and along the public highways, were moved into the cities to places alongside the numerous city churches. In this move the faithful showed where they liked best to be buried. They wanted to be as close as possible to the House of God, and to the relics of the saints. The sacred relics of the martyrs were the first to be moved into the cities. Their remains were deposited in the various churches, until very shortly there was no church which did not have its saintly relics.[1]

Almost at the same time there can be found the beginning of a practice which was to become in a few centuries a very serious problem, the practice of burial inside the churches.[2] It was quite natural that bishops should be buried in their churches,[3] and it early became the custom for the clergy to be buried in the churches to which they were attached.[4] It was thought fitting, too, that such a great layman

[1] From c. 7 of the II Council of Nicaea (787) it can be seen that it was not only the custom for churches to have relics of the saints, but that it was the law: "Quaecumque templa consecrata sunt absque sacris reliquiis martyrum, in iis fieri statuimus reliquiarum depositionem cum consuetis precibus; episcopus autem, post haec, templum consecrans sine sanctis reliquiis, deponatur, ut qui ecclesiasticas traditiones transgressus sit."—Mansi, *Sacrorum Conciliorum Nova et Amplissima Collectio* (53 vols. in 59, Parisiis, 1901-1927), XIII, 751, to be hereafter cited as Mansi.

[2] By the church here it is meant to include also the vestibule and the porch and such other parts of the building that were closely associated with the actual body of the church. At first "burial in church" meant only burial in the outlying parts of the building, not in the church proper. But as time went on, it became the usual practice to bury indiscriminately even the faithful in the body of the church.

[3] Socrates, *Historia Ecclesiastica,* lib. IV, c. XLV—*MPG,* LXVII, 835.

[4] Speaking of burial, St. Ambrose (ca. 340-397) in a letter to his sister said that he had prepared a sepulcher under the altar, a place which was most fitting for priests. "Hunc ego locum," he said, "praedestinaveram mihi. Dignum

as the first Christian Emperor, Constantine the Great, should merit the distinguished honor of having a resting place in church.[5] High civil dignitaries frequently were afforded burial in some church in Rome and in other cities of the Empire.[6]

In the Code of Justinian [7] as well as in many Councils of France, Spain and Germany efforts were made to discourage burial in Churches.[8] But while the trend was checked at certain times and in various localities, it was never stopped altogether. In fact, even as these Councils were attempting to limit the use of churches as places of burial, the custom was growing ever more strong. It reached its logical conclusion in the twelfth and thirteenth centuries, when any Catholic, lay, cleric or religious, could be buried in church.[9] The legislation during the next four hundred years little by little put the matter of church burial in the hands of the bishops, so that it became increasingly difficult for persons to be buried in church. The *Rituale Romanum* of Paul V, issued first in 1614, expressed the desire of the Church that cemeteries and not churches be the ordinary place of burial.[10]

During the time when the custom of burial in church was so general, little difficulty is experienced in studying the manner of the blessing of cemeteries. For if the cemetery was as a rule coextensive with the physical structure of the church, such a cemetery would,

est enim ut ibi requiescat sacerdos, ubi offerre consuevit."—*Epist.* XXII, n. 13—*MPL,* XVI, 1023. Cf. Wernz, *Ius Decretalium,* III, n. 468.

[5] Eusebius, *De Vita Constantini,* lib. IV, cc. 58-60; 70—*MPG,* XX, 1210; 1223, 1226.

[6] St. John Chrysostom (ca. 344-407) alludes to this practice: *Homil. XXVI in Epist. II ad Cor.*—*MPG,* LXI, 582.

[7] (1, 2) 2.

[8] I Council of Braga (561), c. 18—Hardouin, *Acta Conciliorum et Epistolae Decretales ac Constitutiones Summorum Pontificum* (12 vols., Parisiis, 1715), III, 352 (hereafter: Hardouin); VI Arles (813), c. 21—*MGH, Legum Sectio III: Concilia Aevi Merovingici* (Tom. I, recensivit F. Maassen, Hannoverae et Lipsiae, 1893), I, 252 (hereafter cited as *MGH, Leges, III*); Council of Mainz (813), c. 52—*MGH, Leges, III,* I, 272; Council of Meaux (845), c. 72—Hardouin, IV, 1496; Council of Tribur (895), c. 17—Mansi, XVIII, 141.

[9] C. 17, C. XIII, q. 2; cc. 5, 6, X, *de sepulturis,* III, 28.

[10] *Rituale Romanum Pauli V Pontificis Maximi iussu editum* (Romae, 1652), tit. *De Exsequiis* (hereafter cited as *Rituale Romanum Pauli V*).

along with the church, have been consecrated or blessed with one and the same sacred rite.[11]

However, it does not follow that all the burials, even during this period, took place in churches. Cemeteries apart from the church still existed. And it was at this time (ca. 745) that the first extant rite of the blessing of a cemetery is to be placed. This rite is to be found in the *Liber Pontificalis* of Egbert, Archbishop of York (732-766).[12] The Pontifical of Egbert is one of the most ancient books of its kind that has been preserved to the present day.[13] Some would even say that there is every reason to believe that it is the world's most ancient Pontifical.[14]

Since this ceremony of the blessing of a cemetery is the earliest and only indication of what such a ceremony must have been in the days preceding and immediately following the time of Egbert, it is desirable to reproduce it from Martène:[15]

"*Primitus cum aqua benedicta episcopus cum clericis suis circumdare debeat omne coemeterium cum psalmo* Misere mei Deus, *et antiphona* Asperges me. *Postea litania, deinde dicat:* Dominus vobiscum, *in Orientali angulo coemeterii:* Deus qui es totius orbis conditor et humani generis redemptor, etc. *In australi angulo coemeterii:* Domine sancte, Pater omnipotens, trina maiestas, etc. *Item in occidentali angulo coemeterii:* Omnipotens Dominus, qui es custos animarum, etc. *Oratio in medio poliandri.* Adesto quaesumus, Domine, officio servitutis, etc."

The Pontifical of Egbert is but an example of perhaps many other Pontificals of that day. There was no general and uniform rite of blessing. Bishops adopted the one which suited them best, usually the one which was traditional in their locality.

Martène (1654-1739) reproduces other rites of blessing of ceme-

[11] Moulart, *De Sepulturis et Coemeteriis,* p. 101.

[12] Martène, *De Antiquis Ecclesiae Ritibus,* lib. II, c. 20, Vol. III, 361.

[13] F. Cabrol, "Egbert (Pontificale d')," *DACL,* IV, 2214; J. F. Goggin, "Pontificale," *Catholic Encyclopedia,* XII, 231.

[14] Maskell, *Monumenta Ritualia Ecclesiae Anglicanae* (3 vols., Oxford, 1882), II, 77.

[15] *Loc. cit.*

eteries,[16] rites that were used in various parts of the Church in centuries after Egbert, Archbishop of York. These are a little fuller than the one reproduced above, but in substance they are quite similar. The later ones, of course, resemble more closely the solemn and simple blessing of a cemetery found in the *Pontificale Romanum* and in the *Rituale Romanum*.[17]

[16] *De Antiquis Ecclesiae Ritibus,* lib. II, c. 20, Vol. III, 362-368.

[17] See Catalanus, *Pontificale Romanum,* pars 2, tit. 6, nn. 25-32, where the author treats of the early vestiges of cemetery consecration and blessing.

CHAPTER III

THE BLESSING OF CEMETERIES FROM THE TIME OF GREGORY IX (1227-1241) TO THE PRESENT CODE

ARTICLE I. THE NECESSITY OF BLESSING

1. *During the Pre-Reformation Era*

IN the fourth century cemeteries were very likely consecrated along with the churches to which they were joined. As it came to be required that all churches should be consecrated, this same obligation applied also to their adjacent cemeteries.[1] In the sixth century there seemed to be no question that the ground in which the faithful were to be buried should be blessed ground. "What shall we do," asked the Abbess of a monastery in Poiters of St. Gregory, Bishop of Tours, "when the bishop of the city cannot come, and the place where Radegunde ought to be buried is not as yet consecrated with the sacerdotal blessing?" It was seen how St. Gregory of Tours left his own diocese and came to Poitiers to bless that burial place.[2]

By the thirteenth century a cemetery was required either to be consecrated or at least to be blessed. It was not enough that the remains of the dead were buried in a cemetery to render it a *locus sacer*,[3] it was necessary that the bishop designate the cemetery for the burial of the faithful by blessing it.[4] After it was blessed it

[1] Cf. *supra*, p. 14.

[2] Cf. *supra*, pp. 15-18.

[3] Ioannes Andreae, glossa ad c. 1, *de sepulturis*, III, 7, in Clem., v. "coemeteriis."

[4] C. 9, D. I, *de cons*. See also: Barbosa, *Collectanea Doctorum tam Veterum quam Recentiorum in Ius Pontificum Universum* (5 vols., Lugduni, 1656), lib. III, tit. 40, c. 7, n. 6 (hereafter cited as *Collectanea Doctorum*); Murga (De), *Disquisitiones Morales et Canonicae de Sepulturis* (2 vols., Lugduni, 1666), tract. 1, disq. 1, nn. 11-12; Samuellius (*De Sepulturis Ecclesiasticis* [Lucae, 1650], tract. I, disp. 1, controv. 3, concl. 2, n. 3): "Coemeterium idem est, ac locus, qui deputatur sepulturis; et dicitur deputatum per D. Episcopi benedictionem, non vero ante; cuius appellatione non continetur Ecclesia, nec sufficit, quod ibi sit sepultus aliquis, nisi fit ab Episcopo benedictum." Cf. Baruffaldus, *Ad Rituale Romanum Commentaria* (2 vols., Florentiae, 1847), tit. 34, n. 153.

became a *locus sacer,* and not before. So much was this the case that if to an already blessed cemetery the bishop added a new piece of ground which he meant to incorporate in the blessed cemetery, the newly added ground did not become a *locus sacer* until the bishop had blessed it.[5]

It is impossible to say exactly when the rite of the simple blessing of cemeteries began. Authors seem to have taken no notice at all of the interesting question. The blessing of churches, as a rite different in solemnity from that of consecration, existed, it is likely, in the time of Gregory IX (1227-1241). In his decretals Gregory at times assumed that not all churches were consecrated, even though consecrated churches seemed to be the ordinary rule. He said, for example, of these unconsecrated churches, that they were sacred, that they enjoyed the privilege of ecclesiastical immunity,[6] that they could be violated, and that if they were violated they needed to be reconciled.[7] Ordinary profane places are not in law considered sacred and immune, subject to violation or in consequent need of reconciliation. Thus it is presumed that such unconsecrated churches were blessed. And if churches at this time (thirteenth century) were blessed simply and not always consecrated, it is very probable that cemeteries also were being simply blessed as well as solemnly blessed or consecrated.

Because the faithful were to be buried in sacred ground, it followed that cemeteries should be consecrated or blessed. The obligation, however, which made it necessary for Catholics to use blessed ground is not so evident as the prohibition of the burial of the unworthy in sacred ground. As time went on, especially from the sixth century, certain classes of persons were excluded from Christion burial.[8] Infidels, Jews, pagans, unbaptized infants and catechumens, notorious heretics, schismatics, apostates, the publicly excommunicated and interdicted, suicides, those who participated in

[5] Samuellius, *op. cit.,* tract. 1, controv. 16, concl. 5, nn. 10-12.

[6] C. 9, X, *de immunitate ecclesiarum, coemeterii et rerum ad eas pertinentium,* III, 49.

[7] C. 10, X, *de consecratione ecclesiae,* III, 40.

[8] This term included also, besides the burial itself in ground set apart and blessed by the bishop, the conveying of the body to the church and the religious rites which took place at the church.—Kerin, *The Privation of Christian Burial,* p. xiv; Many, *De Locis Sacris,* n. 222.

duels, robbers, public sinners, and many others were excluded from Christian burial, some of these even during the first three centuries of the Church.[9] Their exclusion from burial in Catholic cemeteries followed from the fact that these cemeteries were designated by the bishop for the use of the faithful departed and blessed by him and thereby made sacred.[10] By the twelfth century the principle had been crystalized that all baptized persons could and should be buried in sacred ground unless they were specifically prohibited by law.[11] This is just another way of saying that the Church provided cemeteries which she blessed and dedicated for the exclusive use of the faithful departed.

2. *During the Post-Reformation Era*

After the so-called Reformation, however, it was not always possible for the Church to have her own cemeteries, and when she possessed them it was not so easy for her to keep them exclusively for the burial of her own. Often, especially in small districts which were notably Protestant or non-Catholic, the Church had to be satisfied with one common cemetery, wherein both Catholics and non-Catholics were buried. In circumstances such as these the Holy See, in keeping with her concern that all the faithful be interred in sacred ground, decreed that wherever Catholics could not have a separate cemetery, provision should be made for them to have a specially defined section of the common cemetery.[12] This section was

[9] Murga (De), *Disquisitiones Morales et Canonicae de Sepulturis*, tract. 2; *Rituale Romanum Pauli V*, tit. *De Exsequiis—Quibus non licet dare Ecclesiasticam sepulturam*; Moulart, *De Sepultura et Coemeteriis*, pp. 266-287; Many, *De Locis Sacris*, nn. 217-224; Wernz, *Ius Decretalium*, III, n. 780; Kerin, *The Privation of Christian Burial*, pp. 14-58, 66-88.

[10] C. 3, X, *de sepulturis*, III, 28.

[11] C. 28, C. XIII, q. 2; c. 28, D. I, *de cons.*

[12] The Sacred Congregation of the Propagation of the Faith on August 29, 1763, n. 4, reissued a decree of the Sacred Congregation of the Council (*Catharen.*, July 13, 1635), which had been issued over one hundred years before, and which covered just such a situation—*Codicis Iuris Canonici Fontes cura Emi. Petri Card. Gasparri editi* (9 vols., Romae [postea Civitate Vaticana]: Typis Polyglottis Vaticanis, 1923-1939. Vols. VII-IX ed. cura et studio Emi. Iustiniani Serédi), n. 4542. This work will hereafter be cited as *Fontes*. Cf. also S. C. de Prop. de Fide (*ad Ep. Rosen.*), 16 apr. 1862—*Fontes*, n. 4856.

to be blessed and to have all the privileges of a blessed cemetery.[13] It was to have also a separate entrance,[14] thus likening it as near as possible to an exclusively Catholic cemetery.

It happened all too frequently in those difficult times that not even a section of the common cemetery was allowed to be reserved exclusively for Catholic burials. The Church, however, was ready to take care of the situation with a special rite which it included in the Ritual,[15] by means of which the priest, immediately before consigning the body of the deceased to the grave, would bless that grave.[16]

There have been a number of decrees and official pronouncements on the matter of the burial of non-Catholics in blessed cemeteries. There were many instances particularly of families in which one or several of the members were Catholics. The question that frequently came up may be phrased thus: were the Catholics to be buried alongside their relatives in non-Catholic cemeteries; and if not, was it possible for the non-Catholic husband, wife, son, daughter, mother,

[13] S. C. S. Off., instr. (*ad Ep. Scepusien.*), 16 aug. 1781—*Fontes,* n. 843.

[14] S. C. de Prop. Fide, 29 mart. 1830—*Fontes,* n. 4747.

[15] *Rituale Romanum Pauli V,* tit. *De exsequiis*; and in all the subsequent editions of the *Rituale Romanum,* tit. 6, c. 3, nn. 12, 13; c. 7, n. 3.

[16] Cf. S. C. de Prop. Fide, 29 aug. 1763, n. 4—*Fontes,* n. 4542; S. C. de Prop. Fide (*ad Ep. Rosen.*), 16 apr. 1862—*Fontes,* n. 4856. The Holy Office (S. C. C. Off., 12 febr. 1862—*Fontes,* n. 969) issued a very clear-cut decree outlining the manner of proceeding: "1. Curandum est Episcopo ut Catholici coemeterium habeant a coemeterio acatholicorum distinctum. 2. Si id effici non possit, experiendum est utrum saltem in eodem coemeterio distinctus locus pro tumulatione Catholicorum haberi possit. 3. Si neque id possible sit, usquedum praedicta facultas non obtineatur, singulis vicibus, cum Catholici cadaver ad sepulchrum deferatur, sepulturae locus debet benedici." The Sacred Congregation of Rites (*Briocen.,* 4 sept. 1880, ad 1—*Fontes,* n. 6125) stipulated that this blessing for individual graves was to be used only where the cemetery as a whole was not blessed. In blessed cemeteries there was no need to bless single graves unless there was a tomb or vault that was composed of material that was not included in the original blessing of the cemetery. Once this added structure was blessed, the blessing was not to be repeated even if other burials were made in it.—S. R. C. *Ruremunden.,* 27 maii, 1 iun. 1876, dubium 5—*Fontes,* n. 6091.

father, etc., to be buried with the Catholic in the blessed ground of a Catholic cemetery. The policy had always been that the Catholic was to be buried in the Catholic cemetery; and the non-Catholic in his own cemetery. However, when this worked a hardship on the Catholic, or made for hard feelings among the non-Catholic relatives, or created resentment against the Church, the Holy See allowed a relaxation of the law, but in as far as possible only in individual instances and at the careful discretion of the bishop.[17] These provisions carried out what has always been the practice of the Church, namely to provide blessed ground for the burial of the faithful, and to this end even to make certain concessions in favor of certain non-Catholics when greater good would accrue thereby to the faithful.

Article II. The Minister of Solemn Blessing

1. *The Bishop of the Place*

In the solemn blessing of a cemetery the minister was the bishop. As was noted in examining the testimony of St. Gregory of Tours,[18] the sole minister of the solemn blessing of a cemetery was the bishop. The ordinary minister was the bishop of the place where the cemetery or burial place was located; the extraordinary minister was a bishop from another diocese.

Martène in his *De Antiquis Ecclesiae Ritibus* [19] has given several examples of the rite of solemn blessing of cemeteries as used in various localities from the 8th to the 15th centuries. The minister is always a bishop. In the *Pontifical Romanum* of Clement VIII [20] and in all

[17] S. C. S. Off. instr. (*ad Ep. Scepusien.*), 16 aug. 1781—*Fontes,* n. 843; S. C. de Prop. Fide—*Collectanea S. C. de Prop. Fide* (2 vols., Romae, 1907), n. 1089; S. C. S. Off., 30 mart. 1859—*Fontes,* n. 949. Cf. also: art. 387—*Concilii Plenarii Baltimorensis II Decreta* (Baltimorae: Murphy, 1875), pp. 201-202; art. 317—*Decreta Concilii Plenarii Baltimorensis Tertii* (Baltimorae: Murphy, 1886), pp. 182-183.

[18] Cf. *supra,* p. 17.

[19] Lib. II, cap. 20, Vol. III, 361-368.

[20] *Pontificale Romanum Clementis VIII Pontificis Maximi iussu Restitutum atque Editum* (Antverpiae, 1627), tit. *De Coemeterii Benedictione.*

later Pontificals [21] it was taken for granted throughout the rite of the solemn blessing of a cemetery that a bishop was the one to perform the rite.

It is quite logical that this should be so, since the solemn blessing of cemeteries has always followed the procedure in the consecration of churches,[22] and in the case of the latter the bishop is the proper minister. In the *Decretum* of Gratian, in the special part where he treats extensively of the consecration of churches,[23] it is often stated and always presumed that the minister is one who has episcopal orders.

The question was asked of Gregory VI (1045-1046) [24] what was to be done when it was difficult to determine who was the proper minister of the consecration of a church belonging to a religious community. The difficulty had arisen because it was not certain in whose diocese the church stood.[25] Gregory answered that the religious were to investigate to see what bishop it was that exercised episcopal rights over the inhabitants of that place, and was in charge of administering the sacraments, during the time previous to the building of their church. This would determine who the bishop of the territory was, and accordingly, who had the right to consecrate the church in question.

This example serves to show that while at times there may have been some difficulty in the fact of determining which of two or more bishops was the bishop of the place, there was no question that the

[21] *Pontificale Romanum Clementis VIII primum nunc denuo Urbani VIII auctoritate recognitum* (editio tertia, Parisiis, 1683), tit. *De Coemeterii Benedictione*; *Pontificale Romanum Summorum Pontificum iussu editum et a Benedicto XIV Pontifice Maximo recognitum et castigatum* (Mechliniae, 1862), tit. *eodem*; *Pontificale Romanum Summorum Pontificum iussu editum a Benedicto XIV et Leone XIII Pontificibus Maximis recognitum et castigatum*, tit. *eodem*.

[22] Many, *De Locis Sacris*, n. 144: "Minister consecrationis quoad validitatem et liceitatem est idem omnino ac pro consecratione ecclesiae, quia, in usu universali Ecclesiae, aequo gradu ponuntur consecratio ecclesiae et consecratio coemeterii."

[23] Pars Tertia (D. I, *de cons.*).

[24] C. 1, X, *de religiosis domibus*, III, 36.

[25] *Glossa Ordinaria*, ad c. 1, X, *de religiosis domibus*, III, 36, v. "nunc autem."

local bishop had every right by common law to consecrate all the churches, and therefore all the cemeteries, in his territory.[26]

A bishop outside his diocese was not the ordinary minister of the solemn blessing. In the time of St. Gregory of Tours it was found that this prelate went out of his own diocese into the diocese of Poitiers to consecrate ground for burial. It was an emergency, and he was entreated to do so; he therefore presumed the permission of the bishop of Poitiers.[27] It was not that a bishop outside his own territory could not consecrate a church or cemetery validly, but it was illicit for him so to act without being invited at least implicitly by the ordinary of the diocese or the religious superior.[28] The Church has always insisted that the bishop by the very nature of the episcopal office is appointed for his own diocese, and it is his right and duty to care for his flock in everything a bishop can do. When he himself is for some reason incapacitated or prevented, he may invite another bishop to perform what he is unable to do, but the latter should in no way usurp the rights of the bishop of the place.[29]

In the *Decretum* of Gratian there was provision for the severe punishment of a bishop who, without the necessary permission, performed acts of consecration in the diocese of another bishop.[30] Such

[26] Religious superiors were sometimes by a very special apostolic indult given the power of consecrating their own churches, but this was most rare. Cf. Giraldi, *Expositio Iuris Pontificii iuxta Recentiorem Ecclesiae Disciplinam* (3 vols. in 2, Romae, 1829-1830), pars I, sect. 598, Vol. I, 412 (hereafter cited as *Expositio Iuris Pontificii*); Benedictus XIV, *De Synodo Dioecesana Libri Tredecim* (4 vols., Lovanii, 1763), lib. XIII, c. 15, n. 3 (Vol. IV, 47).

[27] Cf. *supra*, pp. 16, 17.

[28] Pope Gelasius II (1118-1119)—c. 26, C. XVI, q. 7; c. 1, X, *de religiosis domibus*, III, 36.

[29] "Loquendo de iure," says Reiffenstuel (*Ius Canonicum Universum* [5 vols. in 7, Parisiis, 1864-1882], lib. III, tit. 40, n. 3 [hereafter cited as Reiffenstuel]), "solus episcopus loci rite consecrare potest ecclesiam. . . . Dicitur rite; quia licet episcopus alterius dioecesis ecclesiam valide consecrare valeat, tamen id rite, seu licite non facit. . . . Quia quamvis non possit episcopus munus consecrandi ecclesiam committere alicui presbytero, poterit tamen idem committere alteri episcopo."

[30] III Council of Arles (455)—c. 28, C. 7, q. 1.

a bishop was to be deprived of the privilege of celebrating Mass for the period of one year. The Council of Trent (1545-1563) for the same violation decreed *ipso iure* a suspension from the exercise of sacred pontifical functions.[31]

The Roman Pontiffs from time to time did make exceptions to the general rule. Pope Honorius IV (1285-1287) in his Constitution *Ex parte vestra* in 1286 ruled for the Friars Minor that, should the bishop of the diocese delay beyond four months to consecrate a church after he had been humbly asked to do so, the superior was empowered to invite an outside bishop for that purpose.[32] John XXII (1316-1334) granted the same privilege to the Carmelites;[33] Boniface IX (1389-1404) to the Dominicans; and other Pontiffs to various other regulars.[34]

In his Constitution *Dum intra,* published in the V General Lateran Council, December 19, 1516,[35] Pope Leo X, extending this privilege to all Regulars, decreed: *"Nec ab alieno Episcopo consecrationem ecclesiae, vel altaris, aut coemeterii benedictionem petere . . . nisi ubi Ordinarius bis, aut ter cum debitis reverentia, et instantia requisitus, sine legitima causa id recusaverit."*

Although certain authors held that the decree of the Council of Trent,[36] which under pain of suspension forbade bishops to consecrate a church in the diocese of another, "cuiusvis privilegi praetextu," without the permission of the latter, was a revocation of the former decree of Leo X, it was generally held by most of the authors after

[31] Sess. VI, *de ref.*, c. 5: "Nulli episcopo liceat, cuiusvis privilegii praetextu, pontificalia in alterius dioecesi exercere, nisi de Ordinarii loci expressa licentia. . . . Si secus factum fuerit, episcopus ab exercitio pontificalium . . . sit ipso iure suspensus." Beyond all doubt and in the opinion of all, the consecration of churches and cemeteries must be enumerated among pontifical functions.—Many, *De Locis Sacris,* n. 12.

[32] Augustinus a Virgine Maria, *Privilegia Omnium Religiosorum* (Lugduni, 1661), p. 60; Sbaralea, *Bullarium Franciscanum* (7 vols., Romae, 1759-1904. Vols. V-VII compiled by C. Eubel.), III, 555, n. 24.

[33] Const. *Merita vestrae,* 1331—*Privilegia Omnium Religiosorum,* p. 186.

[34] Const. *Sacrae Religionis,* 27 apr. 1402—*Privilegia Omnium Religiosorum,* p. 187.

[35] *Fontes,* n. 72.

[36] Sess. VI, *de ref.*, c. 5.

the Council of Trent that the former decree still obtained.[37] These authors maintained that this concession of Leo X was not a privilege, but rather a general law which regulated *in perpetuum* the relations between bishops and regulars. Moulart, however, did not consider the above concession a general law, but rather a privilege. Accordingly he held that it was very doubtful that this privilege survived the decree of the Council of Trent.[38]

2. *The Vicar General*

Because the act of the consecration of a church and of the solemn blessing of a cemetery was an act of episcopal orders in the sense explained above,[39] and not an act depending on jurisdiction, the vicar general, who was the *alter ego* of the bishop in matters of jurisdiction and not of orders, could not consecrate a church or cemetery.[40] And even when the vicar general was himself a bishop, he was not permitted to consecrate a cemetery nor commission another bishop to perform the act of consecration without first receiving from the ordinary of the place the power so to act.[41]

3. *The Vicar Capitular or Administrator*

When the episcopal see was vacant, the vicar capitular or administrator, though he never had power by reason of his office to consecrate a church or cemetery, could nevertheless call in any bishop of the same rite,[42] to consecrate not only ground for the burial of the

[37] Barbosa, *Iuris Ecclesiastici Universi Libri Tres* (Lugduni, 1660), lib. II, c. 2, n. 33 (hereafter cited as *Iuris Ecclesiastici Universi*); Schmalzgrueber, *Ius Ecclesiasticum Universum* (5 vols. in 12, Romae, 1843-1845), lib. III, tit. 40, n. 14 (hereafter cited as Schmalzgrueber); Giraldi, *Expositio Iuris Pontificii,* pars I, sect. 598 (Vol. I, 412-413).

[38] *De Sepultura et Coemeteriis,* p. 106.

[39] P. 28. Cf. also *infra,* p. 34.

[40] Giraldi, *Expositio Iuris Pontificii,* pars I, sect. 598 (Vol. I, 412); Moulart, *De Sepultura et Coemeteriis,* pp. 102-103; Many, *De Locis Sacris,* nn. 144, 12.

[41] Giraldi, *loc. cit.*; Benedictus XIV, *De Synodo Dioecesana,* lib. II, c. 7, n. 2; Moulart, *op. cit.,* p. 103.

[42] The Holy Office, asked whether a Coptic Catholic bishop could consecrate churches of the Latin rite, answered: "Non expedire."—16 iun. 1831—*Fontes,* n. 870.

faithful, but churches as well.[43] Should, however, the vicar capitular or administrator of a vacant see be a bishop, he could validly and licitly consecrate churches and cemeteries of the diocese, and then there was no need of calling in another bishop for such functions of consecration.[44]

4. *The Regular Superior*

By the common law of the Church all houses, churches and territory of religious were subject to the jurisdiction of the bishop of the place unless proof to the contrary obtained in some excepted cases.[45] All churches and cemeteries of religious had, therefore, to be consecrated, if they were to be consecrated at all, by the bishop of the place in which they were located.[46] While this was the general rule, it sometimes happened that religious superiors requested and obtained the necessary delegation to consecrate or solemnly bless their own cemeteries. The delegation always came from the Roman Pontiff. This concession was very rarely granted, and only under very special circumstances. Pope Paul III, for example, on December 18, 1542,[47] granted to the Abbot Louis of a monastery in Einsiedeln, Switzerland, and to those who followed him as abbot of the same monastery, the faculty of consecrating churches, oratories and cemeteries as long as certain conditions of heresy persisted. Pope Pius IV, twenty years later in 1562, confirmed the former faculty conceded to this same monastery and laid down the same conditions.[48]

[43] Moulart, *De Sepultura et Coemeteriis,* p. 103.

[44] Many, *De Locis Sacris,* n. 12.

[45] V Council of Arles (554), c. 2—c. 17, C. XVIII, q. 2; I Council of Orleans (511), c. 19—c. 10, C. XVI, q. 7; cc. 6, 7, X, *de religiosis domibus,* III, 36.

[46] Reiffenstuel, lib. III, tit. 36, n. 4; tit. 40, n. 9; Schmalzgrueber, lib. III, tit. 36, n. 13.

[47] Cf. Benedictus XIV, *De Synodo Dioecesana,* lib. XIII, c. 15, n. 3.

[48] "Quod ipse Ludovicus, et pro tempore existens Abbas Monasterii huiusmodi, durantibus dictis haeresibus, praefatum Monasterium, et quaecumque ad illud pertinentia, ecclesias, oratoria, coemeteria, et loca hactenus consecrata, et benedicta, quovis modo pro tempore polluta, reconciliare, et nondum consecrata, et benedicta, necnon calices, patenas, libros, vestimenta et alia mobilia ac etiam tabernacula custodiae Eucharistiae consecrare et benedicere."—Cf. Benedictus XIV, *De Synodo Dioecesana,* lib. XIII, c. 15, n. 3.

Benedict XIV (1740-1758) in his *De Synodo Dioecesana*[49] and in his letter *Ex tuis precibus*,[50] explained the general law on consecration, and mentioned a few exceptions to the general rule, when, namely, non-bishops were allowed to consecrate churches and cemeteries. The few instances of the granting of this privilege serve to show the reluctance of the Roman Pontiffs to allocate this power, which was proper only to those who were endowed with episcopal orders, to others than the inherently authorized ministers of consecration. The granted privilege was not of a communicable character.[51] In cases wherein the local ordinary refused repeatedly for no sufficient reason to consecrate a cemetery, the Roman Pontiffs granted regular superiors the faculty of inviting an outside bishop to perform the rite.[52]

5. *The Simple Priest*

Because it was always the bishop who consecrated churches and cemeteries from the time of the first real evidence of the consecration of sacred places, it does not necessarily follow that episcopal orders in the minister were absolutely indispensable to the validity of the act of consecration. A priest with the proper delegation could consecrate a church or cemetery, the reason being that it was not strictly an act belonging so exclusively to episcopal orders that it could not be given to those who were not bishops. For if it were, then such a consecration would be entirely beyond the power of any simple priest ever to perform. Yet priests have received the power to consecrate churches and cemeteries from the Roman Pontiff.[53]

Some authors have made the misleading assertion that the act of consecrating a church or cemetery was an act which a bishop alone, because of his power of orders, could perform; and then in the next sentence they have admitted that with delegation from the Roman

[49] *Loc. cit.*

[50] 16 nov. 1748—*Fontes*, n. 393.

[51] Moulart, *De Sepulturis et Coemeteriis*, p. 105.

[52] Cf. *supra*, p. 30.

[53] Benedictus XIV, *De Synodo Dioecesana*, lib. XIII, c. 15, n. 3; ep. *Ex tuis precibus*, 16 nov. 1748, §§ 1, 8-12—*Fontes*, n. 393; const. *Suprema*, 26 apr. 1749, § 1—*Fontes*, n. 397; Giraldi, *Expositio Iuris Pontificii*, pars I, sect. 598 (Vol. I, 415-416).

Pontiff a simple priest could validly and licitly consecrate a church or cemetery. They offered no explanation as to how this was possible. These statements would seem at first sight to be somewhat inconsistent on their part in view of what has been said immediately above, namely, that if the consecration of a sacred place depended on the power of episcopal orders, then a simple priest without the sacred orders of a bishop could not, even though delegated by the Pope himself, perform the rite of consecration. But some explanation is needed, even if most authors do not discuss this apparent contradiction.[54]

When the power of episcopal orders is spoken of, it must be remembered that there are two sources of this power to be distinguished: the one deriving from the divine law, the other from the human law; the former directly from God and intrinsic to the sacred orders of bishops, the latter from the Church and extrinsic to the orders themselves. But as far as the powers of episcopal orders are concerned, no matter from which source they spring, they are proper to the bishop alone. However, though the Supreme Pontiff cannot grant any power which is proper to bishops *e iure divino,* for example the power of ordaining priests, he can and often does confer on a simple priest some power which belongs to a bishop *e iure ecclesiastico.* St. Thomas discussed the question of the power of bishops to confer confirmation and minor orders. He concluded that a simple priest, delegated by the Roman Pontiff, could validly and licitly administer confirmation and minor orders.[55] Pope Benedict XIV (1740-1758) enumerated the privilege of consecrating a church among those of which St. Thomas spoke as a power that could be extended to a priest.[56] And Moulart added the consecration or solemn blessing of a cemetery to this list.[57]

[54] Reiffenstuel treats this question to some extent in lib. III, tit. 40, n. 26. Many in *De Locis Sacris,* n. 11, alludes to it. Benedict XIV has a fine discussion of this matter: ep. *Ex tuis precibus,* 16 nov. 1748, §§ 9, 1, 8—*Fontes,* n. 393.

[55] *Praeclarissima Commentaria in Quatuor Libros Sententiarum Petri Lombardi* (2 vols., Parisiis, 1659), lib. IV, dist. 7, quaest. 3, art. 1, quaestiunc. 3.

[56] Ep. *Ex tuis precibus,* 16 nov. 1748, § 9—*Fontes,* n. 393. This papal letter was sent to Abbot Engelbert of the Monastery of Kempten in Bavaria.

[57] *De Sepultura et Coemeteriis,* p. 103.

It logically followed then that the Roman Pontiff, since he alone had the plentitude of power to say when and in what circumstances and under what conditions the powers given to a bishop by ecclesiastical law might be exercised by a priest, was the only one who could grant to a priest, otherwise lacking episcopal powers, the privilege of consecrating a cemetery.[58] The bishop, although he had the power himself, could not give to a priest the power of consecrating a church or cemetery: "quia licet episcopus committere valeat quae iurisdictionis existunt, quae ordinis tamen episcopalis sunt, non potest inferioris gradus clericis demandare." [59] The II Council of Seville (619) made it a law that all further delegation of a priest to consecrate a church solely on the authority of the bishop be prohibited as a practice contrary to the traditional ecclesiastical discipline.[60] That bishops cannot delegate a simple priest to consecrate a church or cemetery, but that this is within the power of the Roman Pontiffs alone all canonists are agreed.[61]

ARTICLE III. THE MINISTER OF THE SIMPLE BLESSING

The ordinary minister in the rite of blessing a new cemetery was a priest delegated by the bishop.[62] Therefore, even if he would have acted illicitly, a priest had the power by reason of his sacerdotal orders to bless a cemetery even without the delegation of the bishop of the place.[63]

In his Constitution *Religionis suadet* of February 3, 1514,[64] Leo X

[58] Benedictus XIV, *De Synodo Dioecesana*, lib. XIII, c. 15, n. 2; Fagnanus, *Commentaria in Quinque Libros Decretalium* (4 vols., Venetiis, 1696-1697), lib. III, c. 9, n. 5 (hereafter to be cited as *Commentaria*).

[59] Gregory IX (1227-1241)—c. 9, X, *de consecratione ecclesiae*, III, 40.

[60] C. 7—Hardouin, III, 560.

[61] Benedictus XIV, ep. *Ex tuis precibus*, 16 nov. 1748, § 2—*Fontes*, n. 393.

[62] S. R. C., *Cameracen.*, 9 febr. 1608, ad 2—*Fontes*, n. 5235; *Rituale Romanum Pauli V*, tit. *Ritus Benedicendi Novum Coemeterium per Sacerdotem ab Episcopo Delegatum*.

[63] Petra, *Commentaria in Constitutiones Apostolicas* (5 vols. in 2, Venetiis, 1729), III, const. VI Urbani IV (*Ecclesia*), n. 21 (hereafter cited as *Commentaria*).

[64] *Privilegia Omnium Religiosorum*, pp. 63-64.

granted to the Order of Friars Minor the privilege of blessing their churches, cemeteries and oratories without seeking the permission of the bishop of the place, a privilege which by communication has been extended to all Regulars.[65]

The use of the expression *"solemni benedictione"* in the grant of Leo X has given rise to much discussion among authors. Does the "solemn blessing" mentioned here mean consecration? [66] It has already been pointed out that general permission to Regulars, allowing them without further delegation from the Roman Pontiff and without any permission of the bishop of the place to consecrate their churches and cemeteries, would be entirely contrary to the policy of the Church in this matter. In fact, Benedict XIV (1740-1758) [67] made it quite plain that the delegation to consecrate sacred places was indeed granted by the Roman Pontiff to regular superiors and to simple priests, but it was done only rarely and for very special reasons, and hardly ever for more than one occasion at a time. Furthermore, Leo X not three years after he had issued the constitution granting the privilege in question, decreed in the V Lateran Council in the year 1516 that regulars were not to call in an outside bishop to consecrate church, altar or cemetery, unless the bishop of the place had himself neglected to take care of the consecration.[68] This would hardly have been necessary if these regulars had been in possession of the privilege of consecrating their churches and cemeteries. Authors are generally agreed that this "solemn blessing" in the text of Leo X cannot be taken to mean consecration, but must be understood simply in the sense of blessing.

[65] " . . . generalibus, provincialibus, ac custodibus et guardianis Fratrum Minorum pro tempore existentibus, ut omnia et singula eorum Ordinis, ecclesias, coemeteria, capitula et oratoria, ubicumque existentia, receptas et recepta, recipiendas et recipienda, ac paramenta et ornamenta ac alia quaecumque ad divinum cultum et usum eorum necessaria, in quibus chrisma non intervenit, pro eorum usu tantum, solemni benedictione, ac etiam per vicarium seu guardianos, aut alios ad hoc in capitulis generalibus provide deputandos, benedicere . . . libere et licite valeant."—*Privilegia Omnium Religiosorum, loc. cit.*

[66] Petra, *ibid.*, nn. 15-19; Ferraris, *Bibliotheca*, v. *"ecclesia,"* art. 4, n. 8; Moulart, *De Sepultura et Coemeteriis*, pp. 103-104.

[67] Ep. *Ex tuis precibus*, 16 nov. 1748, esp. §§ 14-19—*Fontes*, n. 393.

[68] Const. *Dum intra*, 19 dec. 1516, n. 12—*Fontes*, n. 72.

ARTICLE IV. THE PROOF OF THE BLESSING

Blessing was not to be presumed; it was a fact which had to be proved. The proof could be in writing,[69] or by means of witnesses. Even as early as the 5th century Pope St. Leo the Great stated that if others were lacking, one reliable witness who was above suspicion could be considered sufficient in the proof of the reception of baptism,[70] and this doctrine has been made applicable with reference to the question of the proof of the blessing conferred on a church.[71] The best witness, of course, was one who was an eye-witness to the blessing itself; next best, the one who knew it from a well-informed and altogether trustworthy source, from one's father, uncle, grandfather, etc.; and even, according to some, a witness who had it from heresay that the blessing had taken place could furnish sufficient proof when other proofs were lacking.[72]

There were, however, two presumptions that carried the weight of adequate proof. If a church was certainly known to have been consecrated, then the adjoining cemetery was presumed to be blessed, even though cemeteries were wont to be blessed separately from churches.[73] And again, a place where the bodies of the faithful had been buried with ecclesiastical permission, that is, with the acquiescence of the bishop, and which by all was thought to be an ecclesiastical cemetery, was presumed to be a place not only destined for the burial of the faithful departed but also blessed by the bishop.[74]

ARTICLE V. THE REPETITION OF THE BLESSING

The general principle with regard to the consecration of a church, and therefore of a cemetery, was that the consecration should never be repeated.[75] However, since there was the other principle that

[69] Glossa ordinaria ad c. 16, D. I, *de cons.*, v. "scriptura."

[70] *Epistola CLXVI ad Leonem—MPL,* LIV, 1193; C. 112, D. IV, *de cons.*

[71] Glossa ordinaria ad c. 16, D. I, *de cons.*, v. "nec certi testes."

[72] Schmalzgrueber, lib. III, tit. 40, n. 22.

[73] Barbosa, *Iuris Ecclesiastici Universi,* lib. II, c. 9, n. 8.

[74] Barbosa, *Collectanea Doctorum,* lib. III, tit. 40, cap. 7, n. 6.

[75] C. 20, D. I, *de cons.*; Glossa ordinaria ad c. 6, X, *de consecratione ecclesiae vel altaris,* III, 40, v. "parietibus."

consecration was never to be presumed but had to be proved, it often happened, in days when records were not kept as in the present day, that a consecration or blessing could not be proved. In that case the consecration was to be repeated [76] absolutely.[77]

[76] C. 16, D. I, *de cons.*: "De ecclesiarum consecrationibus quoties dubitatur, et nec certa scriptura, nec testes existunt, a quibus consecratio sciatur, absque ulla dubitatione scitote eas esse sacrandas; nec talis trepidatio facit iterationem, quoniam non monstratur esse iteratum, quod nescitur factum." This canon comes originally from St. Gregory the Great, *Epistolarum Liber XIV, epistola XVII* [ad Felicem]—*MPL,* LXXVII, 1325-1326. Cf. also: c. 18, D. I, *de cons.*

[77] Benedictus XIV, ep. *Iam inde,* 12 maii 1756, nn. 2-5—*Fontes,* n. 440. In the Council of Rome in 1725 (tit. 25, cap. 3—*Acta et Decreta Sacrorum Conciliorum Recentiorum* [*Collectio Lacensis*], [7 vols., Friburgi Brisgoviae, 1870-1890], I, 386), it was decreed that any church about whose consecration there was a doubt which could not be removed should be consecrated *absolutely.* Cf. Many, *De Locis Sacris,* n. 29.

CHAPTER IV

THE ECCLESIASTICAL IMMUNITY OF CEMETERIES

A PLACE that had been set aside for the burial of the faithful had a destiny different from that of other places. It was little by little to be peopled with the human remains which today were nothing, but which tomorrow would be partakers with the soul in the exquisite privilege of seeing God face to face.[1] And not only was it because of the purpose it served, but also because of its special dedication to God by liturgical blessing, that a cemetery was taken out of the category of merely profane places, and was considered as a place specially deserving the respect and reverence of civil as well as ecclesiastical authorities. The ground itself, while before it was no different from the ground touching its four boundaries, had by a solemn or simple blessing become transformed from something that was quite ordinary to something that was religious and sacred.

Because of their sacred character, cemeteries, like churches and other sacred places, came to enjoy immunities from civil authority and civil obligations, as well as the right to freedom from the commission of all acts that were out of harmony with the reverence so necessarily a part of such a sacred place. Perhaps the most frequently mentioned single immunity that cemeteries enjoyed was that of the right of asylum (*ius asyli*). Churches enjoyed ecclesiastical immunity from the fourth century, but specific inclusion of cemeteries in this privilege is rarely to be found in Church legislation until the twelfth century.[2]

ARTICLE I. IMMUNITY FROM PROFANE AND UNBECOMING ACTS

In the Decretals of Gregory IX (1227-1241) and in the *Liber Sextus* of Boniface VIII (1294-1303) there is a whole title devoted to the immunity of church and cemetery. In this part, as in so many others in the Decretals, what is said of churches is said also for

[1] I Cor. xiii, 12.

[2] C. Th. (9, 45) 4; C. (1, 12) 3. As to the antiquity of the ecclesiastical immunity of churches, cf. Devoti, *Institutionum Canonicarum Libri IV*, II, 340-341; Bargilliat, *Praelectiones Iuris Canonici*, n. 1328; Wernz, *Ius Decretalium*, III, n. 472; Coronata, *De Locis et Temporibus Sacris*, n. 42.

cemeteries, though the latter is often not expressed in an explicit way.[3]

Named principally among the immunities was the right to freedom from worldly business transactions, and from trials of civil and criminal cases.[4] When Our Divine Lord, so justly provoked at the tiresome worldliness of men, drove the buyers and the sellers, and their sheep and oxen as well, out of the Temple in Jerusalem, exclaiming that His house was a house of prayer and not a den of thieves,[5] He was but repeating what His Father had long ago established, namely, that all places consecrated or dedicated to God were to be treated with the most profound reverence.[6] They were to be entirely free and immune from the mercenary businesses of men, however fitting these activities might be in another place.

The cemetery as well as the church in the middle ages had become a significant place for people to gather. People came to these places to pray. Men with more concern for money in their purse than grace in their heart took advantage of these occasions to display and sell their wares, until the Church had to forbid them by law from exercising such acts. The church or cemetery[7] was certainly not the place for business transactions or for the noisy bickering and bargaining that properly belonged to the market place.[8]

[3] Glossa ordinaria ad c. 5, X, *de immunitate ecclesiarum, coemeterii, et rerum ad eas pertinentium,* III, 49, v. "coemeteriis;" Reiffenstuel (lib. III, tit. 40, n. 11): "Coemeteria iisdem gaudent privilegiis, quibus ecclesia." Cf. also: Barbosa, *Iuris Ecclesiastici Universi,* lib. II, c. 3, n. 63.

[4] "Cessent in ecclesiis earumque coemeteriis," ordered Gregory X in c. 25 of the II General Council of Lyons (1274)—Hardouin VII, 717; "negationes et praecipue nundinarum ac fori cuiusque tumultus: omnis in eis saecularium iudiciorum strepitus conquiescat, nulla inibi causa per laicos criminalis maxime agitetur."—C. 2, *de immunitate ecclesiarum,* III, 23, in VI°.

[5] John ii, 14-16; Matt. xxi, 13.

[6] III Kings ix, 3; Isaias lvi, 7; Gen. xxviii, 17; Exod. iii, 5.

[7] Glossa ordinaria ad c. 2, *de immunitate ecclesiarum,* III, 23, in VI°, v. "coemeteriis."

[8] The gloss at the word "processus" in c. 2, *de immunitate ecclesiarum,* III, 23, in VI°, points out that such contracts of sale or of business were indeed valid but nonetheless unlawful and unbecoming in a sacred place. In the 17th century the Sacred Congregation of the Council (*Atrebaten.,* 27 maii 1623) refused to allow any carrying-on of business or court trials in a church or cemetery.—*Fontes,* n. 2440.

The sale of articles of a religious nature for the sake of increasing piety among the faithful was not forbidden, for this practice was *sine verborum strepitu et contentione pretii,* and did not interfere with the devotion of the faithful.[9]

Also prohibited were public meetings of a kind that was concerned primarily with temporal and not spiritual matters; as were political addresses and discussions, and any and all activities that distracted the faithful in their prayer or detracted from the reverence and the peace that should be the atmosphere of a holy place.[10]

Trials, both civil and criminal, were necessary, it is true, but the church or the cemetery was not the place where such tribunals should be set up.[11] Gregory X (1271-1276) did not stop at a condemnation of such trials, but added to his prohibition the penalty of nullity. Both the acts and the sentence of these trials he declared to be null and void.[12] Lucius III (1181-1185) forbade secular judges to conduct criminal trials in churches or cemeteries under pain of excommunication.[13]

[9] Schmalzgrueber, lib. III, tit. 40, no. 82.

[10] "Nullus in locis eisdem, in quibus cum pace ac quiete vota convenit celebrari, seditionem excitet, conclamationem moveat impetumve committat. Cessent in locis illis universitatum et societatum quarumlibet concilia, conciones et publica parlamenta. Cessent vana et multo fortius foeda et profana colloquia. Cessent confabulationes quaelibet. Sint postremo quaecumque alia, quae divinum possunt turbare officium, aut oculos divinae maiestatis offendere, ab ipsis prorsus extranea . . ."—C. 2, *de immunitate ecclesiarum,* III, 23, in VI°.

[11] "Omnis in eis ecclesiis earumque coemeteriis saecularium iudiciorum strepitus conquiescat, nulla inibi causa per laicos criminalis maxime agitetur."—c. 2, *de immunitate ecclesiarum,* III, 23, in VI°.

[12] "Processus iudicum saecularium, ac specialiter prolatae sententiae in eisdem locis omni careant roboris firmitate."—C. 2, *de immunitate ecclesiarum,* III, 23, in VI°.

[13] "Saeculares iudices causas, ubi de sanguinis effusione, et corporali poena agitur, in ecclesiis vel coemeteriis agitare sub interminatione anathematis prohibemus."—C. 5, X, *de immunitate ecclesiarum et coemeterii et rerum ad eas pertinentium,* III, 49. According to the common teaching this excommunication was not a *latae* but a *ferendae sententiae* penalty.—Gloss s. v. "anathematis." Councils also decreed this excommunication. See, for example, the Council of London (1175), c. 6—Mansi, XXII, 149.

The Council of Trent (1545-1563), realizing that earthly princes were ignoring many of the immunities of the Church, repeated all the immunities and ordered them to be observed by all, especially by civil magistrates.[14] Since the time of the Council of Trent most of the legislation and also the decrees of the Popes and the Roman Congregations on ecclesiastical immunities have centered around one immunity in particular, the *ius asyli.*

Article II. The Right of Asylum

The right of asylum (*ius asyli*) may be defined as the right of security or immunity from forced arrest and from bodily harm befalling those who, when accused of evildoing, take refuge in a church, cemetery or other sacred place.[15] Although many local and plenary Councils had legislated before the twelfth century concerning the right of asylum enjoyed by churches, there was really no mention of cemeteries until the X Ecumenical Council, which was the II General Council of the Lateran, held under Pope Innocent II in the year 1139. We ordain, the Council decreed in canon 15, that on those who take refuge in a church or cemetery no one dare to lay a hand. If this order is violated by any one, let him be excommunicated.[16]

During the first twelve centuries cemeteries indeed had the privilege of the *ius asyli.* But it is very likely that Church law, at least during the greater part of these centuries, did not grant the right of asylum to cemeteries as such. For if cemeteries possessed the right of asylum at all it was only because of their close proximity to

[14] Sess. XXV, *de ref.*, c. 20.

[15] Reiffenstuel defines the right of asylum thus: "Ius, seu immunitas asyli, est ius ecclesiis et sacris, necnon aliis quibusdam locis competens, confugientibus ad ea malefactoribus securitatem praestans ad hoc, quod inde violenter extrahi non possint, nec in vita, nec in membris puniri valeant."—Lib. III, tit. 49, n. 20.

[16] "Praecipimus etiam, ut in eos, qui ad ecclesiam vel coemeterium confugerint, nullus omnino manum mittere audeat. Quod si fecerit, excommunicetur." —Mansi, XXI, 530. Cf. H. J. Shroeder, *Disciplinary Decrees of the General Councils, Text, Translation and Commentary* (London, St. Louis: B. Herder Book Co., 1937), pp. 204-206.

churches which had the privilege. The first cemeteries, no doubt, to enjoy the *ius asyli* were the churchyard cemeteries. Even as early as the fourth century the Emperor Theodosius the Younger (408-450) in his Code (438) interpreted the civil law that granted the right of asylum to churches as including in this immunity not only the church building itself, but also everything between the church and the outer walls: the porches, the bishop's and priests' residences, the gardens and the cemeteries.[17] However, since cemeteries were not always in the vicinity of churches, but existed sometimes at great distances from the churches which they served, there would have been many cemeteries which could not possibly have shared the right of asylum that was afforded to churches and their immediate environs. These cemeteries would not have enjoyed the right of asylum until cemeteries as well as churches were given this privilege. Just when cemeteries as such began to enjoy in their own right the *ius asyli* it is impossible to know. This much is certain, by the twelfth century cemeteries, as far as the law was concerned, were put on an equal basis with churches in regard to the possession of the right of asylum.[18] Both were *loca sacra,* not only because they were deputed for divine worship by authority of the bishop, but also because they received the blessing of the Church. And at this time all *loca sacra* (churches and cemeteries) as well as *loca religiosa* (monasteries, houses of regulars, etc.) enjoyed the right of asylum by Church law.[19] Even cemeteries about whose blessing there was some doubt were considered to possess the *ius asyli,* if it could be established that the bishop of the place knew that the faithful were being buried there,

[17] C. Th. (9, 45) 4. Cf. also Justinian's interpretation in his Code (1, 12) 3. The amended and revised Code of Justinian *(Codex repetitae praelectionis),* which alone has survived, appeared in 534. The initial redaction had appeared in 529.

[18] II General Council of the Lateran (1139), canon 15—Mansi, XXI, 530; Schroeder, *op. cit.,* pp. 204-206. This conciliar law was incorporated in the *Decretum* of Gratian under c. 29, C. XVII, q. 4.

[19] Glossa ordinaria ad c. 5, X, *de immunitate ecclesiarum et coemeterii et rerum ad eas pertinentium,* III, 49, v. "coemeteriis." Cf. also Gregory XIV, const. *Cum alias,* 24 maii 1591, §§ 2-3—*Fontes,* n. 172; Benedictus XIII, const. *Ex quo,* 8 iun. 1725, § 4—*Fontes,* n. 290.

for in that case there was a presumption in favor of the blessing as having been conferred.[20]

The right of asylum, it is easy to see, left the way open to abuses. Criminals would use this privilege for the furtherance of their crimes and for the mitigation of their prosecution by law. Gregory XIV in 1591 listed those criminals who were not to be given the right of asylum: public robbers, murderers, highwaymen, pillagers, those who killed or mutilated others in a church or a cemetery, and those who were guilty of heresy or of crimes against the sovereign power.[21] Pope Benedict XIII (1724-1730), explaining this list of evildoers drawn up by Gregory XIV (1590-1591), defining in clear terms just what each category was meant to embrace, and adding some others of his own, decreed that it should pertain to the bishop to decide whether the criminal had committed a crime which disqualified him from the use of the right of asylum.[22]

Pius IX (1846-1878) put the violation of the *ius asyli* among those delicts to which was attached a *latae sententiae* excommunication reserved to the Roman Pontiff.[23] Notwithstanding the Consti-

[20] Pope Lucius III (1181-1185)—c. 5, X, *de immunitate ecclesiarum et coemeterii et rerum ad eas pertinentium,* III, 49; also c. 10; Barbosa, *Iuris Ecclesiastici Universi,* lib. II, c. 3, n. 63; Fagnanus, *Commentaria,* lib. III, c. 10, n. 1; Schmalzgrueber, lib. III, tit. 49, n. 107.

[21] "Ut laicis, ad ecclesias, locaque sacra, et religiosa praedicta confugientibus, si fuerint publici latrones, viarumque grassatores, qui itinera frequentata, vel publicas stratas obsident, ac viatores ex insidiis aggrediuntur, aut depopulatores agrorum, quive homicidia, et mutilationes membrorum in ipsis ecclesiis, earumve coemetriis committere non verentur, aut qui proditorie proximum suum occiderint, aut assassinii, vel haeresis, aut laesae Maiestatis in personam ipsiusmet Principis rei, immunitas Ecclesiastica non suffragetur."—Const. *Cum alias,* 24 maii 1591, § 3—*Fontes,* n. 172. Cf. Benedictus XIII, const. *Ex quo,* 8 iun. 1725, § 4—*Fontes,* n. 290; Benedictus XIV, const. *Officii Nostri,* 15 mart. 1750, §§ 1-15—*Fontes,* n. 406.

[22] ". . . omnimoda cognitio, atque iudicium de criminibus . . . exceptis, . . . ad episcopos tantum privative quoad omnes alios perpetuo spectet, atque spectare debeat."—Const. *Ex quo,* 8 iun. 1725, § 7—*Fontes,* n. 290.

[23] "Immunitatem asyli ecclesiastici violare iubentes, aut auso temerario violantes . . ."—Const. *Apostolicae Sedis,* 12 oct. 1869, II, n. 5—*Fontes,* n. 552. Cf. S.C.S. Off., instr. *(ad Vic. Ap. Myssurien.),* 1 febr. 1871, n. 1—*Fontes,* n. 1014.

tution of Pius IX, the observance of the right of asylum was disregarded and neglected in many regions. From time to time, in order to preserve at least the substance of this immunity, the Roman Pontiffs made concessions and relaxed the *ius asyli* in some details.[24] At the beginning of the present century the condition of the *ius asyli* was such that it was practically a non-existent immunity: it still existed as a Church law both for churches and cemeteries, but it was ignored by the civil authorities for whom it was intended. And without civil co-operation this immunity availed little.[25]

[24] Bargilliat, *Praelectiones Iuris Canonici,* n. 1284.

[25] Cf. Wernz, *Ius Decretalium,* III, nn. 472, 448. Cf. also S. C. S. Off. *(Ratisbonen.),* 22 dec. 1880, ad IV—*Fontes,* n. 1068.

CHAPTER V

THE VIOLATION, THE RECONCILIATION AND THE INTERDICT OF CEMETERIES

ARTICLE I. THE VIOLATION OF CEMETERIES

THE violation or *pollutio* of a cemetery was the suspension of some of the effects of consecration or blessing which automatically followed the perpetration in the cemetery of certain base acts branded as such by ecclesiastical law. The main effect of consecration or blessing remained: the cemetery did not lose its sacred character.[1] In a violated cemetery, however, the faithful were not to be buried until the cemetery was properly purged or reconciled.[2]

The following were the ways by which a cemetery would be violated:

1. *The violation of a contiguous church.* When a church had been violated, then a cemetery which adjoined the church was also violated.[3] Authors were agreed that the *coemeterium contiguum* was one which was in direct contact with the walls of the church.[4] A cemetery which was not contiguous to the violated church, but remote

[1] Moulart, *De Sepultura et Coemeteriis*, p. 118.

[2] C. 1, *de consecratione ecclesiae*, III, 21, in VI°.

[3] Boniface VIII, in c. 1, *de consecratione ecclesiae*, III, 21, in VI°, stated: "Si ecclesiam pollui . . . contingat: ipsius coemeterium, si contiguum sit eidem, censetur esse pollutum. Unde, antequam reconciliatum fuerit, non debet in eo aliquis sepeliri; secus, si remotum fuerit ab eadem. Non sic quoque in casu converso sentimus, ut videlicet polluto coemeterio, quamvis ecclesiae contiguo, debeat ecclesia reputari polluta, ne minus dignum maius, aut accessorium principale ad se trahere videatur. Non unum, sed plura coemeteria esse noscuntur, quae, quamvis sibi cohaerentia, pariete tamen medio seiunguntur. Ideoque, violato eorum altero, alterum, licet de uno ad aliud per portam intermediam habeatur accessus, non propter hoc reputabitur violatum."

[4] Glossa ordinaria ad c. 1, *de consecratione ecclesiae*, III, 21 in VI°, v. "contiguum;" Moulart, *De Sepultura et Coemeteriis*, p. 119; Bargilliat, *Praelectiones Iuris Canonici*, n. 1330; Wernz, *Ius Decretalium*, III, n. 471; Many, *De Locis Sacris*, n. 147.

from it, was not violated, even though it was intimately connected with that church in every other but in a physical way. A church, however, was immune from the violation of even a contiguous cemetery. The reason was: *quia coemeterium est accessorium ecclesiae, et accessorium sequitur principale, non principale accessorium.*[5]

Where there were two cemeteries adjoining each other, separated by a partition or wall, the violation of one did not involve the violation of the other, even though the two were joined by a gate.[6] The wall established a true separation, making them two distinct cemeteries.[7]

Schmalzgrueber (1663-1735) asked the question: what if an act which is capable of violating a cemetery took place at the gate between the two cemeteries? [8] He answered, as did Pirhing (1606-1679) [9] before him, that if the gate was closer to one than the other, it was the closer cemetery that was violated, and not the other. Should the gate be mathematically equidistant from both, the cemetery for which the wall was built and the gate made was the one which underwent the *pollutio*. When there was doubt as to which cemetery was originally meant to be served by the wall and the gate, both were to be considered violated. This serves to give us the mind of the Church, which did not want to multiply any more than was necessary situations that were odious: *Odia restringi et favores convenit ampliari.*[10]

It has been the common teaching of the decretalists [11] and all

[5] Glossa ordinaria ad c. 1, *de consecratione ecclesiae,* III, 21, in VI°, v. "ecclesiam;" and Reg. 42, R. J. in VI°: "Accessorium naturam sequi congruit principalis."

[6] C. 1, *de consecratione ecclesiae,* III, 21, in VI°.

[7] Barbosa, *Iuris Ecclesiastici Universi,* lib. II, c. 9, n. 10; Pirhing, *Ius Canonicum Nova Methodo Explicatum* (5 vols. in 4, Dilingae, 1674-1678), lib. III, tit. 40, n. 33 (hereafter cited as Pirhing); Schmalzgrueber, lib. III, tit. 40, n. 70.

[8] Lib. III, tit. 40, n. 71.

[9] Lib. III, tit. 40, n. 34.

[10] Reg. 15, R. J. in VI°.

[11] Barbosa, *Iuris Ecclesiastici Universi,* lib. II, c. 9, nn. 9, 13; Fagnanus, *Commentaria,* lib. III, c. 9, nn. 21, 22; Pirhing, lib. III, tit. 40, n. 31; Reiffenstuel, lib. III, tit. 40, n. 29; et al.

other canonists after them [12] that a cemetery was violated by the same acts which effected the violation of a church.[13] They based their argument on a deduction from a gloss found in the Decretals of Gregory IX,[14] and also on the above quoted passage from the *Liber Sextus* of Boniface VIII.[15] In the *Liber Sextus* it was provided, as already noted, that if an act were performed that was sufficient to violate a church, the adjoining cemetery was without any additional cause also violated. In the decretals of Gregory IX the gloss states that, in the instance there mentioned, the cemetery did not need a new blessing but a reconciliation, just as would be necessary for a church in the same circumstances.

2. *Homicide.*[16] By the term "homicide" was meant any willful, sinful taking of human life, whether it be another's life or one's own. The method used, even though there was no shedding of blood, did not matter from the point of view of the violation.

The homicide was required to fulfill three conditions: it must have been willful or voluntary, unjust or sinful (*iniuriosum*), and have taken place in the cemetery. It was willful if directly intended, for example, if one attacked or mortally wounded another according to a plan,[17] or if one deliberately took his own life. The taking of life would not have been deliberate if death occurred accidentally, or in self-defense. Should an animal, or one who had not the full use of his faculties, as for example a maniac, or one who was manifestly

[12] Cf. Moulart, *De Sepultura et Coemeteriis*, p. 118.

[13] Occult crimes did not violate a church or a cemetery. The acts must have been in some way public and notorious in fact. The consecration or blessing were public acts which could be violated only by public acts. Cf. gloss, v. "pollui" ad c. 1, *de consecratione ecclesiae*, III, 21, in VI°.

[14] Glossa ordinaria ad c. 7, X, *de consecratione ecclesiae*, III, 40, v. "consuluisti."

[15] C. 1, *de consecratione ecclesiae*, III, 21, in VI°. See p. 46 for text.

[16] C. 19, D. I, *de cons.*

[17] Schmalzgrueber (lib. III, tit. 40, n. 79), reflecting the commonly accepted opinion, said that death did not have to take place in the cemetery to cause the violation of the cemetery. It was enough that the victim died as a result of an injury received in the cemetery. Should something else have caused his death, the cemetery then would not have been violated.

under the influence of liquor or drugs, have caused a person's death, the condition of willfulness would not have been present.[18]

The homicide had to be *iniuriosum,* either to the person or to the place. It was *iniuriosum personae* when the person was unjustly attacked, that is, when he did not deserve the wound that caused his death. It was not injurious to the person if he was an unjust aggressor. The homicide was *iniuriosum loco* when the taking of life was justified, but, since it took place in the church or cemetery, was considered as offending the reverence due the sacred place. If a man was found guilty of capital punishment and duly sentenced to death, his death was then entirely warranted, and not *iniuriosum personae,* but it could not take place in a cemetery without the consequent violation of that cemetery, because such a death was injurious to the sacredness of the place.[19]

Death or the mortal wound must have been inflicted within the confines of the cemetery. If leading to the cemetery there was a roadway or an entrance which was not included in the blessing, or if there was any part that was not sacred ground, then homicide occurring in one of these places did not cause the violation of the cemetery. The killing of a man who was inside the cemetery by another who was outside violated the cemetery; on the other hand, the homicide of one outside the cemetery by one who was actually within the confines of the cemetery did not violate the cemetery.[20] The latter case would have been unchanged as far as the violation of the sacred place was concerned even if the man, mortally wounded, would have dragged himself into the cemetery and then died there.[21]

3. *Considerable Shedding of Blood.* This specific cause of the *pollutio coemeteriorum* was different from the foregoing, which required the unjust taking of human life with or without the shedding of blood. The decretals speak of a copious flow of blood from a

[18] Barbosa, *Collectanea Doctorum,* lib. III, tit. 40, c. 4, nn. 3-4; Reiffenstuel, lib. III, 40, n. 19; Engel, *Collegium Universi Iuris Canonici* (ed. nona, cui adiectae sunt annotationes Caspari Barthel, 3 vols., Beneventi, 1760), lib. III, tit. 40, n. 15. Hereafter cited as Engel.

[19] C. 2, *de immunitate ecclesiae,* III, 23, in VI°.

[20] Engel, lib. III, tit. 40, n. 18.

[21] Reiffenstuel, lib. III. tit. 40, n. 19; Schmalzgrueber, lib. III, tit. 40, n. 78.

wound which did not necessarily cause death.[22] The expression which they used, *"effusio sanguinis,"* must be interpreted to mean not a moderate bleeding from a wound, but a bleeding in quantities as from a severed artery or vein.[23]

The wound involving such bleeding was required to have been inflicted willfully and with grave culpability on the part of the aggressor. Persons, therefore, who accidentally wounded another, or who had not the full possession of their faculties, did not cause the violation of a cemetery even though they inflicted a wound which bled severely.[24]

Furthermore, the *effusio sanguinis* must have taken place in the cemetery. An injury which was sustained in the cemetery but which did not bleed profusely until the victim was removed from the cemetery did not cause violation. Should one have received a wound outside the cemetery and have taken refuge in a blessed cemetery, and there suffered a serious bleeding, there would have been no violation according to Pirhing (1609-1679),[25] Reiffenstuel (1641-1703),[26] Giraldi (1692-1775),[27] and others.

4. *Seminis Humani Effusio.* Again, what was said in the preceding division about *effusio* applies in a relative manner here. Therefore, a cemetery was not violated when merely a *distillatio* took place. *"Humani seminis:"* hence a *menstruatio feminae* within the precincts of a cemetery did not cause its violation. The expression used in the decretals is all-embracing: *"seminis humani effusio."* This included all acts involving an *effusio seminis:* bestiality, consummated sodomy whether properly or only improperly so called, self-pollution, adultery, fornication, and also the otherwise lawful carnal

[22] C. 10, X, *de consecratione ecclesiae,* III, 40; c. 1, *de consecratione ecclesiae,* III, 21, in VI°.

[23] Glossa ordinaria ad c. 1, *de consecratione ecclesiae,* III, 21, in VI°, v. "contiguum."

[24] Council of Cologne (1536), pars 9, c. 17—Mansi, XXXII, 1276; Gonzales-Tellez, *Commentaria Perpetua in Singulos Textus Quinque Librorum Decretalium Gregorii IX* (5 vols. in 4, Venetiis, 1699), lib. III, tit. 40, c. 7, n. 6 (hereafter cited as *Commentaria*).

[25] Lib. III, tit. 40, n. 11.

[26] Lib. III, tit. 40, n. 18.

[27] *Expositio Iuris Pontificii,* pars I, sect. 603 (Vol. I, 428-429).

congress between spouses.[28] These acts of course must have taken place in the sacred precincts of a blessed cemetery.

The *effusio,* to effect a violation, had to be voluntary and gravely sinful. Although conjugal congress under other circumstances of place would not have been sinful, yet in a sacred place it was as a general rule sinful and gravely wrong. However, authors recognized the possibility of an exception to this general rule. Reiffenstuel maintained that it was the common teaching of authors that, for example in time of war when homeless people were put up in a church, should married people, in order not to fall a prey to a seriously molesting temptation of sinful incontinence, have engaged in the mutual exchange of their lawfully possessed marital right, then the church would not have been violated through the exercise of such an act.[29] The same principle was applied for any parallel case occurring within the precincts of a blessed cemetery.[30]

5. *The Burial of the Unbaptized: Infidels and Pagans.* The burial of infidel or pagan adults certainly caused the violation of a church,[31] and for the same reason the violation of a cemetery.[32] However, this rule was not extended to include all unbaptized persons. Most of the authors, if understood properly from what they said and left unsaid, can be interpreted as favoring the stand that the burial of catechumens who were about to receive Baptism did not violate the church or cemetery in which they were buried.[33]

The burial of unbaptized infants of infidel parents violated the sacred place where they were laid to rest. But the burial in consecrated or blessed ground of unbaptized fetuses and of infants of baptized parents presented a matter on which the authors were divided in their opinion. They did agree on one point: if the fetus died within the womb of the deceased mother and was not extracted but buried

[28] Engel, lib. III, tit. 40, n. 20.

[29] Lib. III, tit. 40, n. 20.

[30] Moulart, *De Sepultura et Coemeteriis,* pp. 123-124.

[31] Theodorus (690), *Poenitentiale,* c. 1—*MPL,* XCIX, 927; Burchardus, *Libri XX Decretorum,* lib. III, cc. 13, 38—*MPL,* CXL, 676, 679; cc. 27, 28, D. I, *de cons.*

[32] Many, *De Locis Sacris,* n. 147; Wernz, *Ius Decretalium,* III, n. 471, note 159.

[33] Cf. Moulart, *De Sepultura et Coemeteriis,* p. 125.

with her in sacred ground, then the place of burial did not suffer violation. Their reason was that, as far as the burial was concerned, the fetus was not considered as a person apart from the mother.

Reiffenstuel (+1703) [34] and more than twenty others named by Ferraris (+ca. 1760) [35] maintained that infants who died unbaptized were to be included among the infidels and pagans in the matter of burial. Their burial, therefore, in blessed ground caused its violation. Engel (ca. 1634-1674).[36]

Schmalzgrueber (1663-1735) [37] and later authors held this opinion. But Moulart (1832-1904),[38] Wernz (1842-1914),[39] Many (+1922) [40] and others inclined toward the more lenient and perhaps not less tenable view. They held that the unbaptized children of infidels and pagans were to be included in the same category as their parents, because either of themselves or through their parents they detested or opposed the Christian faith. But this was not true of the children of believing parents, for such, if they were not as yet baptized, were admittedly destined by the will of their parents to be baptized. Death, however, had intervened, and thus baptism had become impossible. Therefore these latter were not to be considered included in the canons referring to infidels and pagans, especially when there was question of a *res odiosa*.[41]

[34] Lib. III, tit. 40, n. 21.

[35] Cf. *Bibliotheca*, v. "ecclesia," art. 4, n. 52.

[36] Lib. III, tit. 40, n. 13.

[37] Lib. III, tit. 40, n. 74.

[38] *De Sepultura et Coemeteriis*, pp. 127-128.

[39] *Ius Decretalium*, III, n. 471, note 159.

[40] *De Locis Sacris*, n. 34.

[41] The *Rituale Romanum Pauli V* (tit. *De Sacramento Baptismi rite Administrando—De Baptizandis Parvulis*) and the later editions of the Ritual stated that infants who were baptized *in utero matris* and then were delivered dead were to be given burial *in loco sacro*. Infants, however, of baptized parents, when such infants died before they reached the use of reason, were to be buried in an unblessed section of the cemetery. Cf. also the Provincial Council of Avignon (1725), tit. 29, c. 3—*Collectio Lacensis*, I, 513. It must be remembered that those whose burial was prohibited in blessed ground were not necessarily to be identified in their status with those whose burial caused a cemetery's violation. The *Rituale* specified that unbaptized infants should not be buried in blessed ground, but nowhere did it expressly state that the burial of unbaptized infants violated the place of their burial.

6. *The Burial of Excommunicated Persons.* Regarding the *pollutio* following the burial of excommunicated persons in consecrated ground the decretals leave no doubt. It is in these decretals that it is learned that a cemetery in which excommunicates have been buried must be reconciled.[42] Did the burial of all excommunicated persons have the same grave results? Innocent III (1198-1216) in explaining this point (1213), set the limits at what one would consider today as *excommunicati vitandi,* that is, persons who had been cut off from the unity of the Church in such a way that the faithful were not to have anything to do with them, and who, by dying without being reconciled, were to be separated from the faithful in death as well as in life. *"Quibus viventibus non communicavimus, mortuis communicare non possumus."* [43]

Some question arose as to just what persons were to be considered in the class of *excommunicati vitandi.* For in the days of Innocent III, and for as long as two hundred years after him, all excommunicates were to be avoided and shunned by the faithful.[44] Any one who did communicate with an *excommunicatus vitandis* was not thereby a *vitandus* himself, but he was considered excommunicated in a limited sense, incurring a minor excommunication as it was then called, being still in union with the Church but forbidden to receive the sacraments.[45]

Pope Martin V in 1418, in his constitution *"Ad evitanda,"* [46] though without using the terms, classified excommunicates into two

[42] C. 7, X, *de consecratione ecclesiae,* III, 40.

[43] St. Leo the Great, *Epistola CLXVII*—Jaffé, *Regesta Pontificum Romanum ab condita Ecclesia ad Annum post Christum Natum MCXCVIII* (2 vols. in 1, ed. secundam correctam et auctam auspiciis Gulielmi Wattenbach curaverunt F. Kaltenbrunner (ad annum 590), P. Ewald (anno 590-882), S. Lowenfeld (anno 882-1198), Lipsiae, (1885-1888), n. 544. In c. 12, *de sepulturis,* III, 28, Innocent III ruled: "Sacris est canonibus institutum, et utentium consuetudine approbatum, ut quibus non communicavimus vivis non communicemus defunctis, et ut careant ecclesiastica sepultura qui prius erant ab ecclesiastica unitate praecisi, nec in articulo mortis ecclesiae reconciliati fuerint."

[44] Hyland, *Excommunication, Its Nature, Historical Development, and Effects,* The Catholic University of America Canon Law Studies, n. 49 (Washington, D. C.: The Catholic University of America, 1928), pp. 35-36.

[45] Hyland, *op. cit.* pp. 31-34.

[46] *Fontes,* n. 45.

groups: *excommunicati tolerati* and *excommunicati vitandi.* In the latter group only those were to be included who were excommunicated by name, either by a sentence of a judge or by a special and express public denunciation, and those who were notoriously guilty of laying sacrilegious hands on clerics. Hence after the legislation of Pope Martin V it was only the burial of *excommunicati vitandi,* and not of *excommunicati tolerati,* that necessitated the reconciliation of the cemetery in which the burial took place.[47]

7. *The Burial of Heretics, Schismatics and the Interdicted.* Heretics and schismatics, from what Martin V laid down as the norm to be followed,[48] were not to be considered as *vitandi.* Only after sentence had been pronounced upon them by a judge, or after they had been expressly and publicly denounced as *vitandi,* did their burial in sacred ground effect a violation of that ground.[49] The burial of persons who were under local or general personal interdict likewise did not cause the violation of a cemetery.[50] These could not be considered as coming under the term *excommunicati vitandi,* and therefore any penalties that were applied to the latter were not to be extended to include interdicted persons: *res odiosa restringenda.*[51] However, there was this exception, decreed in 1179 by Pope Alexander III in the III General Council of the Lateran: when a person was interdicted *nominatim,* he was to be considered as a *vitandus.*[52] His interment, therefore, in a Catholic cemetery caused its violation.

Article II. The Reconciliation of a Violated Cemetery

While a cemetery remained violated no burials were to be made in it. This is clear from the decretal of Boniface VIII: "Coeme-

[47] Benedictus XIV, *De Synodo Dioecesana,* lib. XII, c. 5, n. 4; Gonzales-Tellez, lib. III, tit. 40, c. 7, n. 8.

[48] Const. *Ad evitanda,* 1418—*Fontes,* n. 45.

[49] Petra, *Commentaria,* ad const. XVIII Innocentis IV *(Fidelibus),* nn. 42-50, III, 108.

[50] Pirhing, lib. III, tit. 40, n. 13.

[51] Reg. 15, R. J. in VI°. Suarez, *Commentaria ac Disputationes in Tertiam Partem Divi Thomae* (5 vols., Lugduni, 1608-1828), pars 3, quaes. 83, art. 3, disp. 81, sect. 4.

[52] C. 9—c. 3, X, *de privilegiis et excessibus privilegiatorum,* V, 33.

terium . . . pollutum . . . antequam reconciliatum fuerit, non debet in eo aliquis sepeliri." [53] This reveals also the urgency of the reconciliation of the cemetery. For if the reconciliation was delayed, the remains of the faithful departed had to be laid to rest elsewhere in an unblessed, temporary grave, and later on exhumed and transferred to the reconciled cemetery. There was no penal legislation which affected those who disregarded this injunction by bringing about a burial in a violated cemetery, but Suarez did not hesitate to say that they committed a grave sin of disobedience against the lawful authority which set up this law, and a serious sin against religion which decried such irreverence.[54]

Before any reconciliation could take place the removal of the body or bodies of infidels, pagans and *excommunicati vitandi* whose burial had caused the violation of the cemetery was necessary. Only when the body of such a one could not be distinguished from the bodies of the faithful buried there was the reconciliation to be made without its removal.[55]

1. *The Rites of Reconciliation*

Before a cemetery was to be reconciled it was necessary to determine which of four rites was to be used. When the cemetery alone was violated and the cemetery had been consecrated or solemnly

[53] C. 1, *de consecratione ecclesiae,* III, 21, in VI°.

[54] *Commentaria ac Disputationes in Tertiam Partem Divi Thomae,* pars 3, quaest. 83, art. 3, disput. 81, sect. 4.

[55] C. 12, X, *de sepulturis,* III, 28: ". . . si contingat interdum, quod vel excommunicatorum corpora per violentiam aliquorum, vel alio casu in coemeterio ecclesiastico tumulentur, si ab aliorum corporibus discerni poterunt, exhumari debent, et procul ab ecclesiastica sepultura iactari." Also, c. 7, X, *de consecratione ecclesiae,* III, 40: "Coemeteria in quibus excommunicatorum corpora sepeliri contingit, reconcilianda erunt aspersione aquae solemniter benedictae, sicut in dedicationibus ecclesiarum fieri consuevit . . ." And the gloss ad v. "consuluisti" in the same passage states that after the bodies of the excommunicates have been removed from the cemeteries, the latter are to be reconciled with blessed water such as is used in the reconciliation of churches. This *aqua benedicta,* it is to be noted, was the same for the consecration of churches and for the reconciliation of both churches and solemnly blessed or consecrated cemeteries.

blessed, the proper rite was contained in the *Pontificale Romanum;*[56] if the cemetery had been blessed with the rite in the *Rituale Romanum,* then the rite of reconciliation was to be taken from the Rituale.[57] There were also two other rites, one in the Pontifical when the cemetery had been solemnly blessed,[58] and one in the Ritual when the cemetery had been simply blessed,[59] which took care of the situation which required the reconciliation of both a violated church and its violated contiguous cemetery.

While at one time the reconciliation of a cemetery, like its consecration or blessing, was very likely included in the act of the reconciliation of the adjacent church, this view could not be maintained after the thirteenth century. Gregory IX (1227-1241) pointed out that violated cemeteries were to be reconciled with water solemnly blessed as in the dedication and as in the reconciliation (gloss at the word "consuluisti") of churches.[60] The gloss states: " . . . sicut ecclesia reconciliatur, ita et coemeterium." Gregory IX had in mind, quite evidently, a distinct ceremony for the reconciliation of a cemetery. And yet, a number of authors, even in spite of the Pontifical and the Ritual, held the mistaken notion that, since a cemetery was violated because of some act which violated the adjoining church, the cemetery was reconciled automatically with the reconciliation of the church,[61] basing their opinion on the principle: *Accessorium naturam sequi congruit principalis.*[62] But this was not the case.[63] While the Pontifical and the Ritual made one rite serve the purpose of the reconciliation of both the church and the cemetery when both were violated, it did not follow that only the church was to be reconciled

[56] Tit. *De Reconciliatione Coemeterii sine Ecclesiae Reconciliatione.*

[57] Tit. VIII, c. 30, *Ordo Reconciliandi Coemeterium Violatum, sive Contiguum sit, sive Separatum, ubi Ecclesia non est Polluta.*

[58] Tit. *De Ecclesiae et Coemeterii Reconciliatione.*

[59] Tit. VIII, c. 28, *Ritus Reconciliandi Ecclesiam Violatam, si nondum erat ab Episcopo Consecratam.*

[60] C. 7, X, *de consecratione ecclesiae,* III, 40.

[61] Barbosa, *Iuris Ecclesiastici Universi,* lib. II, c. 9, n. 11; Passerini, *De Ecclesiarum Reconciliatione* (Parmae, 1694), disp. 3, c. 6, n. 4; Giraldi, *Expositio Iuris Pontificii,* pars I, sect. 603 (Vol. I, 428).

[62] Reg. 42, R. J. in VI°.

[63] Moulart, *De Sepultura et Coemeteriis,* pp. 133-134.

directly, the cemetery being reconciled indirectly or by way of participation. An examination of the rite will reveal that instead of being just one rite, there were really two rites in one. Some of the ceremonies and prayers the minister performed and read in the church for the reconciliation of the church; but there were others which the rubrics directed the minister to use in the cemetery for the reconciliation of the cemetery.

2. *The Minister of the Reconciliation of a Solemnly Blessed Cemetery*

(1) The Bishop of the Place

Broadly considered the minister of reconciliation was the same as the minister of the consecration and the blessing of the cemetery. The bishop of the place was the ordinary minister of the reconciliation of a consecrated cemetery. The act was considered like the act of consecration, an act of episcopal orders.[64] And therefore if the bishop of the place was legitimately prevented from performing this duty, he had to ask another bishop to do it for him.[65] He could not appoint a priest to act as the minister of this rite unless he did so by apostolic indult.[66]

(2) The Regular Superior

To the Friars Minor and by communication in their prerogative there came to the other exempt regulars the privilege of reconciling their own cemeteries, as well as their churches and oratories, from

[64] C. 9, X, *de consecratione ecclesiae,* III, 40. See also: Catalanus, *Pontificale Romanum,* pars 2, tit. 7, § 2, n. 1; Pirhing, lib. III, tit. 40, n. 32. Cf. *supra,* pp. 28, 34.

[65] The Sacred Congregation of Rites put this very clearly when it declared: "Ecclesiae consecratae et coemeterii reconciliationem proprio Episcopo impedito vel absente, committendam esse alteri Episcopo."—*Cameracen.,* 9 febr. 1608—*Fontes,* n. 5235.

[66] C. 9, X, *de consecratione ecclesiae,* III, 40. Cf. also in regard to a simple priest as the minister of the reconcilation of a consecrated cemetery: Fagnanus, *Commentaria,* lib. III, tit. 40, c. 9, n. 6; Pirhing, lib. III, tit 40, n. 20; Giraldi, *Expositio Iuris Pontificii,* pars I, sect. 602 (Vol. I, 427); Benedictus XIV, *De Synodo Dioecesana,* lib. XIII, c. 15, n. 2.

Pope Leo X on February 3, 1514, in his Constitution *Religionis saudet:*

> "*Praelati regulares, vel alii sacris in capitulis generalibus deputati, suas ecclesias, coemeteria et oratoria qualibet sanguinis aut seminis effusione, seu alias quomodolibet pollutas, seu polluta, quoties opus fuerit, aqua per eos (praesertim in locis remotis, ubi Episcopum aquam benedicentem per duas dietas adire non poterunt) benedicta reconciliare libere et licite valeant.*" [67]

Regulars therefore were given the privilege of reconciling their own consecrated cemeteries, and if they were forty miles (*duae dietae*) [68] from the bishop of the place they could even bless the water they were to use in the rite of conciliation. Reiffenstuel [69] and Many [70] extended this permission to include the case wherein the episcopal see was vacant through the death, resignation, or deposition of the incumbent; or even when the bishop was absent from his episcopal city.

(3) The Simple Priest

When by apostolic privilege a simple priest or a regular superior reconciled a consecrated church they were to use the rite found in the Pontificale Romanum.[71] It is certainly justified, in the light of all that has been seen heretofore concerning the close parallelism between church and cemetery in the matter of the consecration, the blessing, the violation and the reconciliation, to conclude that a simple priest or a regular, when reconciling a cemetery that had been solemnly blessed with the rite in the *Pontificale,* had to use the rite of reconciliation of the Roman Pontifical.[72]

[67] *Privilegia Omnium Religiosorum,* pp. 63-64.

[68] See glossa ordinaria ad c. 28, X, *de rescriptis,* I, 3, v. "ultra duas dietas."

[69] Lib. III, tit. 40, n. 27.

[70] *De Locis Sacris,* n. 42.

[71] At the end of c. 28, *Ritus Reconciliandi Ecclesiam Violatam,* in any of the Roman Rituals, may be found this direction: "Simplex sacerdos tantum ex privilegio Sedis Apostolicae potest ecclesiam ab episcopo consecratam reconciliare, et tunc utatur ritu in Pontificali praescripto . . . cum aqua ab episcopo ad hunc usum rite benedicta."

[72] Moulart, *De Sepulturis et Coemeteriis,* p. 134.

3. *The Minister of the Reconciliation of a Simply Blessed Cemetery*

The ordinary minister of the reconciliation of a cemetery that was blessed with the rite of the *Rituale Romanum* was a priest who probably did not need the delegation of the bishop of the place. The text, upon which the burden of the proof that a priest was the ordinary minister rests, is one which refers directly to the reconciliation of a blessed church, and by inference only to the reconciliation of a blessed cemetery.[73] A violated church that was blessed, not consecrated, was to be reconciled instantly and without delay ("*protinus*"). But, as authors maintained, this necessarily meant that a priest was to do it, for it would have been unreasonable to expect that a bishop, with his multifarious other duties, could attend to this matter immediately. Furthermore, they argued, holy water ("aqua exorcizata" of the text) had to be used, and this could be blessed by any priest. Churches were to be reconciled without any delay in order that the worship of God might continue uninterruptedly. For an equally urgent reason, namely the necessity of the Christian burial of the faithful, cemeteries were reconciled as soon as it was morally possible.

Great discussion arose as to whether or not the priest had to be delegated by the bishop to perform the rite of reconciliation as found in the Roman Ritual. The Ritual itself, in the rite of the reconciliation of a church and a cemetery, had the rubric: "Ecclesiae violatae reconciliatio *per sacerdotem ab episcopo delegatum* fiat hoc modo. . . . " And again, in the rite of the reconciliation of a violated cemetery, there was the rubric: "Mane diei, qua facienda est reconciliatio coemeterii, *sacerdos, si ab episcopo facultatem habeat. . . .*" [74] Thus it seemed that a delegation by the bishop was necessary.

A few years previous to the issuing of the *Rituale Romanum* of Paul V (1614), in the year 1608, the Sacred Congregation of Rites published a decree which stated that a simple priest invested with an ecclesiastical dignity could reconcile a blessed church or cemetery, but before he could do it independently of the bishop he was required

[73] C. 10, X, *de consecratione ecclesiae,* III, 40.

[74] *Rituale Romanum Pauli V,* as also all the later Rituals.

to have an apostolic indult as for the solemn blessing of a church, for it was an act of episcopal jurisdiction.[75]

However, in spite of these powerful authorities, most of the authors followed the opinion that a delegation was not necessary. Among these authors may be mentioned Barbosa (1589-1649),[76] Pirhing (1606-1679),[77] Reiffenstuel (1641-1703),[78] Schmalzgrueber (1663-1735),[79] Ferraris (+ca. 1760),[80] Benedict XIV (1675-1758),[81] Catalanus (+after 1760),[82] and Many (+1922).[83] Among those holding for the necessity of the delegation were principally: Catalanus in his *Rituale Romanum* (1760) in which he apparently changed his previous stand on the question,[84] Giraldi (1692-1775),[85] Moulart (1832-1904)[86] and Wernz (1842-1914).[87]

One very good reason in favor of those who held that a delegation was not necessary was that by the time the priest reached the bishop, and received from him the delegation to perform the rite of reconciliation of the cemetery, several days would have been consumed. Thus, from the viewpoint of the necessitated delay, the situation would scarcely have differed from the case in which the bishop him-

[75] *Cameracen.*, 9 febr. 1608: "Simplex reconciliatio ecclesiae, seu coemeterii non consecrati, potest committi presbytero in dignitate constituto; et ad eam peragendam independenter ab episcopo requiritur privilegium apostolicum, sicut et ad ipsam ecclesiam eodem modo solemniter benedicendam; sunt enim actus iurisdictionis episcopalis."—*Fontes*, n. 5235.

[76] *De Officio et Potestate Episcopi* (Lugduni, 1656), alleg. 28, n. 27.

[77] Lib. III, tit. 40, n. 19.

[78] Lib. III, tit. 40, n. 28.

[79] Lib. III, tit. 40, n. 84.

[80] *Bibliotheca*, v. "ecclesia," art. 4, n. 71.

[81] *De Synodo Dioecesana*, lib. XIII, c. 15, n. 2.

[82] *Pontificale Romanum*, pars 2, tit. 7, § 2, n. 7.

[83] *De Locis Sacris*, n. 42.

[84] *Rituale Romanum Benedicti XIV iussu Editum et Auctum* (2 vols., Patavii, 1760), tit. 8, c. 30, n. 1.

[85] *Expositio Iuris Pontificii*, pars I, sect. 603 (Vol. I, 428); sect. 598 (Vol. I, 416).

[86] *De Sepultura et Coemeteriis*, pp. 136-138.

[87] *Ius Decretalium*, III, n. 471.

self performed the ceremony, as in the case of a cemetery that had been solemnly blessed. And yet in the case of the cemetery which required the reconciliation of the *Rituale Romanum* it was distinctly specified in the law that the reconciliation was to be effected without delay.[88]

Another strong reason in support of the less exacting doctrine was that Benedict XIV, a Pontiff high on the list of the most famous canonists, adhered to the opinion that a delegation was not necessary. It is to be remembered, too, that this Pontiff is numbered among the few Popes who revised the *Rituale Romanum*. His words in this matter are very clear: "Si simpliciter benedicta fuerit (ecclesia), tunc idem Gregorius IX . . . statuit, *nulla praeobtenta delegatione, per simplicem sacerdotem,* adhibita aqua benedicta, quam sanctam sive lustralem vocant, posse ecclesiam pollutam reconciliari" et addimus, coemeterium pollutum.[89]

Article III. The Interdict of Cemeteries

The local interdict, which affects a place directly and the people in that place only indirectly, dates back to the eleventh century and very probably to an earlier era.[90] When a cemetery was interdicted, the burial of the faithful in it was strictly forbidden,[91] and the interdict was rarely relaxed in those early days. Innocent III allowed clerics who were not personally interdicted and who were in no way responsible for the local interdict to be buried in the cemetery provided that all solemnity was foregone.[92] This same Pontiff also allowed other worthy exceptions.[93] However, the exceptions were few,

[88] C. 10, X, *de consecratione ecclesiae,* III, 40.

[89] *De Synodo Dioecesana,* lib. XIII, c. 15, n. 2.

[90] Cf. Wernz, *Ius Decretalium,* VI, n. 219; Ayrinhac-Lydon, *Penal Legislation in the New Code of Canon Law* (New York: Benziger Bros., 1936), nn. 128-130; Coronata, *Institutiones,* n. 1784.

[91] C. 16, *de sententia excommunicationis,* V, 11, in VI°; also the gloss ad v. "interdicti."

[92] C. 11, X, *de poenitentiis et remissionibus,* V, 38; c. 18 of the Synod of Cologne (1280)—Hardouin, VII, 834. Cf. Murga (De), *Disquisitiones Morales et Canonicae de Sepulturis,* tract. 2, disq. 4, dubium 1.

[93] C. 24, X, *de privilegiis et excessibus,* V, 33.

and the privation of the burial of even the innocent among the faithful [94] was rigorously carried out, any violation of the interdict being punished with excommunication.[95]

[94] Samuellius, *De Sepulturis Ecclesiasticis,* tract. 2, disp. 1, controv. 11, concl. 8, n. 12.

[95] C. 16, *de sententia excommunicationis,* V, 11, in VI°; c. 1, *de sepulturis,* III, 7, in Clem.; Synod of Cologne (1280), c. 11—Hardouin, VII, 834.

PART TWO

CANONICAL COMMENTARY

CHAPTER VI

THE SOLEMN BLESSING OF CEMETERIES

ARTICLE I. THE TERMS: "CONSECRATION" AND "SOLEMN BLESSING"

STRICTLY taken cemeteries are not consecrated, but are at most solemnly blessed. To speak of the "consecration of a cemetery," or of a "consecrated cemetery" is not an altogether unfamiliar mode of expression. In fact, many authors before the Code [1] used the word *consecration* quite as freely as they used the term *solemn blessing* when they referred to the rite in the Roman Pontifical which is entitled *"De Coemeterii Benedictione."* Post-Code authors, however, following the terminology of the Roman Pontifical and the Code, seldom refer to the consecration of a cemetery; it is almost always the solemn blessing. Nevertheless, canonists who have written in English use the term *"consecration"* perhaps just as often as the

[1] Martène (*De Antiquis Ecclesiae Ritibus,* lib. II, c. 20 [Vol. III, 362-368]) gives a number of rites of solemn blessings of cemeteries, the earliest dating back to the eighth century, and several of which he calls "consecrations." See also: Moulart, *De Sepultura et Coemeteriis,* p. 101; Bargilliat, *Praelectiones Iuris Canonici* (1891 ed.), II, n. 1328; Many, *De Locis Sacris,* n. 144. Rivet (*Institutiones Iuris Canonici Privati* [Romae: Ex Typographia Pontificia in Instituto Pii IX, 1914], n. 49) says "Ex antiquissima consuetudine benedici debet coemeterium, quae benedictio eodem modo fit ac ecclesiae dedicatio, vel ab Episcopo aut sacerdote a R. Pontifice delegato iuxta ritus Pontific. Rom. (et dicitur *consecratio*) vel ab Episcopo aut sacerdote ab Episcopo aut Superiore Regulari deputato . . . iuxta ritus Ritualis Rom. (et est *benedictio*)."

phrase *"solemn blessing."* [2] The interchangeable use of these two terms is somewhat bewildering to one who wishes to know precisely whether the rite in the Roman Pontifical is technically (that is liturgically and canonically) to be called a solemn blessing or a consecration.

It is important at the outset, therefore, to define these terms. Consecration and blessing, it must be declared, have both general and strict meanings. In general, consecration is an act by which a thing is transformed from a common and profane to a sacred use, or by which a person or thing is dedicated to the service and worship of God by prayers, rites and ceremonies.[3] Blessing in its wide sense is the less solemn dedication or sanctification of a person or thing to serve some sacred purpose.

Coming to the strict definition of these terms, one may define consecration as an act performed by a duly qualified minister, usually a bishop, who by the use of certain prayers and by the anointing of the person or object with holy oils constitutes the same as something

[2] Augustine (Bachofen), *A Commentary on the New Code of Canon Law* (8 vols., St. Louis: Herder, 1925-1938. Vol. II, 6. ed., 1936; Vol. VI, 3. ed., 1931; Vol. VIII, 3. ed., 1931), VI, 101, 102, 105, 110, 111 (hereafter cited as *Commentary*); O'Reilly, *Ecclesiastical Sepulture in the New Code of Canon Law*, The Catholic University of America Canon Law Studies, n. 18 (Washington, D. C.: The Catholic University of America, 1923), pp. 14-17; Ayrinhac-Lydon, *Penal Legislation in the New Code of Canon Law*, n. 269; Kerin, *The Privation of Christian Burial*, pp. 107, 108, 109, 110, etc.; Rev. James H. Murphy, in *The Ecclesiastical Review* (originally, *The American Ecclesiastical Review*, Philadelphia, 1889—), in an article entitled: "Parish Priests and Christian Burial"—LXVII (1922), 12-25; also author (unnamed) of article "The Disposal of Lots in Consecrated Cemeteries," *The Ecclesiastical Review*, LXXVIII (1928), 430-432, and many other articles in the same *Review;* the Benedictine author of the article "The Consecration of a Cemetery"—*The Homiletic and Pastoral Review*, XXX (1930), 976-982; Woywod, *A Practical Commentary on the Code of Canon Law* (6. printing, 2 vols., New York: Wagner, 1941), nn. 1192, 1195, hereafter cited as *A Practical Commentary;* also Woywod in various articles in *The Homiletic and Pastoral Review*, such as "Burial of Catholics in Non-Catholic Cemeteries," XXXVII (1936-1937), 79-81; "Several Points on the Desecration of Cemeteries," XXV (1924-1925), 171-173, and many others.

[3] Cf. Augustine, *Commentary*, III, 565-566.

sacred and dedicated permanently to the service of God. On the other hand, blessing is an act performed by a duly qualified minister, usually a priest, who by the use of certain prayers and by the sprinkling of the person or thing with holy water constitutes[4] the same as sacred and dedicated permanently to the service of God.[5] Purposely in the above definitions both have been worded in as far as possible in a parallel way so that the differences and similarities can more readily be recognized.

In both consecration and blessing, therefore, the object passes from its original profane or common state to a new state, that of being a sacred object. This new state is permanent, whether it be brought about by a consecration or by a blessing. The ceremonies of a consecration are more elaborate and more solemn than those of a blessing. Holy oils are always used in a consecration; holy water is usually employed in a blessing.[6] The ordinary minister of a consecration is a bishop;[7] the ordinary minister of a blessing is a priest.[8]

The Roman Pontifical contains both consecrations and blessings. In it one finds, for example, the consecration of a bishop; the bless-

[4] The blessing which is defined here is the constitutive blessing. This is the one with which the present treatise will be concerned. There is also an invocative blessing which does not render sacred the object blessed, such as the blessing of food, houses, ships, etc. Cf. De Herdt, *Sacrae Liturgiae Praxis Iuxta Ritum Romanum* (10. ed., 3 vols., Lovanii, 1902-1903), III, n. 291.

[5] Cf. Ferraris, *Bibliotheca,* v. "benedictio," art. 1, n. 1; Wernz, *Ius Decretalium,* III, nn. 436, 760; Baruffaldus, *Ad Rituale Romanum Commentaria,* II, 66; Le Vavasseur, *Ceremonial Selon Le Rit Romain d'apres Baldeschi et Favrel* (6. ed., 2 vols., Paris, 1882), I, nn. 297-299; Van der Stappen, *Sacra Liturgia* (3. ed., 5 vols., Mechliniae: H. Dessain, 1912), IV, Q. 318-319.

[6] Cf. Wernz, *Ius Decretalium,* III, 760; Coronata, *De Locis et Temporibus Sacris,* n. 4; Vermeersch-Creusen, *Epitome,* II, n. 470; Cappello, *Tractatus Canonico-Moralis de Sacramentis* (3 vols. in 6, Taurini: Marietti, 1932-1939. Vol. I, 3. ed., 1938) I, n. 111; Augustine, *Commentary,* VI, 3; Wapelhorst, *Compendium Sacrae Liturgiae Iuxta Ritum Romanum* (11. ed., Neo-Eboraci: Benziger Fratres, 1931), n. 415; Baier, *Catholic Liturgics* (translated and adapted from the German of Richard Stapper, Paterson, New Jersey: St. Anthony Guild Press, 1935), p. 322.

[7] C. 1147, § 1.

[8] C. 1147, § 2.

ing of an abbot; the consecration of a church, of a fixed altar, of a portable altar, of a chalice and paten; the blessing of a cornerstone, of vestments, of a cemetery. As a matter of fact there are in the Roman Pontifical more formulas for blessings than for consecrations. The Pontifical is the bishop's book and most of the consecrations and blessings found therein were once and for the greater part still are reserved to the bishop. The Roman Ritual contains many more blessings. The latter is the priest's manual and the priest is competent, unless it is otherwise indicated, to perform the blessings the formulas of which are contained in it.

The blessing of a new cemetery is a blessing to be found in the Roman Ritual.[9] Its minister, according to the Ritual, is any priest delegated by the bishop. There is a form of the blessing of a cemetery, as above indicated, also in the Roman Pontifical.[10] This, while yet a blessing, is a more solemn blessing than the one contained in the Ritual, and the rubrics in the Pontifical indicate throughout that the minister of this more solemn blessing is a bishop.

The formula of the solemn blessing of a cemetery, although contained in the Pontifical, connotes a blessing, and not a consecration. In this ceremony there is an abundant use of holy water, but there is no anointing with holy oils. The Code never speaks of the "*consecratio*" of a cemetery, while it does speak of the "*consecratio*" of churches,[11] oratories,[12] fixed altars,[13] portable altars,[14] chalices and patens.[15] All of these latter are real consecrations, and in the ceremony holy oils are used. The Code calls the rite in the Roman Pontifical the solemn blessing of cemeteries; the rite in the Roman Ritual, the simple blessing.[16]

Authors, therefore, who use the expression "*coemeterii consecratio*" or "*coemeterium consecratum,*" are making use of the term

[9] Tit. VIII, cap. 29, *Ritus Benedicendi Novum Coemeterium.*
[10] Tit. *De Coemeterii Benedictione.*
[11] Cc. 1165-1168.
[12] C. 1191.
[13] C. 1197.
[14] C. 1197.
[15] Cc. 1305; 294, § 2.
[16] Cf. c. 1205, § 1.

consecration in its broader meaning, referring always, of course, to the rite of solemn blessing as found in the Roman Pontifical. It was quite natural, especially in the earlier days of the Church, to speak of the consecration and blessing of cemeteries instead of their solemn and simple blessing, for there was the consecration and blessing of churches, and the legislation regarding cemeteries followed closely in the wake of the legal enactments concerning churches not only in its juridical development but also in its borrowed legal terminology.

And so, in this work "*consecration*" and "'*solemn blessing*" are terms that are used interchangeably. It will always be understood, however, that cemeteries are never consecrated in the strict sense of the term. As has been said,[17] most of the authors who have written in English use *consecration* very liberally in their treatment of cemeteries, and it is not an incorrect term if it be understood in the meaning in which it is intended to be employed.

Article II. The Rite of the Solemn Blessing

The rite of the solemn blessing of cemeteries is found in the *Pontificale Romanum* under the title: *De Coemeterii Benedictione.* Before the Code this rite was also called the rite of the *consecration* of cemeteries, but, as has already been pointed out in the preceding article, the term "*solemn blessing*" is the more correct term. The minister of this solemn blessing is not free to use or not to use the rite of the *Pontificale Romanum;* he must use the formula exactly as he finds it.[18] Episcopal orders are generally required in the minister of the solemn blessing of cemeteries.[19] There are, however, exceptions to this general rule, as will be seen in the subsequent article. But whoever may legitimately act as the minister of this rite, even though he be not a bishop, must use the rite of the Pontifical, disregarding only those rubrics which evidently refer exclusively to bishops.

[17] *Supra,* pp. 63-64.

[18] Cf. c. 1148.

[19] Cf. cc. 1205, § 1, and 1155, § 1.

Article III. The Minister of the Solemn Blessing

1. *Local Ordinaries*

Canon 1205, § 1, which directs that all Catholic cemeteries are to be blessed with a solemn or simple blessing, states that the minister of the ceremony of the solemn blessing is to be governed by an earlier canon. The canon referred to is canon 1155, which specifically treats of the minister of the consecration of sacred places. There it is established that sacred places, that is to say, churches, oratories, altars and cemeteries,[20] even those belonging to exempt regulars, are to be consecrated by the local ordinary [21] in whose diocese the place to be consecrated is located. This ordinary, however, if he is to be able to consecrate, must be a bishop. A vicar or prefect apostolic, for example, even though he is a local ordinary,[22] cannot consecrate sacred places unless he has the episcopal character.[23] In a word, therefore, the Code [24] determines that even though the solemn blessing of cemeteries is not strictly a consecration,[25] nevertheless the law (c. 1155) which determines the valid and licit minister of the consecation of sacred places is to be the same law that establishes the competent minister of the solemn blessing of cemeteries.

Canon 1155, § 1, makes the episcopal ordinary of the territory in which the cemetery is located the valid and licit minister of the solemn blessing of cemeteries.[26] This is true even when the cemeteries of exempt religious are concerned. Since this law is of a

[20] C. 1154.

[21] In canon 1155, §§ 1, 2, the Code uses the term *"Ordinarius territorii"* instead of its usual term *"Ordinarius loci."* Augustine (*Commentary*, VI, 5) implies that *ordinarius territorii* has a wider meaning than *ordinarius loci*, for he says that the former term includes all local ordinaries, whether their territories are large or small, and also includes such abbots and prelates *nullius* whose territory consists of less than three parishes, and who are otherwise in the legislation of the Code, not included with those abbots and prelates *nullius* whose territory consists of three or more parishes. Cf. cc. 319 and 198.

[22] C. 198.

[23] Cf. *infra*, p. 71.

[24] C. 1205, § 1.

[25] Cf. *supra*, pp. 63-67.

[26] Cf. c. 1205, § 1.

universal nature and contained in the Code, no other may be the minister of such a solemn blessing unless the Code itself gives him this power,[27] or unless the Roman Pontiff by special indult grants such faculties to non-bishops.[28] The reservation of the solemn blessing of cemeteries to local ordinaries in episcopal orders has always been the practice of the Church.[29] Heretical and schismatical bishops, and those who are under censure, provided that they are validly consecrated bishops, are valid ministers of this solemn rite, although, of course, they act illicitly.[30]

Besides the power of orders required in the ordinary minister of the solemn blessing of cemeteries, there is also required ecclesiastical jurisdiction.[31] The jurisdiction that is necessary is the jurisdiction that a local ordinary has over the territory under his care. So much is this jurisdiction of the local ordinary required that even the cemeteries of exempt religious are under that jurisdiction as far as the solemn blessing of such cemeteries is concerned.[32] This jurisdiction is such that, even in cases wherein the ordinary of the place is not himself a bishop, and therefore cannot perform the blessing, his permission is to be sought and obtained by any one who in his territory wishes to bless a cemetery solemnly.[33]

Thus, for example, a local ordinary who is not a bishop (v. g., a vicar capitular or the administrator of a vacant see) has the right to expect regulars, even though they are exempt, to apply to him when they wish to have their cemeteries solemnly blessed, and he, the local ordinary, shall designate the bishop who is to bless their cemetery. Likewise, Cardinals outside the territory of their jurisdiction, and bishops outside their dioceses, must obtain the permission of the ordinary of the place (even though he may be without

[27] Cf. cc. 1155, § 1; 239, § 1, 20°; 323, § 2.

[28] Cf. cc. 80, 81.

[29] Cf. *supra*, pp. 27-31.

[30] Coronata, *De Locis et Temporibus Sacris*, n. 5; Augustine, *Commentary*, VI, 5.

[31] C. 1155.

[32] C. 1155.

[33] Cc. 1155, § 2; 1157; 239, § 1, 20°.

episcopal orders) each time they wish to bless solemnly a cemetery under his jurisdiction.[34]

Bishops who are members of clerical exempt orders, although they live permanently in his territory must have the permission of the local ordinary, even when the latter is without the episcopal character, in order that they may bless cemeteries belonging to their own institute with the rite of the Roman Pontifical.[35] This jurisdiction which the local ordinary exercises with regard both to the consecration of sacred places and to the solemn blessing of cemeteries in his territory affects the licitness of the act, and not its validity.[36]

2. *Cardinals*

There is special provision in the Code [37] to allow cardinals, even when they are not bishops, the privilege and the power of blessing cemeteries with the rite of a solemn blessing as found in the Roman Pontifical. No special legislation would be necessary if cardinals were all bishops, for then they could validly consecrate all sacred places, including cemeteries in the territory of their own jurisdiction and also wherever else they wished, provided that they obtained (for licitness) the permission of the ordinary of the place.[38] But not all of the cardinals are bishops. The six cardinal bishops and the fifty cardinal priests are all endowed with episcopal orders; the fourteen cardinal deacons, however, are as a rule priests only.[39]

Canons 239, § 1, 20°, and 1155 have made it clear that as far as the consecration of sacred places is concerned all cardinals, whether or not they be bishops, have the same rights and privileges. They may solemnly bless cemeteries, therefore, in their own territories; they may also solemnly bless cemeteries anywhere, but in this

[34] Cc. 1155, § 2; 1157. Cf. also Coronata, *De Locis et Temporibus Sacris*, n. 5.

[35] Tit. *De Coemeterii Benedictione*.

[36] Coronata, *De Locis et Temporibus Sacris*, n. 5.

[37] Cc. 1155, § 1; 239, § 1, 20°.

[38] Cf. cc. 1147, 1155, 1157.

[39] Chelodi, *Ius de Personis iuxta Codicem Iuris Canonici* (2. ed., Tridentini: Libr. Edit. Tridentinum, 1927), n. 156 (hereafter cited as *Ius de Personis*).

latter case they must be either invited [40] or permitted [41] to do so by the ordinary of the place, and if there be question of the cemeteries of exempt regulars, then consent must also be obtained from the respective major superior.[42] It is commonly agreed among authors that the permission and consent of both the local and the religious ordinary, as required by canons 239, § 1, 20°, 1155 and 1157, is demanded for licitness only. Obviously a cardinal should not act without this permission and consent.[43]

3. *Vicars and Prefects Apostolic*

Vicars and prefects apostolic, being local ordinaries [44] and being included therefore under the term "*ordinarii territorii*" of canon 1155, are beyond doubt capable of solemnly blessing cemeteries if they have received episcopal orders.[45] But frequently enough, more often with regard to prefects apostolic than with reference to vicars apostolic,[46] these prelates are not bishops. It is when this is the case that some doubts are raised as to the ability of these local ordinaries solemnly to bless cemeteries. The important canon in any discussion of this situation is canon 294.

This canon states: vicars and prefects apostolic enjoy in their respective territories the same rights and faculties as residential bishops in their dioceses, unless the Apostolic See has made some restriction in a particular case. Even though they may not be in episcopal orders, they are competent, within the limits of their territory and during the tenure of their office, to perform all blessings reserved to bishops, the pontifical blessing alone excepted. They can, moreover, consecrate chalices, patens and portable altars with the sacred oils blessed by a bishop.

Does canon 294, § 2, bespeak for vicars and prefects apostolic the power solemnly to bless cemeteries even when they are not

[40] C. 1155, § 2.

[41] C. 1157.

[42] C. 1157.

[43] Coronata, *Institutiones*, n. 724, note 5. Cf. *infra*, p. 83.

[44] C. 198.

[45] Coronata, *Institutiones*, n. 373.

[46] Vermeersch-Creusen, *Epitome*, I, n. 402.

bishops? The answer must be that this canon does give these prelates this power, for it states explicitly that they are able to perform *all blessings reserved to bishops*, even though they themselves may not have episcopal orders. The only blessing excepted is the pontifical blessing itself. Canon 1155, § 1, certainly makes the solemn blessing of cemeteries a reserved blessing, reserved to local ordinaries who are bishops. Canon 294, § 2, therefore, taken together with canons 1205, § 1, and 1155, § 1, makes vicars and prefects apostolic who lack episcopal orders the valid and licit ministers of the solemn blessing of cemeteries.[47]

4. *Vicars General*

Specific mention is also made of vicars general in the canons which specify the minister of the solemn blessing or consecration of a cemetery.[48] Mention is made of them in this connection, however, so as to exclude them from being ministers of this sacred rite unless certain requirements are fulfilled.

A vicar general is either a bishop or he is not a bishop. If he is a bishop, so far as jurisdiction is concerned he is still only a vicar, one taking the place or acting in the name of the ordinary of the diocese, and he may not solemnly bless a cemetery licitly (although he can validly)[49] without having previously obtained a special mandate from the bishop who rules over the diocese.[50] This mandate may be given either verbally or in writing.[51] A vicar general

[47] Augustine, *Commentary*, II, 311-312; Vermeersch-Creusen, *Epitome*, I, n. 406; Coronata, *Institutiones*, n. 373; Blat, *Commentarium Textus Codicis Iuris Canonici* (5 vols. in 7, Romae: Collegio "Angelico," 1921-1938. Vol. II, 2. ed., 1921; Vol. III, pars II, 2. ed., 1934), II, n. 310.

[48] Cc. 1205, § 1; 1155, § 1.

[49] Consecration of a place and solemn blessing of a cemetery by any bishop wherever it is performed, even if for one reason or another it should be illicit is always valid. This can be inferred from c. 1147, §§ 1 and 3. Cf. Wernz, *Ius Decretalium*, III, n. 437; Augustine, *Commentary*, VI, p. 5; Coronata, *De Locis et Temporibus Sacris*, n. 5; *Institutiones*, n. 724; Gasparri, *Tractatus Canonicus de Sanctissima Eucharistia* (2 vols., Parisiis, 1897), I, n. 156 (hereafter to be cited as *De SS. Eucharistia*).

[50] C. 1155, § 1.

[51] Chelodi, *Ius de Personis*, p. 330, note 3; Coronata, *Institutiones*, n. 421.

who is not a bishop, even though he is listed in the Code as a local ordinary,[52] cannot validly bless a cemetery solemnly even with a special mandate, because episcopal orders are essential in the minister of a solemn blessing,[53] as long as such an act is not authorized, either by the law itself or in consequence of an apostolic indult, for performance by a non-bishop.[54] A vicar general, therefore, in order that he may consecrate or solemnly bless a cemetery, must have the episcopal character if his act of consecration or of solemn blessing is to be valid, and he must moreover possess a mandate which he has received from his bishop if such an act of consecration or of solemn blessing is to stand as a lawful act.

5. *Abbots and Prelates "Nullius"*

Canon 1155, which deals with the minister of the consecration of sacred places, does not specifically mention abbots and prelates *nullius* as ministers of consecration. Nevertheless a previous canon does make them valid and licit consecrators of sacred places (c. 323, § 2), and this canon must be understood as an exception to canon 1155, § 1. Canon 323, § 2, states that any abbot or prelate *nullius* who is a bishop may consecrate sacred places, and that even an abbot or prelate *nullius* who is not a bishop also can consecrate sacred places. In the latter case, however, it does make this provision, namely, that when an abbot or prelate *nullius* (who is not a bishop) is required by apostolic prescription or by the constitutions of his religious institute to receive the abbatial blessing from some bishop of his choice, he must receive this blessing before he may consecrate sacred places. If, however, the abbot or prelate *nullius* is not obliged to receive this blessing, he enjoys the privilege of the act of consecrating without previously receiving the abbatial blessing.[55]

[52] C. 198, § 2.

[53] Cc. 1205, § 1; 1155. Cf. Augustine, *Commentary,* VI, 4; Coronata, *De Locis et Temporibus Sacris,* n. 5; *Institutiones,* n. 724.

[54] C. 1147, § 1.

[55] Vermeersch (*Epitome,* I, n. 438): "Horum Praelatorum alii charactere episcopali insigniuntur, alii non; alii sunt benedicendi, non autem alii; prioribus benedictio est condicio quorundam privilegiorum." Cf. also Coronata, *Institutiones,* n. 389.

Therefore, abbots and prelates *nullius,* those namely whose territory comprises at least three parishes (c. 319, § 2), can validly and licitly consecrate or solemnly bless cemeteries, provided that they received the abbatial blessing, if they are required to receive it. This privilege must be exercised within the limits of their territory, where they can be considered as *"ordinarii territorii,"* the term used in canon 1155, § 1. Abbots and prelates with a territory of less than three parishes do not have from the Code by virtue of canon 323, § 2, the power to consecrate sacred places, because the Code does not legislate for them.[56] But when this power is given them by particular law or by apostolic indult, they are included under the term *"ordinarius territorii"* of canon 1155, § 1, and can therefore solemnly bless cemeteries in their own territory without seeking the permission of any one.[57]

The question of whether or not abbots and prelates *nullius* were able validly to consecrate churches and to solemnly bless cemeteries outside the territory of their jurisdiction was discussd by authors since the Code. Cappello, in his consideration of the question, was of the opinion that they could not validly consecrate sacred places outside their own territory.[58] The question was finally put before the Code Commission and the answer, given on January 29, 1931, was a confirmation of Cappello's stand, namely that abbots *nullius* were not competent by virtue of canon 323 to consecrate churches (and therefore also cemeteries) validly outside their territory.[59]

6. *Apostolic Administrators*

The apostolic administrator is, in the definition of canon 198, § 1, an *"ordinarius loci."* The extent of his powers will be determined in large part by his letter of appointment.[60] Therefore, in the matter

[56] C. 319, § 2.

[57] Cc. 1155, § 1; 1157. Also see Augustine, *Commentary,* VI, 5.

[58] "De Consecratione Ecclesiarum," *Periodica de Re Canonica et Morali utili praesertim Religiosis et Missionariis* (Brugis, 1905—; ab anno 1927: *Periodica de Re Morali, Canonica, Liturgica*), XIX (1930), pp. 139 ff.

[59] *Acta Apostolica Sedis, Commentarium Officiale* [AAS] (Romae, 1909—), XXIII (1931), 110.

[60] C. 314.

of the solemn blessing of cemeteries, his letter of appointment must first be consulted. Provided that the letter of appointment does not augment the powers which attach to his status in virtue of the common law, the apostolic administrator may consecrate or solemnly bless cemeteries only if he is endowed with episcopal orders.[61] If he is not a bishop, he may, since he is an *"ordinarius territorii,"* invite some bishop of his own rite solemnly to bless any cemetery that requires such a blessing.[62]

There are two types of apostolic administrators: temporary apostolic administrators, and permanent apostolic administrators.[63] The permanent apostolic administrator is always a bishop, and almost always the neighboring bishop or metropolitan;[64] the temporary apostolic administrator, on the other hand, is generally a bishop, and sometimes only a priest.[65] It can be said therefore that, since most apostolic administrators are bishops, they as a rule are able to take care of all consecrations in the dioceses which are committed to their administration. The temporary apostolic administrator who is a priest usually has no need for the faculty to consecrate sacred places, for his office is of its nature short-lived. He is nevertheless permitted to call in an outside bishop for any consecrations that may be necessary, for in this he is likened to the vicar capitular.[66] When the situation requires it, the Holy See is wont to grant many additional faculties to temporary apostolic administrators who are not in episcopal orders, so that they may the more easily serve the needs of the territories under their jurisdiction. Never, however, are such faculties to be presumed.[67]

[61] Cc. 1205, § 1; 1155, § 1.

[62] C. 1155, § 2.

[63] Cf. c. 315, §§ 1-2.

[64] Toso, *Ad Codicem Iuris Canonici Commentaria Minora* (5 vols., Romae: Marietti, 1920-1934), II, 137.

[65] Cf. Vermeersch-Creusen, *Epitome,* I, n. 431; Wernz-Vidal, *Ius Canonicum,* II, n. 557; Coronata, *Institutiones,* n. 379.

[66] Cf. cc. 315, § 2, 1°; 435, § 2; 1155, § 2.

[67] McDonough, *Apostolic Administrators* (The Catholic University of America Canon Law Studies, n. 139, Washington, D. C.: The Catholic University of America Press, 1941), p. 111.

7. *Vicars Capitular or Administrators*

Enumerated among the local ordinaries are the vicar capitular and the administrator of a vacant diocese.[68] Vicars capitular and administrators, who as a rule are not bishops, may not solemnly bless cemeteries, but they may invite a bishop of their own rite to perform the blessing.[69] A vicar capitular or an administrator who is a bishop, since he is juridically an *"ordinarius territorii,"* may validly and licitly bless cemeteries solemnly during the time of their legitimate administration.[70]

8. *Religious Superiors and Religious Bishops*

Religious superiors as such have no power solemnly to bless cemeteries. They are neither bishops nor are they *"ordinarii territorii."* [71] It does happen at times that there may be living in a religious community one of their number who is a bishop. This religious bishop, of course, may validly and licitly consecrate or solemnly bless cemeteries of the religious society, congregation or order, or even other cemeteries, provided that he has obtained the permission of the local ordinary, even though the latter himself lacks episcopal orders.[72] It is not unheard of that from time to time the Holy See allows some religious superior the privilege of consecrating sacred places.[73] In this case, however, such a superior must inform the ordinary of the place, both of his faculties from Rome, and of his intention solemnly to bless a certain specified cemetery.[74]

9. *Priests*

If the solemn blessing of cemeteries were really a consecration in the technical or juridical sense,[75] then a simple priest, or even one

[68] C. 198.
[69] C. 1155, § 2.
[70] Cc. 1155, § 1; 198; 435.
[71] Cc. 1155, § 1; 198, § 2.
[72] Cc. 1147, § 1; 1205, § 1; 1155; 1157; Vermeersch, *Epitome*, II, n. 471.
[73] Cf. *supra*, pp. 32-33.
[74] C. 1155.
[75] For a discussion of this point cf. *supra*, pp. 63-67.

delegated by his local ordinary or religious superior, certainly could not validly consecrate cemeteries, because he lacks the necessary power of episcopal orders for an act of consecration.[76] Since, however, the solemn blessing of cemeteries is not a consecration in the strict sense, the very pertinent question arises: would the solemn blessing of a simple priest, or of a priest delegated by his ordinary, be valid, even when it might be illicit?

The Code takes up the question of the minister of the solemn blessing of cemeteries in three canons. In canon 1147, § 2, the principle is stated that a priest is the ordinary minister of blessings unless the blessing is reserved to the Roman Pontiff or to bishops. Even when blessings are reserved, paragraph 3 goes on to say, the blessing by a priest is valid, although without the proper permission it will be illicit, except when in the reservation it is clear that it would be invalid for a priest to perform the reserved blessing without getting the proper faculties.

Now, canon 1205, § 1, makes it incontestably clear that the minister of the solemn blessing of cemeteries is one of those mentioned in canon 1155. This latter canon lays down the two conditions necessary in the minister of the consecration of sacred places, and of the solemn blessing of cemeteries (c. 1205, § 1). The first condition is that the minister be an *"ordinarius territorii,"* and a priest as such is not an ordinary in the sense of canons 198 and 1155. The second condition is that the minister have episcopal orders—and no simple priest meets this requirement.

That the solemn blessing of cemeteries, therefore, is a reserved blessing is clear from canon 1205, § 1, reserved to the local ordinary who is a bishop. The crux of the matter now is: Does canon 1155, § 1, (to which the above canon refers) reserve this blessing to the local ordinary who is in episcopal orders in such a way that it would be invalid if it were performed by any one less than a bishop? Or, to apply the question more directly to our case: Can a priest, acting without apostolic delegation, validly perform this ceremony in virtue of the ruling of canon 1147, §§ 2 and 3, which canon states that a priest is the ordinary minister of blessings and validly performs even

[76] Cc. 1147, § 1; 1155, § 1.

reserved blessings unless in the reservation it is clear that the blessing cannot validly be performed by a priest?

The two important clauses in the reservation of this solemn blessing of cemeteries (c. 1155, § 1) are these: *"spectat* (benedictio solemnis) *ad Ordinarium territorii"*; and *"dummodo Ordinarius charactere episcopali sit insignitus."* The first clause, while it points unmistakably to the local ordinary and to none other, does not seem to be a clause which, taken by itself, excludes all other ministers *under pain of invalidity.*[77] The second clause has a greater excluding force, since it is a *"dummodo"* clause. It is expressly stated in the law with regard to rescripts that a *"dummodo"* clause must be considered as a condition essential to the validity of the rescript.[78] This law on rescripts cannot as such be applied to all the laws of the Code. However, in canon 11 there is enunciated the general principle to be applied throughout the Code, which states that laws must be *expressly* or *equivalently* invalidating or incapacitating if they are to be considered as engendering an effect of invalidity or of nullity.[79]

An invalidating law commands that a certain act be regarded as invalid, and an incapacitating or disqualifying law orders that a certain person be considered disqualified and incapable of performing certain acts.[80] A law is *expressly* invalidating or incapacitating when

[77] Cf. c. 11.

[78] C. 39.

[79] C. 11: Irritantes aut inhabilitantes eae tantum leges habendae sunt, quibus aut actum esse nullum aut inhabilem esse personam expresse vel aequivalenter statuitur.

[80] Cicognani, *Canon Law* (2. revised ed., authorized English version by J. O'Hara and F. Brennan, Philadelphia: The Dolphin Press, 1935), p. 558. Since this study is concerned with disqualifying laws (*leges inhabilitantes*) the following definitions of such laws may be given: "Lex inhabilitans non afficit directe actus veluti lex irritans, sed immediate in *personam* dirigitur, quam incapacem reddit ad quosdam valide actus efficiendos."—Maroto, *Institutiones Iuris Canonici ad normam Iuris Canonici* (2. vols., Romae, 1919-1921. Vol. I, 3. ed., Romae: Apud Commentarium pro Religiosis, 1921), I, n. 223 (hereafter cited as *Institutiones Iuris Canonici*). Michiels explains it thus: "Lex inhabilitans ea dicitur, quae directe respiciens personam agentem, hanc personam ad ponendos quosdam actus iuridicos ita facit absolute vel relative inidoneam eiusve voluntatem ita reddit inefficacem, ut eiusmodi actus, quamvis per se validi essent, invalidi fiant eo quod a tali persona peraguntur."—*Normae Gene-*

it is so stated in so many words; it is *equivalently* invalidating or incapacitating when the law determines the form or formalities certain acts must embrace, or when in the law there are determined certain conditions as requisite for the possession or recovery of personal capacity. Sometimes these forms, formalities and conditions are required for the validity of the act involved, that is, when they are essential to the act itself; at other times the act is valid but illicit, that is, when the law is not fulfilled in its complete detail.[81] Coronata[82] explicitly enumerates a *dummodo* clause as one which expresses so essential a condition to a law that if the condition of that *dummodo* clause is not fulfilled the act is invalid or the person juridically incapable of performing the act.

The law governing the minister of the solemn blessing of a cemetery (cc. 1205, § 1 and 1155, § 1) states that it is the right of the ordinary of the territory in which the cemetery is situated to bless that cemetery, provided that *(dummodo)* the local ordinary just mentioned is endowed with the episcopal character. There seems to be no room for speculation. A non-bishop according to canons 1155, § 1, and 1147, § 1, cannot validly consecrate a church, oratory or altar, and a non-bishop cannot validly bless a cemetery solemnly in virtue of the ruling of canons 1205, § 1, 1155, § 1, 1147, §§ 2, 3. Nor may a priest be delegated by his ordinary to perform the solemn blessing or consecration of a cemetery, for a delegation of this sort would entail a dispensation from the common law,[83] the power to

rales Iuris Canonici (2 vols., Lublin-Polonia: Universitas Catholica, 1929), I, 268.

[81] "*Expresse* irritatio vel inhabilitatio constat quando aptis verbis sancitur, *aequivalenter* quando determinantur forma aut solemnia quibus actus perfici debent vel conditiones quae ad capacitatem habendam sive recuperandam requiruntur. Animadvertendum tamen est, quod sive in forma vel solemniis, sive in conditionibus requisitis a iure, distingui debet id quod est *substantiale* (forma vel conditiones substantiales) et id quod est *accidentale* (forma, etc., accidentales). Si forma vel conditiones substantiales negligantur, actus erit invalidus; non vero si negliguntur accidentalia solemnia vel conditiones."—Maroto, *Institutiones Iuris Canonici,* I, n. 225. Cf. also: Van Hove, *De Legibus Ecclesiasticis,* nn. 160-161.

[82] *Institutiones,* n. 21.

[83] Cc. 1205, § 1; 1155, § 1.

grant such is not given to ordinaries by the Code. Such a dispensation must come from the Roman Pontiff himself.[84]

Accordingly, a priest (i. e., a non-bishop) who attempts solemnly to bless a cemetery without the delegation of the Code [85] or of the Roman Pontiff acts not only illicitly but invalidly. This has always been the unanimous teaching of canonists. It will be remembered that, according to the first known record of the solemn blessing or consecration of cemeteries, St. Gregory was called to go from his own diocese of Tours into the diocese of Poitiers to bless ground for burial. It was quite evident then that a priest could not perform this blessing; otherwise this trip of St. Gregory of Tours would have been unnecessary.[86]

Throughout the history of the solemn blessing of cemeteries from the time of St. Gregory of Tours (+594) until the advent of the Code the valid and licit minister of the solemn blessing of cemeteries was the same as for the consecration of churches.[87] The Code itself incorporated among its canons the pre-Code law on the minister of solemn blessings of cemeteries, as was seen above.[88] And all post-Code authors agree that bishops are the ordinary ministers of this solemn blessing; and that priests are rarely ministers of this rite, and then only with apostolic delegation.[89] Since, then, the Code

[84] Cc. 80, 81.

[85] There are cases in the Code wherein this kind of power is given to persons who are not bishops: to Cardinal-deacons, c. 239, § 1, 20°, and c. 1155, § 1; to vicars and prefects apostolic, c. 294, § 2; to abbots and prelates *nullius*, c. 323, § 2.

[86] Cf. *supra*, pp. 15-17.

[87] Reiffenstuel, lib. III, tit. 40, n. 29; Moulart, *De Sepultura et Coemeteriis*, pp. 101-102. Many (*De Locis Sacris*, n. 144) says: "Minister consecrationis (coemeterii) quoad validitatem et liceitatem est *idem omnino* ac pro consecratione ecclesiae, quia, in *usu universali Ecclesiae*, aequo gradu ponuntur *consecratio ecclesiae et consecratio coemeterii*." (The italics are the author's.)

[88] Cf. *supra*, pp. 68-69.

[89] Coronata, *De Locis et Temporibus Sacris*, n. 145; *Institutiones*, n. 795; De Meester, *Juris Canonici et Juris Canonico-Civilis Compendium* (ed. nova, 3 vols. in 4; Brugis: Desclée, 1921-1928), n. 1115 (hereafter cited as *Compendium*); Augustine, *Commentary*, VI, 104; Rossi, *La "Sepultura Ecclesiastica" e l'"Ius Funerum" nel Diritto Canonico* (Bergamo: Arnoldi, 1920), n. 24; Bargilliat, *Praelectiones Iuris Canonici*, n. 1462; Prümmer, *Manuale Iuris Ca-*

has not changed the pre-Code law on the minister of the solemn blessing of cemeteries, the unanimous opinion of pre-Code authors that episcopal orders are required in the minister must be retained. Canon 6, § 2, expressly legislates for just such a situation.

There are some authors, however, who may *seem* to say that a simple priest, that is, one not delegated by the Code or by the Roman Pontiff, is capable of being the valid and licit minister of the solemn blessing of cemeteries. The texts of Cappello and of Vermeersch-Creusen invite inspection on this point. This is what Cappello says: The solemn and the simple blessing of a cemetery is to be given by him who is the legitimate minister of the blessing of sacred places in general, that is, either by the ordinary (the local ordinary or the major superior of exempt clerics) or by a priest delegated by him.[90] Cappello *seems to say* that the same persons who are the valid and licit ministers of the simple blessing are also the valid and licit ministers of the solemn blessing. In effect, therefore, if this were true, he would be saying that if a bishop wished to have a cemetery solemnly blessed with the rite contained in the Roman Pontifical he could either bless it himself or he could in virtue of the ruling of canon 1156 (which deals with the blessing of sacred places) appoint one of his priests to perform the solemn blessing. By the same token a major superior of exempt regulars could solemnly bless, or appoint one of his priests to bless solemnly a cemetery under his jurisdiction.

But this is certainly not what Cappello wished to say. For this

nonici, n. 373; Woywod, *Commentary,* nn. 1195; 1192; O'Reilly, *Ecclesiastical Sepulture in the New Code of Canon Law,* pp. 15-17; Blat, *Commentarium Textus Codicis Iuris Canonici,* III, pars II, n. 62; Cocchi, *Commentarium in Codicem Iuris Canonici* (8 vols., Taurinorum Augustae: Marietti, 1931-1940. Vol. V, 3. ed., 1932), V, n. 49; Wernz-Vidal, *Ius Canonicum,* IV, n. 566; Beste, *Introductio in Codicem* (Collegeville, Minn.: St. John's Abbey Press, 1938), p. 585.

90 "Benedictio sollemnis et simplex coemeterii dari debet ab eo qui est minister legitimus benedictionis locorum sacrorum in genere, i. e., vel ab Ordinario (Ordinario loci aut Superiore maiore religionis clericalis exemptae) vel a sacerdote ob eo delegato."—*Summa Iuris Canonici* (3 vols., Romae: Universitas Gregoriana, 1936-1939, Vol. II, 3. ed., 1939), II, n. 714.

latter interpretation would be irreconcilable with canon 1205, § 1, which clearly points out that the minister of the solemn blessing of cemeteries is to be the same as for the consecration of churches, oratories and altars; and that the minister of the blessing of cemeteries is the same as the minister of the blessing of sacred places. The explanation of this passage must be, therefore, that Cappello distinguishes the two kinds of blessings of cemeteries, the solemn and the simple, but does not distinguish precisely just who is the qualified minister of the solemn blessing, and who is the minister of the simple blessing, but names all those who are involved in the blessing (solemn and simple) of cemeteries.[91]

The passage in Vermeersch-Creusen is one similar to that of Cappello. They speak of a threefold blessing as found in the liturgical books: the solemn blessing of cemeteries, the simple blessing of cemeteries, and the blessing of individual graves. Then immediately they mention the ministers of the *blessing of cemeteries,* without distinguishing one blessing from another.[92] The same, therefore, must be said of these authors as was said of Cappello, that though they do distinguish the different kinds of blessings, they do not speak in precise language of the minister of each blessing.

[91] The quotation from Cappello, if properly amplified, can be read as follows: "Benedictio sollemnis et simplex coemeterii dari debet ab eo qui est minister legitimus benedictionis [blessing in the general sense, a term which includes both consecration and blessing] locorum sacrorum in genere [cc. 1155, 1156], i. e., vel. ab Ordinario (aut Ordinario loci [for the solemn blessing—cc. 1205, § 1, and 1155, § 1; for the simple blessing—cc. 1205, § 1, and 1156] aut Superiore maiore religionis clericalis exemptae) vel a sacerdote ab eo delegato [cc. 1205, § 1, and 1156]." When something as complex as the determination of the minister of the solemn and the simple blessing is put into a few words or concentrated in one sentence, it is understandable that the author may possibly be misinterpreted.

[92] "Coemeterium in quo fideles sepeliendi sunt benedicemdum est. Triplex benedictio in libris liturgicis invenitur, sc. benedictio sollemnis (*Pont. Rom.*, p. II) aut simplex (*Rit. Rom.*, VIII, c. 29) totius coemeterii et benedictio simplex tumuli (*Rit. Rom.*, VI, c. 3, n. 12). Ius benedicendi coemeterium pertinet privative ad Ordinarium loci, nisi de coemeteriis religionis clericalis exemptae agatur, quae ab Ordinario proprio eiusve delegato benedici possunt."—*Epitome,* II, n. 514.

Article IV. The Permission of the Local Ordinary and of the Religious Ordinary

The solemn blessing of cemeteries is a blessing reserved to the ordinary of the place *(ordinarius territorii)*.[93] Whenever the local ordinary does not himself perform the solemn blessing, his invitation, permission or consent, ***whether he is a bishop or not a bishop,*** must be obtained by the one who does solemnly bless a cemetery in his territory.[94] This permission (*licentia*—c. 1155, § 2) or consent (*consensus*—c. 1157) will be necessary as often as the following situations occur:

(1) When the vicar general, being a bishop, is to bless solemnly a cemetery in his own diocese. The special *mandatum* he must have provides the necessary permission;[95]

(2) When an outside bishop wishes to bless solemnly a cemetery within the territory of another;[96]

(3) When a cardinal solemnly blesses a cemetery outside his own territory and within the territory of the local ordinary;[97]

(4) When religious, even exempt regulars, wish to have their cemeteries blessed;[98]

(5) When a religious bishop residing within or outside the territory of the local ordinary wishes to bless solemnly a cemetery within the sphere of the latter's jurisdiction;[99]

(6) When, by virtue of an apostolic indult, a priest has the power solemnly to bless ground for burial, and wishes to do so within the territory of his own or another ordinary *(ordinarius territorii)*.[100]

[93] Cc. 1205, § 1; 1155.

[94] Canon 1155, § 2; Ordinarius territorii, licet charactere episcopali careat, potest cuilibet eiusdem ritus Episcopo *licentiam* dare consecrationes peragendi in suo territorio.

[95] Cc. 1155, §§ 1-2; 1157.

[96] C. 1157.

[97] Cc. 239, § 1, 20°; 1157.

[98] C. 1155, § 1.

[99] Cf. cc. 1155, § 1; 1157.

[100] C. 1157.

The local ordinary who is not a bishop (e. g., the vicar capitular or administrator of a vacant diocese), since he cannot solemnly bless a cemetery,[101] must call in a bishop to perform this ceremony.[102] It is, of course, only for the licitness of the blessing, but nonetheless a strict obligation, that he must invite only a bishop of the same rite as his own.[103] Accordingly a local ordinary of the Latin rite may invite only a bishop of the Latin rite to perform the solemn blessing of cemeteries in his territory. Should there be a cemetery belonging to some Oriental rite (v. g., to the Greek or Ruthenian Catholics) within the borders of a Latin diocese, the local ordinary is not solemnly to bless that cemetery, but is to call in the proper Oriental bishop. If this is impossible, the Latin episcopal ordinary of the place may solemnly bless that cemetery, but not without previously obtaining the permission of the Sacred Congregation for the Oriental Church.[104]

It is only for the licitness of his act that an outside bishop must have the permission or the invitation of the ordinary of the place before he attempts the solemn blessing of any cemetery outside his own territory.[105] However, the local ordinary's permission is due on another count, since this solemn blessing requires the use of pontificals (crosier and miter),[106] and since bishops are expressly forbidden by the Code,[107] as they were once forbidden by the Council of Trent,[108] to perform pontifical functions outside their own diocese and in the territory of another without the express, or at the very least the reasonably presumed, permission of the local ordinary.

When religious cemeteries of exempt clerical institutes are involved, the consent of the religious ordinary [109] must be obtained (for licitness) in addition to the permission of the ordinary of the place

101 Cc. 1205, § 1; 1155, § 1.

102 C. 1155, § 2.

103 Augustine, *Commentary,* VI, 5. Cf. also Cappello, *Summa Iuris Canonici,* II, n. 662.

104 Vermeersch-Creusen, *Epitome,* II, n. 471.

105 Cf. c. 1147; § 1.

106 C. 337, § 2.

107 C. 337, § 1.

108 Sess. VI, *de ref.,* c. 5.

109 Cc. 198, § 1; 488, 8°.

in instances of the solemn blessing of these cemeteries.[110] For the solemn blessing of the cemeteries of other religious [111] the permission of the ordinary of the place suffices.[112] All religious, exempt or non-exempt, who have the special privilege of being able to consecrate sacred places, must, before they exercise this power, obtain the permission of the ordinary of the place, unless they themselves are local ordinaries, or unless an exemption from this obligation is included in their privilege.[113]

Pope Leo X, in his constitution *Dum intra* of December 19, 1516,[114] gave to all regulars the privilege of selecting their own consecrator when the ordinary of the place had been petitioned two or three times to perform the consecration of their church or cemetery and had for no good reason refused to do so. Whether the regulars are to be considered as enjoying this privilege today, since it is an exception to or at least a qualification of canon 1155, § 1, is a controverted question. Authors are divided on the question. Some hold that regulars can exercise their choice of a bishop should the occasion arise to use the privilege;[115] others strictly deny them this

[110] Cc. 1155; 1157.

[111] The distinction here made between the religious of exempt clerical institutes and the religious of other institutes amounts to this: The ordinary of the place has the full right to consecrate or solemnly bless (or, if he is not a bishop, to appoint a bishop to consecrate or solemnly bless) all cemeteries in his territory, whether they be parochial, interparochial or religious (c. 1155). When there is question of the cemeteries of exempt regulars, however, the local ordinary has not the same *full right* (though he has the right—c. 1155) to the solemn blessing, inasmuch as he must for the licitness of his act have the consent of the major superior (c. 1157). If an outside bishop is solemnly to bless the cemetery of exempt religious, he will need both the permission of the local ordinary (c. 1155) and the consent of the religious ordinary (c. 1157).

[112] Cc. 1155, § 1; 1157; 198, § 1.

[113] Cf. Coronata, *De Locis et Temporibus Sacris,* n. 5.

[114] *Fontes,* n. 72; cf. *supra,* p. 30.

[115] Bondini, *De Privilegio Exemptionis seu de Regularium Immunitate ab Ordinariorum Locorum Iurisdictione prout in Novo Iuris Canonici Codice Sancitur* (Romae, 1919), pp. 111-112; Augustine, *Commentary,* VI, 4; Coronata, *Institutiones,* n. 726; *De Locis et Temporibus Sacris,* n. 5; O'Reilly, *Ecclesiastical Sepulture in the New Code of Canon Law,* p. 17; Cappello, *Summa Iuris Canonici,* II, n. 662.

privilege;[116] still others say that this right is extremely doubtful.[117] A study of canon 1155 reveals that the ordinary of the place has not only the power (if he is a bishop) but also the right to consecrate all the sacred places in his territory, and to bless solemnly all cemeteries (c. 1205, § 1). This is true even of places belonging to and destined for the exclusive use of regulars, for this case is given specific consideration in the canon.[118] The Code, therefore, must be taken in its obvious and unmistakable meaning, namely, that when regulars have a cemetery to be blessed solemnly, they must notify the ordinary of the place, whose right and duty it is to see that the cemetery is blessed. But the point at which the commentators part company is where the local ordinary has been notified several times of the necessity of solemnly blessing a cemetery belonging to regulars, and has without legitimate cause refused to see that the cemetery is blessed. Some say that the privilege accorded to regulars by Leo X in the year 1516, namely of calling in an outside bishop in such a case, has survived the Code, and some maintain that it has not. The privilege of Leo X was to the effect that regulars who had, with all due reverence, asked the ordinary of the place to consecrate a church or altar, or to bless a cemetery, as many as two or three times, and had been refused by him, could ask an outside bishop to perform the consecration or blessing.[119]

Vermeersch-Creusen hold that the privilege of Leo X was taken away from the regulars just a few years after it had been extended to all of them, at the time, namely, of the Council of Trent (1545-1563), when in the strong language of that Council bishops were

[116] Blat, *Commentarium Textus Codicis Iuris Canonici,* III, pars II, 3; Vermeersch-Creusen, *Epitome,* II, n. 471.

[117] Melo, *De Exemptione Regularium* (The Catholic University of America Canon Law Studies, n. 12, Washington, D. C.: The Catholic University of America, 1921), p. 133; Cocchi, *Commentarium in Codicem Iuris Canonici,* V, n. 1.

[118] "Consecratio alicuius loci, *quanquam ad regulares pertinentis,* spectat ad ordinarium territorii. . . ."

[119] "Nec ab alieno Episcopo consecrationem ecclesiae, vel altaris, aut coemeterii benedictionem petere . . . nisi ubi Ordinarius bis, aut ter cum debitis reverentia, et instantia requisitus, sine legitima causa id recusaverit."—Const. *Dum intra,* 19 dec. 1516, n. 12—*Fontes,* n. 72.

unqualifiedly forbidden the use of pontificals in the diocese of another without the latter's permission.[120] Most authors, however, have held that the privilege outlasted the Council of Trent.[121]

With the coming of the Code authors were not all so sure that this privilege of regulars could still be called upon when the occasion arose. In the first place the Code reiterated the law of the Council of Trent when it decreed in canon 337, § 1, that a bishop could not conduct pontifical functions outside his diocese without the express or the reasonably presumed consent of the ordinary of the place. In the second paragraph of this same canon the Code defined just what was meant by conducting pontifical functions *("exercere pontificalia")*. This term meant in law the conducting of those sacred functions in which the laws of the sacred liturgy require the use of the pontifical insignia, the use, that is, of the crosier and miter. The solemn blessing of cemeteries, therefore, was made one of the sacred functions prohibited to outside bishops, for in that blessing the Roman Pontifical requires the bishop-minister to use the crosier and miter.[122]

Canon 1155 cannot be said to touch on the privilege of regulars which is the question here. It simply states that all consecrations of sacred places, and the solemn blessing of cemeteries (c. 1205, § 1), are in the hands of the ordinary of the territory in which the place is located. Even though it does not take cognizance of it, this canon cannot be said to have eliminated the privilege of regulars, which was meant to go into effect only when the ordinary of the place had refused, after repeated invitations, to consecrate or solemnly bless a sacred place.

On the other hand, canon 1157 does specifically eliminate and nullify all contrary privileges.[123] This canon declares that, no matter

[120] Sess. VI, *de ref.*, c. 5: "Nulli episcopo liceat, cuiusvis privilegii praetextu, pontificalia in alterius dioecesi exercere, nisi de Ordinarii loci expressa licentia. . . . Si secus factum fuerit, episcopus ab exercitio pontificalium . . . sit ipso iure suspensus." Cf. Vermeersch-Creusen, *Epitome,* II, n. 471.

[121] Cf. *supra,* pp. 30-31; 85-86.

[122] Tit. *De Coemeterii Benedictione.*

[123] "Non obstante quolibet privilegio, nemo potest locum sacrum consecrare vel benedicere sine Ordinarii consensu." Cf. also c. 4.

what privileges were in effect before the Code, no one can consecrate or bless a sacred place now without the consent of the ordinary. From the point of view of the present problem, the important word in this canon is *"Ordinarii."* From canon 198 it is to be seen that while major superiors of exempt clerical institutes are not included in the term *"ordinarii loci seu locorum,"* these regular superiors are included in the term *"ordinarii."* Therefore it cannot be held that canon 1157 removes from the number of privileges which regulars have enjoyed in the past the privilege of selecting their own bishop-consecrator when the local ordinary has failed in his duty. For this privilege can be put into use without in any way violating canon 1157. This latter canon does have this effect on the privilege, however, that when local regular superiors, for example priors who are not major superiors,[124] and therefore are not to be understood as ordinaries,[125] may have been able before the Code to exercise the privilege of calling in an outside bishop to consecrate a sacred place, they must now have the consent of their major superiors (ordinarii) before they act. Canon 1157 does not make it necessary for local or major superiors of exempt clerical institutes to have the permission of the *local* ordinary to call in another bishop to perform the consecration or solemn blessing when the former has refused to do it. The outside bishop, likewise, does not in virtue of the ruling of canon 1157 need the consent of the ordinary of the place before he performs such a consecration or solemn blessing, provided that he has the invitation or consent of the major regular superior.

In conclusion, the following résumé will epitomize the question and give what appears to be the only practical solution. Authors, as has already been pointed out, are divided on the question. The Code, in canon 4, lays down the principle that privileges enjoyed before 1918 continue in force unless "by the canons of this Code they are expressly revoked." Nowhere has this privilege been expressly revoked; therefore it must be considered as still existing. However, in concrete cases, this privilege will seldom be used. Bishops, knowing full well the law of canons 337, § 1, and 1155, § 1, and realizing

[124] C. 488, 8°.
[125] C. 198, § 1.

that the spirit behind these laws is that each bishop is, under the Roman Pontiff, supreme in his diocese, will not be pleased to find themselves invited to perform a ceremony as solemn as the consecration or the solemn blessing of sacred places—rites that are reserved in ordinary circumstances to the local bishop—in the diocese of another, who it may be presumed is utterly unwilling that such a ceremony take place. Practically taken, therefore, the only procedure open to religious, exempt and non-exempt alike, against a local ordinary who is failing in his duty, is to have recourse to the Holy See.[126]

[126] Cf. Vermeersch-Creusen, *Epitome,* II, n. 471.

CHAPTER VII

THE SIMPLE BLESSING OF CEMETERIES

BESIDES the solemn blessing or consecration of cemeteries there is also the simple blessing of cemeteries.[1] This latter is not merely an invocative blessing *(benedictio invocativa)*, but it is really a constitutive blessing *(benedictio constitutiva)*, and by it profane ground becomes sacred. The ceremony is not quite as elaborate as the rite of solemn blessing which is to be found in the Roman Pontifical.[2] The ordinary minister of the simple blessing is a priest delegated by the ordinary of the place or by the regular major superior.[3]

ARTICLE I. THE RITE OF THE SIMPLE BLESSING

The day before the blessing of a cemetery a wooden cross, in height between five and six feet, is set up in the middle of the cemetery. Other things are prepared in the cemetery and in the sacristy (or if the cemetery be not near a church, in a house or shelter nearby), such as candles, a step-ladder, a vessel with holy water, a censer and boat, etc., as directed by the *Rituale Romanum*.[4] In the rite itself most of the prayers and ceremonies take place before this wooden cross which during the course of the ceremony is blessed. At one stage of the cemetery blessing, however, after the litany of the saints, the priest makes a complete circuit of the cemetery and sprinkles holy water throughout the whole area to be blessed. He then returns to the cross in the center of the cemetery, places three candles upon it, one on the vertical piece, and one on each of the horizontal arms, and then incenses and sprinkles the cross with holy water. With this the ceremony is completed.

[1] *Rituale Romanum*, tit. VIII, c. 29.

[2] Tit. *De Coemeterii Benedictione*.

[3] *Rituale Romanum*, tit. VIII, c. 29; cc. 1205, § 1, and 1156.

[4] Tit. VIII, c. 29. Cf. Schulte, *Benedicenda: Rites and Ceremonies to be Observed in some of the Principal Functions of the Roman Pontifical and the Roman Ritual* (New York: Benziger Brothers, 1907), pp. 80-81 (hereafter cited as *Benedicenda*).

Article II. The Minister of the Simple Blessing

Canon 1205, § 1, explicitly determines that the blessing of cemeteries is to be governed as to the minister by canon 1156, which as an introductory canon designates the ministers of the blessing of sacred places. In canon 1156 it is stated that the right of blessing a sacred place belongs either to the ordinary of the place in whose territory the place is located, or to the major superior of exempt religious,[5] or to a priest delegated by one or the other. The ordinary of the place or his delegate will be the proper minister when the place to be blessed is parochial or interparochial, or when it belongs to or is for the use of the secular clergy, of non-exempt religious, or of the laity. It goes without saying that the major superior of exempt regulars or his delegate will be the minister of blessing only when the place to be blessed is under the jurisdiction of that major superior.

In the application of canon 1156 specifically to cemeteries, as canon 1205, § 1, directs, the rule is that the simple blessing of cemeteries pertains to the ordinary of the place or to his delegate for all the cemeteries in his territory except those which belong to exempt religious. Cemeteries of exempt religious may be blessed by the major superior or by his delegate without any permission or consent of the local ordinary.[6] It is to be noted here that in the solemn blessing of a cemetery the permission of the local ordinary is always necessary, no matter who owns the cemetery or who is the minister.[7]

Since the simple blessing of cemeteries requires priestly orders and not the episcopal character, any priest may validly bless a cemetery even though he does it illicitly and acts without the necessary delegation from the local or religious ordinary.[8] Should it happen that superiors of exempt regulars, who are not however major superiors, have the privilege of blessing cemeteries without receiving a specific delegation,[9] then these local superiors would still have to

[5] Cf. cc. 198; 488, 8°.

[6] Cf. cc. 1156; 1157.

[7] Cf. cc. 1155; 1157.

[8] Cc. 1147, § 3; 1156; *Rituale Romanum*, tit. VIII, c. 29.

[9] Such a privilege was granted to the Friars Minor in 1514 by Leo X, for the text of which see *supra*, pp. 35-36.

obtain the consent (not delegation) of their major superiors by reason of canon 1157 for any blessing of cemeteries they wish to perform.[10] This canon (1157) does not revoke any privilege which may have granted to religious superiors the power of blessing their own cemeteries without a specific delegation, but it is very explicit in eliminating any privileges *("non obstante quolibet privilegio")* whereby the *consent* of either the local ordinary or the religious ordinary could be considered as not necessary. This consent is now, since the Code is in force, required in every case for the simple blessing as well as for the solemn blessing or consecration. It is to be understood, of course, that the *delegation* given to a priest by the ordinary of the place or by the religious ordinary in accordance with the requirement of canon 1156 also provides the *consent* of these superiors as demanded by canon 1157.

[10] This consent may be given in a general fashion and in pressing cases may be readily presumed.—Coronata, *De Locis et Temporibus Sacris,* n. 5; *Institutiones,* n. 726.

CHAPTER VIII

THE NECESSITY OF THE BLESSING OF A CEMETERY

ARTICLE I. THE BLESSING OF CEMETERIES OWNED BY THE CHURCH

THE Code, in canon 1239, § 3, states that all the faithful are to be given Christian burial [1] unless it is clear that they are expressly deprived by law (as for example in canons 1239, § 1, and 1240). In canon 1204 the Code defines what it means by Christian burial: the transfer of the remains to the church, the funeral services in the church, and the interment in a place lawfully appointed for the burial of the faithful departed. And just what is considered a place legitimately designated for Catholic burials is very distinctly defined in canon 1205, § 1. This canon states that the bodies of the faithful, that is, of those whose interment is not prohibited (canons 1239-1240), are to be buried in a cemetery, which the Church possesses in her own name (canon 1206, § 1), and which has been blessed either solemnly or simply according to the rites found in the *Pontificale Romanum* or the *Rituale Romanum.*[2] In another place (canon 1154) the Code states that Catholic cemeteries are sacred places assigned by the liturgical consecration or blessing which they receive to the special purpose of receiving the bodies of the faithful.

From the earliest days of the Church, even within the lifetime of the Apostles, there have been Christian cemeteries, that is, cemeteries which were used exclusively for the burial of Christians. Of this fact there is no doubt.[3] But just when the first Christian cemetery was blessed, and exactly at what Council or by the decree of what Roman Pontiff it was made obligatory that all Christian

[1] The Roman Ritual also expresses this rule very clearly (tit. VI, c. 1, n. 18): "Ceterum nemo Christianus in communione fidelium defunctus, extra ecclesiam aut coemeterium rite benedictum sepeliri debet."

[2] Tit. *De Coemeterii Benedictione,* in the former; and in the latter: tit. VIII, c. 29.

[3] Cf. *supra,* pp. 11-12.

cemeteries be blessed, history does not disclose. It is true, however, that by the sixth century the Church had for some time insisted that the bishop of the place bless the burial places of the faithful before Christians were allowed to be buried there. The incident which clearly illustrates this is the one which St. Gregory of Tours recounts in his "*De Gloria Confessorum.*"[4] Radegunde, a one-time queen of the Franks, died a member of a monastery in Poitiers. The place where she was to be buried had not been blessed, and the bishop of the place was away from the city. So important did the abbess of the monastery deem the burial of Radegunde in blessed ground that she called upon the services of the neighboring bishop, St. Gregory of Tours, to make the rather considerable journey from Tours to Poitiers, a distance of at least sixty miles, to bless the ground for the burial.[5]

After the time of St. Gregory of Tours (538-594), one experiences little difficulty in seeing that the mind of the Church was, first that she possess cemeteries of her own, and secondly that these cemeteries be solemnly blessed, and when this was impossible, that they at least be blessed with the rite of the Roman Ritual.[6] The Code, in canons 1206, § 1, and 1205, § 1, reasserts the Church's right to have her own cemeteries, and, possessing them as her exclusive property, to have them blessed with a solemn or simple blessing.

The law of the Code, therefore, is that when the Church owns her cemeteries, these are to be blessed before the bodies of the faithful are to be interred in them.[7] What is not specifically prescribed by the Code is whether the cemetery is to be blessed in the solemn or in the simple form. It is not difficult, however, to know the mind of the Church on this point, if one considers the canonical legislation on the consecration and blessing of churches which in so many of its details parallels the legislation on cemeteries. The Code's first choice is that all churches be consecrated. But, realizing that not all

[4] C. 104—*MGH, Scriptores Rerum Merovingicarum,* I, 815.

[5] *Supra*, pp. 15-16.

[6] Prümmer, *Manuale Iuris Canonici,* n. 373.

[7] Cc. 1154, 1205, § 1. Cf. also Coronata, *De Locis et Temporibus Sacris,* n. 144; Cappello, *Summa Iuris Canonici,* II, nn. 711, 714; Wernz-Vidal, *Ius Canonicum,* IV, n. 562.

churches can fulfill the stringent conditions for consecration, she provides for the blessing of these churches and does not feel that she can require them to be consecrated. She does require cathedral churches to be consecrated, and, if at all possible, also collegiate, conventual and parish churches.[8]

The Church, preferring that whenever possible churches should be consecrated and not just blessed, would seem to have the same prior choice in the matter of cemeteries. It is natural that the Church should wish that her sacred places receive a solemn and not merely a simple dedication to their religious purposes. But inasmuch as the simple as well as the solemn blessing constitutes cemeteries as sacred places and affords them the same juridical effects, one finds today that more often than not cemeteries are blessed with the simple rite rather than with the solemn ceremony.[9]

Article II. The Blessing of Cemeteries not Owned by the Church

It is a frequent occurrence today to find Catholic cemeteries as such a practical impossibility, that is to say, in some localities for one reason or another the Church does not possess her own blessed cemeteries. Sometimes the Church *cannot* have in her own name the ground in which she must bury her faithful departed. There have been and still are, for example, countries where all cemetery property is owned by the State. No private corporaton can possess such property, since by law burial ground can be owned, administered and maintained only by the government.[10] In the United States the

[8] C. 1165, § 3.

[9] Many, *De Locis Sacris*, n. 144.

[10] "It is a well known fact," says Augustine, "that in Rome even Cardinals must be buried in the common city cemetery."—*Commentary*, VI, 106. In France cemeteries are government-owned.—Many, *De Locis Sacris*, n. 143; Bargilliat, *Praelectiones Iuris Canonici* (37. ed., 2 vols., Parisiis: Apud Baston, Berche et Pagis, 1923), n. 1458; cf. also Lucien Crouzil, "Cimetière, VIII: Les Cimetières en Droit Français," *Dictionnaire de Droit Canonique*, III, 741-745. Herbert Thurston in his article "Cemetery" in the *Catholic Encyclopedia* (III, 508), quotes Dr. Peter Lex, *Das kirchliche Begrabnissrecht* (Ratisbon, 1904) as giving the situation in Germany: "From the principles which now obtain in

Church experiences no opposition or restrictions in the ownership and maintenance of her cemeteries. Any private corporation, religious or secular, may own and operate cemeteries.[11]

In other instances, because of the high degree of bigotry and religious prejudice in some Protestant or atheistic communities, the Church *does not* own any cemetery property. Frequently, too, it happens that a separate cemetery for Catholics would be impracticable, when, as is often the case, the Catholics are too few in number or too poor to have their own cemetery.

When the Church, therefore, *can not* or *does not* have her own cemeteries, what is to be said of the blessing of the ground in which Catholics are to be buried? Consistent with the Church's desire that all the faithful be buried in blessed ground, the Code provides three remedies to take care of the three distinct and different situations that may arise: (1) when Catholics are permitted to have their own separate section in the municipal cemetery, this special Catholic section is to be blessed; (2) when Catholics must be buried indiscriminately with non-Catholics in a common cemetery, the whole cemetery is to be blessed provided the Catholic burials outnumber the non-Catholic ones; (3) when Catholics cannot have their own section in the communal cemetery and at the same time non-Catholic burials are in excess of the Catholic, each individual grave is to be blessed at the time of burial.[12]

1. *The Blessing of a Special Section Reserved for Catholic Burials*

Should the Church for one reason or another not possess her own cemetery, her preference would be that she have the exclusive use

German law, the idea of a Catholic churchyard from the point of view of Catholic teaching and practice has been completely suppressed and the cemetery has been degraded into a mere burial-ground belonging to the civil corporation." For the law in Spanish speaking countries cf. Ferreres, *Institutiones Canonicae* (2. ed., 2 vols., Barcinone: E. Subirana, 1920), II, n. 126.

[11] Zollmann, *American Church Law* (St. Paul, Minn.: West Publishing Co., 1933), n. 619: Augustine, *Commentary,* VI, 108; Woywod, *A Practical Commentary,* n. 1238.

[12] C. 1206, §§ 2-3.

of one portion of the common burial-ground.[13] This special section then could and should be blessed,[14] and to all intents and purposes it would be just as private, and just as satisfactory, as though the Church possessed it as her own cemetery. If possible the Catholic section should be fenced off from the remainder of the community cemetery and a separate entrance be made for this reserved plot.[15]

2. *The Blessing of the Whole Municipal Cemetery*

When the Church cannot possess her own cemetery and cannot obtain the exclusive use of one section of the municipal cemetery it is now prescribed by the Code (c. 1206, § 2) that, if the burials are predominently Catholic, the whole cemetery is to be blessed. This is an obligation that each local ordinary is to take care of wherever and whenever such a situation exists in his territory.

The Church in canon 1206, § 2, has in mind a very specific situation. In many countries, especially in Europe, which themselves are largely Catholic or which have many Catholic communities, there is a law that cemeteries are to be under the exclusive ownership of the municipality or the State. No public or private non-governmental corporation may legally own or even operate cemeteries. All cemeteries are public, for the use of all citizens indiscriminately, and no religious or lay group may reserve a plot or section for the exclusive use of its adherents.[16] By law, therefore, in these countries the native right of the Church to possess her own cemeteries has been denied and there exists no immediate hope of changing this situation. In such cases the Code directs bishops to bless or have blessed all cemeteries in their territory where most of the burials are Catholic, provided that this, too, is not prohibited by the civil authorities.

The Church, as has been said, has in mind municipally-owned cemeteries, for she refers to "*coemeteria societatis civilis propria.*"[17]

[13] S. C. de Prop. de Fide, litt. (*ad Ep. Rosen.*), 16 apr. 1862—*Fontes*, n. 4856; Coronata, *De Locis et Temporibus Sacris*, p. 148, note 5.

[14] C. 1206, § 2. Cf. also: S. C. S. Off., instr. (*ad Ep. Scapusien.*), 16 aug. 1781—*Fontes*, n. 843.

[15] S. C. de Prop. Fide (C. G.), 29 mart. 1830—*Fontes*, n. 4747.

[16] Cf. *supra*, p. 95.

[17] C. 1206, § 2.

But what about those cemeteries which are owned by a private individual or by a private or public corporation and in which the greater number of interments are Catholic? Is such a cemetery to be blessed? The answer must be in the negative for two reasons. First, the explicit mention in the Code of "cemeteries owned by the civil authority" contains by that very fact an implicit exclusion of all other types of cemeteries. And secondly, the Church will be effectively denied her native right to possess cemeteries of her own without any hope of recovering that right only through legislation. The important point to remember is that the Church must be *denied* the right to own cemeteries. The fact that she finds it impossible or impracticable (e. g., for economic reasons) to have her own cemetery in a given locality is not sufficient to allow the blessing of the whole cemetery even though most of the burials are of Catholics.

The provision for the blessing of a whole cemetery where many non-Catholics are to be buried as well as Catholics, even though the latter be in a greater number, is somewhat new.[18] Before the Code there was great hesitancy in blessing a municipal cemetery because such cemeteries were so frequently subject to possible violation by the burial of heretics.[19] But the Church seemed willing even as early as 1874 to reckon with the chance of possible violation, since the good to be obtained far outweighed the possible evil that might be sustained. The absolute government control of cemeteries in the 19th century was becoming more and more common in Europe. Some communities made up entirely of Catholics, and other communities which were predominantly Catholic, could not own their own cemeteries. As a result the common cemeteries in these localities were not being blessed. Bishops inquired of Rome if it would not be possible to bless government-owned cemeteries in cases wherein practically all the burials were Catholic, and the Sacred Congregation of the Inquisition replied to the Bishops of Belgium on July 8, 1874, to the effect that such cemeteries should be blessed whenever that was possible.

The Code,[20] therefore, confirming a practice already sanctioned,

[18] Coronata, *De Locis et Temporibus Sacris*, n. 144.
[19] Many, *De Locis Sacris*, n. 143.
[20] C. 1206, § 2.

now instructs ordinaries to bless community cemeteries which are open to all, Catholic and non-Catholic alike, provided that most of the burials were those of the bodies of Catholics. But a relevant question may well be asked: does this mean that the Church wishes that all municipal cemeteries in predominantly Catholic communities are to be blessed in their entirety, or does the Church wish rather that she be given a specific portion of that common cemetery for the burial of her faithful, which portion she will bless to the exclusion of the other section left for non-Catholic burials? For in every locality where the Church cannot or does not have her own cemetery, even though most of the burials are those of Catholics, there are always two possibilities. Either a certain section is allotted to Catholic burials and another to non-Catholic burials, or Catholics and non-Catholics are buried indiscriminately throughout the whole cemetery.

Vermeersch-Creusen, without entering into any discussion of the question, give their opinion that, if in a Catholic community the Church had her choice between the exclusive use of a special section of the municipal cemetery for the burials of her faithful on the one hand and the indiscriminate burial of Catholics among the non-Catholics on the other hand, she would choose the latter. Basing their opinion on canon 1206, § 2, they state that the Church *prefers* to bless the whole civic cemetery where both Catholics and non-Catholics are to be buried rather than in such a case to divide the cemetery into two parts, one for the Catholics and one for the non-Catholics, and to bless the former and not the latter. The reason they give is this: by the blessing of the whole cemetery the right of the Church is better recognized and vindicated than by the blessing of but one part of the cemetery assigned to Catholic burials.[21]

In the sentence following the one just quoted in the accompanying footnote, Vermeersch-Creusen in their 1925 (2nd) edition had this to say: Even in the case when in Catholic communities Catholics

[21] *Epitome* (II, n. 516): "Ex constanti Ecclesiae disciplina, non licet acatholicos in coemeterio benedicto sepelire. At videtur Codex tolerantiam istius mali saparationi coemeterii in varias partes praeferre, ubi cives maiore ex parte sunt catholici. Benedictione enim totius coemeterii ius Ecclesiae melius agnoscitur et significatur, quam si pars tantum ei assignetur."

are buried indiscriminately among non-Catholics, the prescription of canon 1212 should be carried out as far as possible, which prescribes that there should be an unblessed section for the burial of those who may not be given Christian burial.[22] In other words, the above authors, after saying that the Church *prefers* to bless the whole municipally-owned cemetery rather than just a part designated for Catholic burials, added that inasfar as possible a special plot or section is to be set aside which shall remain unblessed, as required by canon 1212, to be reserved for those who may not be given Christian burial. But if one portion is to be unblessed and appointed for those who *are not* to receive Christian burial, then the other section must of a necessity be for those who *are* to be given Christian burial. Therefore, in effect, Vermeersch-Creusen were saying that there should be a Catholic section and a non-Catholic section, the former to be blessed, the latter to remain unblessed, even in those places where the Catholic interments outnumber the non-Catholic. For in the terms of the Code only the faithful who die in communion with the Catholic Church are to be given Christian burial *("sepultura ecclesiastica")*, and all non-Catholics as well as those Catholics who are listed in canon 1240, § 1, may not be given Christian burial.[23]

[22] "Etiam in hoc primo casu [i. e., where the whole cemetery is blessed, and not just one section of it] servandus est quantum fieri potest c. 1212 qui postulat ut locus, non benedictus, humandis iis destinetur qui sepultura ecclesiastica non donantur."—*Loc. cit.*

[23] Kerin (*The Privation of Christian Burial*, pp. 173-187) discusses the interesting question whether material heretics are excluded from Christian burial, that is, those non-Catholics who belong to a heretical sect without knowing that they are acting against the law of the Church. Canon 1240, § 1, 1°, "refuses Christian burial only to those who *notoriously* belong to a heretical sect ("sectae haereticae . . . *notarie addicti*"), and that means that they must appear both to know that what they do is against the law of the Church, and to will to do it nevertheless, and therefore be guilty of a formal delict." After a thorough study of the question, Kerin comes to the conclusion that canon 1240 does not apply to non-Catholics as such, but to Catholics who have deserted their faith and have notoriously become affiliated with some heretical sect; and that all non-Catholics, whether they are formal or material heretics, are excluded. Therefore a distinction, as Vermeersch-Creusen made in their earlier edition, between those who *are* and those who *are not* to be given Christian burial, is nothing else than a distinction between Catholic burials and non-Catholic burials.

In the 1934 (5th) edition, the above contradiction was corrected in favor of the opinion that the Church prefers to have blessed the whole municipal cemetery in which both Catholics and non-Catholics are buried, rather than to have blessed a section devoted solely to Catholic burials in localities where the burials are predominantly Catholic. In this later edition mention of canon 1212 concerning a section for non-Catholic interments is omitted.

There is some foundation for the opinion of Vermeersch-Creusen in the arrangement and wording of canon 1206, § 2. In that canon it is stated that when the right of the Church to have her own cemetery has been violated, and there is no hope of recovering that right, the local ordinaries shall see to it (1) that the civil cemeteries are blessed, provided that the majority of interments there are Catholic burials, or at least (2) that the Catholics have a special section reserved for them, which part is to be blessed.[24] It would almost seem from this canon that the Church did prefer to have the whole civil cemetery blessed when Catholic burials are more numerous than non-Catholic interments, rather than to have a blessed section that is reserved for Catholics. But this is not so. For the whole tradition of the Church has always been that there should be provided separate cemeteries for the burial of the faithful, these cemeteries to be owned and blessed by the Church. No one will deny, either, that it has always been the custom of the Church to exclude all non-Catholics and unworthy Catholics from Christian burial, on the principle that was first enunciated by Pope St. Leo the Great, and later reiterated many times by succeeding Roman Pontiffs: *"Quibus viventibus non communicavimus, mortuis communicare non possumus."* [25]

Hence, in keeping with these traditions and with the principle of St. Leo the Great, the Church, it must be said, would much prefer, in cases when she cannot own her own cemetery, that the common or municipal cemetery be divided into two parts, one for Catholic

[24] C. 1206, § 2: Sicubi hoc Ecclesiae ius violetur nec spes sit ut violatio reparetur, curent locorum Ordinarii ut coemeteria, societatis civilis propria, benedicantur, si, qui in eis condi solent, sint maiore ex parte catholici, aut saltem ut in eis catholici spatium habeant, idque benedictum, sibi reservatum.

[25] *Epistola CLXVII—MPL,* LIV, 1205-1206.

and one for non-Catholic burials. This is true whether the Catholic burials are in the majority or in the minority, whether the percentage of Catholic interments is ninety per cent or ten per cent. If in a Catholic community the Church is allowed to have her way, she will choose to set aside an adequate plot for the burial of unbelievers and heretics and unworthy Catholics. This latter section she will leave unblessed; the larger section which is reserved, therefore, for those who are to receive Christian burial she will bless. It is only in Catholic communities, where the Church is not allowed to possess her own cemeteries and is not permitted to provide separate sections for Catholic and non-Catholic burials, that she permits (but in no wise prefers) the blessing of the whole municipal cemetery, in which Catholic and heretic and unbeliever are laid to rest side by side. It is entirely the exception, says Coronata, that the Church would allow in a cemetery blessed by her sacred rites the interment of unbelievers and heretics. The burial of such persons in sacred ground must be considered an act of mere tolerance on the part of the Church, and not of positive permission, and therefore as often as it *can* be avoided it *must* be avoided *("quoties vitari potest, vitanda est")*.[26] That the blessing of a common municipal cemetery in localities which are for the greater part Catholic is rather a tolerance than a preference of the Church is the opinion of most canonists who express their views on the question.[27]

But can this view be reconciled with the wording of canon 1206, § 2, which says: " . . . *curent locorum Ordinarii ut coemeteria, societatis civilis propria, benedicantur, si, qui in eis condi solent, sint maiore ex parte catholici, aut saltem ut in eis catholici spatium habeant, idque benedictum, sibi reservatum.*" Two different meanings can be had from this part of canon 1206. To indicate the two possible meanings there follows the English equivalent of this part

[26] " . . . exceptio illa qua infideles in coemeterio benedicto sepeliri permittuntur, ut mera tolerantia Ecclesiae consideranda est, non ut positiva permissio, et proinde quoties vitari potest, vitanda est."—*De Locis et Temporibus Sacris*, n. 137.

[27] Coronata, *loc. cit.*; De Meester, *Compendium*, n. 1172; Cance, *Le Code de Droit Canonique, Commentaire Succinct et Pratique* (5. ed., 3 vols., Paris: J. Gabalda et Fils, 1930), III, n. 32, note 2.

of the canon, and in parentheses and in italics an added clause which will help to illustrate the different meanings.

> (1) Local ordinaries are to see to it that municipal cemeteries are blessed if most of the burials are of Catholics, or at least *(where Catholic burials outnumber the non-Catholic)* that Catholics have a special blessed section for themselves.
>
> (2) Local ordinaries are to see to it that municipal cemeteries are blessed if most of the burials are of Catholics, or at least *(where the Church is not allowed to bless the whole cemetery or where the number of Catholic burials is less than that of the non-Catholic)* that Catholics have a special blessed section for themselves.

Apparently Vermeersch-Creusen take the first (1) meaning;[28] Coronata, Wernz-Vidal and the others derive from the canon the second (2) meaning.[29] If the first is the accepted meaning, the canon is saying in effect that the Church prefers to have all Catholics and non-Catholics buried together in a blessed cemetery, rather than to have Catholics buried in a special blessed section even where Catholic burials are more numerous, from which section all non-Catholics are to be excluded. If the second is the meaning to be taken from the canon, then the Code is saying that when Catholic burials predominate, the municipal cemetery is to be blessed; where non-Catholic

[28] *Epitome,* II, n. 516, *ut supra,* pp. 99-101. Prümmer (*Manuale Iuris Canonici,* n. 374) also derives the first (1) meaning from canon 1206, § 2.

[29] *Supra,* p. 102. Wernz-Vidal quite evidently take this second meaning. They say in part: "In hypothesi ergo quod coemeterium sit unicum et sit omnino sub iure auctoritatis civilis, in quo eadem auctoritate cogente fieri debeat sepultura quorumvis civium, sine ulla separatione pro diversis cultibus; primo loco, ubi gravia incommoda non sint timenda, curari debet ut coemeterium benedicatur, pro quo sufficit ut inserviat pro sepultura civium, qui sint maiori ex parte catholici: et solum subsidiarie recurrendum est ad benedictionem cuiusque tumuli vel fossae. *At antequam recurratur ad huiusmodi media, curandum est* ut in coemeterio necessario, in quod ius proprietatis Ecclesia non habeat, pars specialis, eaque benedicta, catholicis reservetur; quae pars reservata et benedicta adhuc est habenda ut coemeterium ecclesiasticum, licet eius proprietatem Ecclesia non sinatur habere."—*Ius Canonicum,* IV, n. 562. Blat also must be included in this opinion: *Commentarium Textus Codicis Iuris Canonici,* III, pars II, n. 63.

burials are in the greater number, the whole cemetery cannot be blessed, but that the ordinary should try to have the cemetery authorities set aside one part of the cemetery for the burial of Catholics, and this section the ordinary will bless.

From what has been said in the pages immediately preceding it will be seen that this second interpretation is juridically the more acceptable one. For, to accept the first is to accept a meaning that goės counter to twenty centuries of Catholic tradition. The Church's first choice has always been that Catholic and non-Catholic be buried each in his own cemetery, the former in blessed ground, the latter in unblessed ground.[80] Furthermore, the first interpretation makes no provision for the situation not uncommon today in many parts of the world in which a Catholic section is set aside in secular or municipal cemeteries in those localities where the Church cannot or does not have her own cemetery. And yet provision for such a situation must certainly be made in paragraph 2 of canon 1206, for paragraph 3 of the same canon takes it for granted that paragraph 2 has provided for that case.

While insisting that in Catholic communities the Church prefers to have an unblessed section for those who are not to receive Christian burial, one must not assume that the whole municipal cemetery is never to be blessed unless an unblessed section can be set aside. Coronata makes special mention of this fact when he states that those who restrict the blessing of municipally owned cemeteries in Catholic communities to those cases only where the non-Catholics can be set apart in an unblessed plot are setting up a restriction which is not in the Code and is not to be understood as being implied by the Code.[81] To impose such a restriction there would be little difference between communities that are largely Catholic and those which are non-Catholic. The Code evidently means in canon 1206, § 2, to give Catholic communities the right to have blessed cemeteries which are not owned by the Church, even in cases when they cannot have a separate section. Such a privilege is not enjoyed by Catholics in non-Catholic areas.

[80] Cf. *supra*, pp. 25-26.

[81] *De Locis et Temporibus Sacris*, n. 144, note 5.

Another question which quite naturally arises is this: In the event that the communal cemetery of a predominantly Catholic community is blessed in accordance with canon 1206, § 2, does the cemetery become violated by the burial of a person who is unbaptized or by one who has been excommunicated by judicial sentence? It stands to reason that in such a cemetery, besides the Catholics who will make up the greater number of burials, it is possible and probable that there will be buried apostates from the Catholic faith, schismatics and heretics, infidels, agnostics, atheists and pagans. In Italy, for example, the law requires that those who must by canon law be deprived of Christian burial are nonetheless to be given burial in blessed ground.[32] In canons 1207 and 1172 the Code specifies that a cemetery, by the burial of an infidel or a person excommunicated by ecclesiastical sentence, is violated and is in need of reconciliation. The first conclusion, therefore, to come to mind is that blessed community cemeteries—ecclesiastically owned cemeteries are not under discussion in this place—are violated by the burial of an infidel or of a judicially sentenced excommunicate.

This was the answer given in the year 1929 in *L'Ami du Clergé*.[33] The unnamed author argued that the burial of unbaptized persons in such a cemetery is inevitable, and therefore violation is inescapable. Canon 1175 orders the removal of the body if that be possible before reconciliation may take place. This important condition for reconciliation would always be impossible, for the State controls the cemeteries, and there would be no other cemetery in which to bury the offending body. Therefore, the writer concluded, to avoid frequent violation, the only practical solution today is to bless the individual graves of those worthy of Christian burial, and not to bless the entire cemetery. Other authors hold that the burials of such persons violate the cemetery, but that this violation must be tolerated in view of the tremendous good to be gained from the opportunity of burying Catholics in sacred ground.[34]

[32] Coronata, *De Locis et Temporibus Sacris,* n. 137.

[33] Vol. XLVI (1929), 174.

[34] DeMeester, *Compendium,* n. 1172; Rossi, *La "Sepultura Ecclesiastica" e l' "Ius Funerum," nel Diritto Canonico,* n. 13.

Wernz-Vidal[35] and Coronata,[36] however, are of the opinion—and their opinion seems much more reasonable—that in canon 1206, § 2, there is contained a partial dispensation from 1172. This would mean that since the Code very plainly allows cemeteries to be blessed when violation because of the burial of unbelievers and sentenced excommunicates is something frequently to be expected, it may be understood that for this particular type of blessed cemetery the burial of such persons does not constitute a violation. The opinion of these authors, therefore, seems very plausible for the reason that the Church must have intended—if that part of canon 1206, § 2, is to offer any practical benefits—that blessed municipal cemeteries would not be violated every time an infidel or excommunicate is buried there. The conditions stipulated in the canon, however, must be observed very strictly if a dispensation is to be considered as implicitly granted therein. These conditions are three; two of them are explicitly contained in canon 1206, § 2, one of them is implicitly included. The first condition is that the Church's innate right to possess her own cemetery is taken away from her with no hope of regaining that right (explicit). Second, the burials in the cemetery are for the greater part Catholic burials (explicit). Third, there is no other place, neither inside the cemetery nor outside of it, provided for the interment of those who are deprived of Christian burial (implicit).

When the Church does not own the cemetery, but allows the whole municipal cemetery to be blessed, or directs that a special section of the common cemetery be blessed and set aside for Catholic burials when that is possible,[37] what kind of blessing does she mean: solemn or simple? From the parallel legislation of the Code on the consecration and blessing of churches,[38] it is evident that the Church, in the circumstances outlined in canon 1206, § 2, means rather the simple and not the solemn blessing of cemeteries. The cemetery property does not belong to the Church but to some one else: to the

[35] *Ius Canonicum,* IV, n. 563.

[36] *Institutiones,* n. 792.

[37] C. 1206, § 2.

[38] Cf. c. 1165.

State; to the municipality; or to some private secular corporation or citizen. The Church is allowed to bless the whole cemetery, but beyond that she is allowed to do little more. She may be allowed the exclusive use of a section of the cemetery, but perhaps only under certain specified conditions and for a certain length of time, which may or may not be determined by contract. At the expiration of the time established, or upon the alleged non-fulfillment of some or all of the conditions, or by a change in the civil law on the matter, or by a change of ownership, the Church stands to lose her exclusive use of her section of the cemetery. Such an unstable and vulnerable "quasi-ownership" makes the thought of solemn blessing inadmissible.

3. *The Blessing of Individual Graves*

Canon 1206, § 3, provides for a third possible situation when the Church does not possess her own cemetery, and when the burials are in greater number non-Catholic. The Code directs that in such a case, attempts to obtain a separate section for Catholic burials having failed,[39] the cemetery is not to be blessed, but individual graves are to be blessed immediately before receiving the remains of the Catholic deceased. This is to be employed only as a last resort, when all previous efforts to have a blessed cemetery, or a blessed section of a municipal cemetery, have proved fruitless. The rite for blessing individual graves is to be found in the Roman Ritual, title VI, chapter 3, n. 12. Authors agree that such a blessing is invocative and not constitutive, that is to say, the ground becomes blessed but it does not become a sacred place *(locus sacer)* by this *benedictio tumuli.*[40] It is to be pointed out that if the cemetery has received a cemetery blessing there is no need for the distinct blessing of the grave, for this rite is meant only for those cases wherein the ground in which one of the deceased faithful is to be buried is as yet unblessed

[39] Cf. c. 1206, § 2.

[40] Many, *De Locis Sacris*, n. 143; Coronata, *De Locis et Temporibus Sacris*, n. 143; *Institutiones*, nn. 792, 795; DeMeester, *Compendium*, n. 1172; Cappello, *Summa Iuris Canonici*, II, n. 714. Wernz-Vidal (*Ius Canonicum*, IV, n. 563) maintain that the *benedictio tumuli* should be considered constitutive.

ground.[41] When, however, it is not just a question of an earth grave in a blessed cemetery, but of a vault or mausoleum (*"sepulcrum aedificatum," "sepulcrum ex lapidibus confectum,"* etc.), the tomb is to be blessed, because the material out of which the vault or mausoleum is made has not been blessed with the ground of the cemetery on which it rests. The rite of blessing such a tomb is the *benedictio tumuli* of the Roman Ritual, title VI, chapter 3, n. 12.[42]

To sum up: the Church has a right to possess her own cemeteries, and these she will bless with either a solemn or a simple blessing. Ecclesiastically owned cemeteries are, of course, the ideal situation. In the United States the Church is perfectly free to have this type of cemetery.[43] If the Church cannot possess her own cemetery, either

[41] *Rituale Romanum,* tit. VI, c. 3, nn. 12, 13. To the Sacred Congregation of Rites was put the following question: "An Sepulcrum, quod novum foditur in coemeterio rite benedicto, prima tamen vice benedicendum sit?" The answer given by the Sacred Congregation was: "Negative."—*Ruremunden.,* 27 maii 1876, ad V—*Fontes,* n. 6091. Cf. also: Many, *De Locis Sacris,* n. 143; Rossi, *La "Sepultura Ecclesiastica" e l' "Ius Funerum" nel Diritto Canonico,* n. 26; Coronata, *De Locis et Temporibus,* n. 144; Wernz-Vidal, *Ius Canonicum,* IV, n. 566.

[42] ". . . an igitur praescriptio haec [Ritualis Romani] tantum respiciat cryptam seu Sepulcrum lapideum in coemeterio vel Ecclesia aedificatum, non autem simplicem foveam in Ecclesia effosam? Affirmative.

"An si benedictionis formula omitti debeat, nihilominus cadaveris et tumuli aspersio ac incensatio servanda sint, quemadmodum pro sepultura parvulorum praescribitur? Serventur Rubricae."—S. R. C., *Ruremunden.,* 27 maii 1876, ad V—*Fontes,* n. 6091. The rubrics prescribe both the aspersion and the incensing.

"Dubium I. Rubrica Ritualis Romani in Ordine Exequiarum quoad benedictionem tumuli sic se habet: *cum autem pervenit ad sepulcrum, si non est benedictum, Sacerdos illud benedicat dicens hanc orationem, etc.* Quaeritur:

"1. An Sacerdos debeat facere hanc benedictionem etiamsi Sepulcrum adsit in Coemeterio iam antea benedicto, adeo ut in omnibus Exequiis fidelium, saltem eorum qui ad usum rationis pervenerint, benedictio Sepulcri sit requisita, excepto solummodo casu Sepulcri iam antea ut talis benedicti? . . . Quoad primam quaestionem: Affirmative, quoties agitur de Sepulcro ex nova materia confecto."—S. R. C., *Briocen.,* 4 sept. 1880—*Fontes,* n. 6125. Cf. also Rossi, *loc. cit.;* Vermeersch-Creusen, *Epitome,* II, n. 516; Coronata, *Institutiones,* n. 795; Beste, *Introductio in Codicem,* p. 586.

[43] Zollman, *American Church Law,* n. 619.

because the civil law of the place makes it impossible, or because the small number or poverty of Catholics makes a separate cemetery impracticable, her preference would be to have a special section of the common cemetery for her own exclusive use. This plot she will bless, and it thereby becomes sacred ground. This is the next best arrangement to having her own cemetery, because the Church can bury her faithful children in sacred ground and exclude from these sacred precincts all those unworthy of Christian burial, since the latter can be buried elsewhere in the unblessed portion of the same cemetery.

When neither of the above situations obtains, two modes of procedure are open. In those places where the Church cannot have cemeteries of her own, she allows the whole public cemetery to be blessed when the number of Catholic burials exceeds the number of non-Catholic interments. In those localities, on the other hand, where the non-Catholic outnumber the Catholic burials, the whole cemetery is not to be blessed, but the graves of all Catholics are to be blessed just before interment. Likewise, this same procedure is to be followed in those Catholic communities where the Church is not permitted either to bless the communal cemetery or to have a special section of her own.

Thus the Church has taken into account every possible situation. In every case she provides for the burial in blessed ground of every member of the faithful departed. This maternal solicitude for Christian burial, as expressed in her legislation, shows what high esteem the Church has for the bodies of her faithful which were once the temples of the Holy Ghost and which on many occasions tabernacled the sacramental Presence of Jesus Christ.

Article III. The Blessing of Additions to Blessed Cemeteries

When a cemetery has been blessed is it necessary to bless each portion that may thereafter be added to it? For example, the original cemetery that was blessed, either solemnly or simply, was a piece of land ten acres in extent. As time went on an addition became necessary and one acre was added to it. Would this additional non-blessed plot have to be blessed separately, or would it be considered blessed when adjoined to the original blessed cemetery?

This question as touching cemeteries is not treated in the Code. Woywod in answering this question in *The Homiletic and Pastoral Review,*[44] applies the legislation on this same point as found in the Code in reference to churches.[45] He says: "It is certain that a church does not lose its blessing or consecration upon enlargement, provided the old part is larger than the addition. When the remodelling has been completed, the new part is considered blessed, because it has become one with the blessed or consecrated edifice. In like manner, when a piece of land adjoining the blessed or consecrated cemetery is acquired by the Church and joined to the cemetery, the whole tract of land is considered blessed or consecrated provided the added piece of land is smaller than the old cemetery. If it is as large or larger than the old cemetery it should be blessed with the cemetery blessing." In substance the same kind of answer was given years before in the publication *L'Ami du Clergé.*[46]

At first glance this may seem to be a very justifiable and logical explanation. It is a general principle that what is not said of the consecration, the blessing, the violation, the reconciliation, or the interdict of cemeteries can be safely drawn, *mutatis mutandis,* from the parallel law of the Code in relation to churches.[47] But it is not just a question of applying to cemeteries the law of churches whenever they seem to demand a similar treatment. One must look to the underlying reasons in the law for churches and see if those same reasons are present to warrant the application of the law to cemeteries.

Let the question at hand be considered. Evidently in the case when a church is repaired, for instance, when the whole inside is renovated by means of new plastering throughout, of new beams and joists, of new woodwork and of a new surface on the floor, the new parts need not be consecrated or blessed, for they are now part of the original church which is substantially the same as it was when it was first blessed. The new part is so integrated with the old that

[44] Vol. XXXVI (1936), 971-972.

[45] C. 1170.

[46] Vol. XXX (1913), 48.

[47] Cf. cc. 1205, § 1; 1207; 20.

the most one can say is that it is the old church renovated, or that it looks like a new church, but one cannot say that it is a new church. And when the repairs do not constitute a new church, that is, when more of the old church (especially the walls—canon 1170) remains than is replaced by the renovation, there is no necessity of a new consecration or blessing. The same holds true of a church which is enlarged. Even though larger now, the church is substantially the same as it was originally, and therefore needs no re-consecration or blessing.[48]

A similar regulation is to be found in the Code relative to renewing a dwindling supply of baptismal water [49] or of the sacred oils.[50] If one or the other of these hallowed materials is lacking in sufficient quantity, but some portion remains, then an unblessed amount something less than the remaining amount of blessed water or consecrated oil may be added, and the whole amount then exists as blessed or consecrated. The fundamental principle on which this fact is based is that the greater part determines what the whole will be: *"Pars maior trahit ad se minorem,"* or *"accessorium naturam sequi congruit principalis."* [51]

When a consecrated or blessed church is repaired or enlarged, or when an addition is made to baptismal water or to the holy oils, that which is the original and that which is added are so intimately intermingled that each loses its separate identity and the two become one substance. Since they are now one, the resultant substance (that is, the enlarged church and the increased quantity of baptismal water and of the holy oils) is either blessed or it is not blessed. The Church has decided in the above cases that the addition need not be blessed. And the reason for the Church's decision is based on the fact that in the finished product, so to speak, the component parts consisting of one blessed and one unblessed part are indistinguishable and inseparably united and that the part that is the greater determines

[48] Cappello, *Summa Iuris Canonici,* II, n. 671; Wernz-Vidal, *Ius Canonicum,* IV, n. 365.

[49] C. 757, § 2.

[50] 734, § 2.

[51] Regula 42, R. J. in VI°.

what the whole shall be. Or to put it another way: the part that has the greater quantity determines the quality of the whole.[52]

But is an addition to a cemetery to be considered as of the same character with additions to baptismal water, to the holy oils or to a church? The answer, it would seem, is that an addition to a cemetery is very different from the additions just mentioned. First of all, the addition and the original section of a cemetery do not coalesce to form *one whole* as do the new and old parts of a church, nor do the two parts of a cemetery unite to become *one substance* as do the blessed and unblessed parts of baptismal water and of the sacred oils. And secondly, the addition to a cemetery does not inherently constitute a case of an *ipso facto* or *automatically* effected participation of the new part in the blessing of the old, for this would entail practical difficulties.

(1) A blessed cemetery is of a definite size. When other land is added to that cemetery, the resultant enlarged cemetery can be called *one* cemetery to be sure, but, though it be one, it consists of *two clearly defined parts,* one blessed, the other unblessed. The parts do not mingle when united; they keep their identity; they lie side by side and do not overlap or become fused. Hence there is not an equal reason, as in the additions to churches, to baptismal water or to the holy oils, for considering the new and lesser part as sharing in the blessing of the adjacent sacred ground.

The doctrine of the liturgist De Herdt (-1883) offers some interesting argumentation on this point.[53] He takes the side that additions to blessed cemeteries must be blessed. He states that if a blessed cemetery is extended beyond its original limits, the addition of necessity is either larger or smaller than the blessed part. If the addition is larger, it cannot be said that the larger section which is unblessed becomes blessed when joined to the smaller section which is blessed, for the lesser part does not determine the condition of the greater part. And if the added part is smaller, even then it is to be separately blessed, for the act of joining it to a blessed cemetery does not cause it to be blessed. If this lesser part were to be considered

[52] Cf. cc. 1170; 757, § 2; 734, § 2.

[53] *Sacrae Liturgiae Praxis Iuxta Ritum Romanum,* III, n. 300.

as blessed, this would obtain either because it is ***mingled*** with the blessed part, after the manner of unblessed water and oil, which when mixed with a greater quantity of blessed water and oil becomes blessed, or because this lesser part is considered to form ***one whole*** *("unum totum")* with the blessed part, after the manner of a church to which is added a smaller portion, which, since it forms one whole *("unum totum")* with the blessed part, must be considered blessed, the greater determining the quality of the lesser part. ***But neither of these can be applied to a cemetery, because the unblessed part is not mingled with the blessed part, as water with water, and oil with oil; nor does the lesser part form one whole ("unum totum") with the blessed part, but keeps its separate and distinct identity.***

The reason for this is quite obvious, De Herdt goes on to say. For, if it be supposed that the unblessed section is much larger than the blessed part, then the latter certainly does not lose its blessing when the two are joined, since there is the principle that a thing remains blessed as long as it remains in the condition in which it was when it received its blessing. The lesser part which was blessed does not change when a larger unblessed part is adjoined to it, and therefore does not lose its original blessing.[54] And if this smaller blessed section does not cease to be blessed when the larger part is added to it, then the opposite is true, namely, that when the unblessed section is smaller than the blessed, it does not become blessed when incorporated with the larger blessed part. Furthermore, De Herdt adds, even though you build a fence or wall around a cemetery and call it *one* cemetery, there can exist in that *one* cemetery one or even several parts that are not blessed.

The logical conclusion from what De Herdt says is that a cemetery is, with reference to additions, vastly different from water, oil and a church building. A blessed section and an unblessed section of a cemetery can never commingle, can never be considered *one* as to quality or blessing. Every new section, whether large or small,

[54] This cannot be said for churches, for baptismal water or for the holy oils. For if in these cases the addition is greater than the original, *the whole* is unblessed because the two parts have formed a substantial unit, and the lesser part follows the condition of the greater part—*pars maior trahat ad se minorem*. Cf. cc. 1170; 757, § 2; 734, § 2.

must be blessed.[55] In this matter De Herdt seems to express the opinion of liturgists in general.[56]

(2) It is not always desirable that the addition of a new part to the sacred ground of an existing cemetery be blessed—something that cannot be said of additions to churches, to baptismal water or to the holy oils. Therefore, additions to cemeteries present a very different case, a case not comparable to the additions made to churches, blessed water and sacred oils.

The Code in canon 1212 prescribes that besides the blessed cemetery the Church should provide if possible an unblessed section for those to whom Christian burial may not be given. In some Catholic cemeteries there will be found three sections: one that is blessed and reserved for the burial of the faithful; a second that is unblessed for the burial of unbaptized infants; and a third unblessed section for non-Catholic adults and for Catholics to whom Christian burial is denied.[57] In such a case wherein three sections are provided, even though the unblessed parts were added after the blessing of the main part, and even when the three sections are contiguous in such a manner that both of the unblessed sections are touching blessed

[55] De Herdt maintains, however, that if the part which is added to the blessed cemetery is so small that it ought not to be even considered, it must be admitted that the larger part (which is blessed) determines what this lesser part will be: ". . . pars addita tam modica sit, ut considerari non debeat; in hoc enim casu admittendum est maiorem partem trahere ad se minorem"—*loc. cit.* Just why he makes such a statement after showing in the very same paragraph that the principle, *pars maior trahit ad se minorem,* has no application to the blessing of cemeteries, it is hard to see. For it would seem that if the principle mentioned cannot be applied when there is question of, e.g., a one-acre addition to a ten-acre blessed cemetery, it cannot be applied to a smaller addition, no matter how small it may be. Practically taken, if a piece of ground about the size of one or two graves were added to a blessed cemetery, that small parcel of land would not be blessed with a separate cemetery blessing, although it could be so blessed, but each grave would be blessed at the time it was to receive the remains of one of the faithful departed. This latter blessing, however, would not render that strip of ground sacred.

[56] Cf. Schulte, *Benedicenda,* pp. 53-55; Van der Stappen, *Sacra Liturgia,* IV, Q. 344.

[57] Cf. cc. 1205, § 1; 1212. Cf. also Coronata, *De Locis et Temporibus Sacris,* n. 141.

ground, the three sections remain distinct. *If by the mere fact of adding adjoining ground to a blessed cemetery it too becomes blessed as long as it was smaller in extent, one could never adjoin ground to a blessed cemetery and keep it unblessed for the purposes of canon 1212.* If repairs are made on a blessed church or a minor enlargement is undertaken, and if pure unblessed water is added to baptismal water, and also if pure unblessed olive oil is mixed with the holy oils, the new part being in smaller quantity than the original cannot be anything else but blessed, for it forms one substantial whole with the original part. The newly acquired piece of land adjacent to a blessed cemetery, if the same rule applied, could not remain unblessed; and therefore the bishop would never be able to realize the provision of canon 1212 unless he bought a plot that was separated from his blessed cemetery.

If, then, in some instances the addition to a blessed cemetery is to remain unblessed and in other cases it is, eventually at least, to become a blessed portion of the original cemetery, it is logical that the *intention* of the bishop is necessary to determine whether it is to be blessed or to remain unblessed. In other words, if the bishop purchased the plot with the intention that it be an addition to the already blessed cemetery, it would be considered *ipso facto* blessed. If he, on the other hand, purchased it, intending that it remain unblessed in order that he might use it for non-Catholic burials, it would remain unblessed. Were this the case, it would be not only the addition of a new plot to a blessed cemetery, but also the intention of the bishop to have its blessing effected, that would determine whether the new land was to partake of the blessing of the cemetery.

In the case of a church that is repaired or enlarged there is definitely no need for any intention on the part of the bishop to effect a status of blessing for the newly constructed part. When a contractor, in preparation for repairing or enlarging a consecrated church, brings his stone and sand and cement and deposits them outside the consecrated church, these materials are not consecrated. But when he fits them into the building and they are lodged in their place to form a physical union with the building, then that stone and sand and cement are a part of the original consecrated church. Because these new materials which were used in the repairing or enlarging of the building make now a physical unit with the already consecrated church, they cannot but be consecrated. There is no need that the bishop or pastor *intend* that the new part be blessed or consecrated; it is blessed or consecrated—one might even say—in spite of what they may intend, and certainly not because of what they actually intended.

Since the intention of the bishop is necessary in relation to additions made to cemeteries, but not in relation to enlargements undertaken for churches, there seems to be no choice but to maintain that the two cases are diverse, and that they cannot be treated alike. Additions to cemeteries, therefore, cannot be considered to share automatically with the blessing of the blessed cemeteries to which they may be adjoined. A distinctly new ceremony is necessary.

Modern canonists seem to take no note of this question.[58] Samuellius (+1660), however, stated very explicitly that a bishop, merely by adding a new piece of ground to an already blessed cemetery, could not consider the added piece blessed thereby. The added ground did not become a sacred place, he added, until it was blessed by the bishop or his delegate.[59] Baruffaldus, an eminent liturgist of the early eighteenth century, followed Samuellius in claiming that the blessing of a cemetery extended only to the boundaries of the original plot and did not include later additions.[60] De Herdt, a liturgist of the later 19th century, also declared [61] that when a blessed cemetery was

[58] For Woywod's opinion, cf. *supra,* p. 110.

[59] "Coemeterium antea benedictum, si postea amplificetur, et maius reddatur per alterius loci additionem privati, cum nova interveniente benedictione, et solemnitate dioecesani, fit locus sacer, alias minime gentium. Probatur: nam ad constituendum locum sacrum requiritur deputatio cum aliis solemnitatibus et dioecesani benedictione. . . . Nam pars addita non est coemeterium: quia coemeterium est locus benedictus, fidelium sepulturae dedicatus."—*De Sepulturis Ecclesiasticis,* tract. 1, controv. 16, concl. 5, nn. 10-12.

[60] ". . . addam quae refert Samuellius . . . circa amplitudinem benedictionis coemeterii, quae non se extendit nisi ad limites primo destinatos, nec comprehendit ampliationes, quae postmodum fieri possunt."—*Ad Rituale Romanum Commentaria,* tit. LXXIV, n. 11.

[61] *Sacrae Liturgiae Praxis Iuxta Ritum Romanum,* III, n. 300.

enlarged the new part had to be blessed by means of a distinct ceremony. The argumentation of De Herdt has already been referred to in the previous pages. Samuellius, Baruffaldus and De Herdt can be said to represent the pre-Code legal thought on the matter of the blessing of annexations to blessed cemeteries. The doctrine that a separate blessing was necessary for additions to cemeteries, but not for additions to churches, was held at a time, therefore, when the legal enactments regarding churches and cemeteries were most intimately related, and when most of the laws on the blessing of churches were to be applied also with relation to cemeteries. And if this separate blessing was held necessary for cemetery additions before the Code, then the same requirement seems all the more to obtain today, when in the positive law of the Code provision is made for cemeteries with an almost independent set of laws.

The opinion of Woywod,[62] therefore, that additions to blessed cemeteries partake of the blessing of the cemeteries to which they are adjoined must be set aside. His opinion is based on the supposition that the addition to a blessed cemetery is directly parallel with the addition to a blessed church. If the two situations were parallel, they would demand a similar treatment. But as has been pointed out, the two cases are not the same, and accordingly demand different treatment. The addition to a blessed church becomes blessed when it is annexed to the church, for it then has been made an inseparable, integral and necessary part of the church building. The church, now that the addition has been made, is no longer complete without that part. The added part cannot any longer be thought of as being complete in itself. Its own identity is lost and its separate status is fortified as soon as that part has become integrated with the original church building. Being an integral part of the church, it partakes of the blessing of the church. This is not true of additions to a cemetery, for a cemetery is quite complete without the additions, and the additions are equally as complete and separate and distinct whether they are still disconnected from or actually connected with the blessed cemetery.

If, however, there are those who would still maintain that there

[62] Cf. *supra*, p. 110.

is solid probability for the argument of Woywod, the conclusion given above would still remain the only safe one in practice, namely, that all additions to blessed cemeteries must be separately blessed. The reason is this: because of the arguments and authorities mentioned in this article there is certainly a positive doubt that the additions which are left to participate in the blessing of the original cemetery are really blessed. And in all cases of positive doubt, so the Code states in canon 1159, § 2, the sacred place (i. e., the part of the cemetery concerning which the doubt exists) must be blessed absolutely and not conditionally.[63]

[63] It will presently be pointed out that the *"ad cautelam"* of canon 1159, § 2, is not to be misconstrued with the terms *"sub conditione"* or *"conditionaliter,"* which terms have an entirely different meaning.. Cf. *infra*, pp. 125-127.

CHAPTER IX

CONCOMITANT OBLIGATIONS

Article I. The Time of the Blessing

Nothing is specified in the Code concerning the time (day and hour) of the blessing of cemeteries. The *Pontificale Romanum*, too, and the *Rituale Romanum* are silent on the question of time. But as far as the day is concerned, it is fitting that such solemn rites should take place on a Sunday or holyday, as the Code requires in the consecration of a church.[1] But since the Code does not make this a hard and fast rule even for churches, it cannot be imposed as an iron-clad rule as regards cemeteries. The most that can be said is that cemeteries which are to be solemnly blessed by the bishop with the rite of the Roman Pontifical[2] should, if it be possible, be blessed on a Sunday or holyday, so as to give the rite its proper solemnity, and to afford the faithful the opportunity of being present in large numbers. Cemeteries which are to be simply blessed with the rite of the Roman Ritual[3] may be blessed on any day.

As to the time of the day, the Pontifical[4] assumes that Mass will be said after the solemn blessing of a cemetery, and therefore that this rite will be performed in the morning. The Ritual says nothing of a Mass following the simple blessing of a cemetery, but liturgists say that the simple blessing also should take place in the morning.[5]

Article II. The Record of the Blessing

Canon 1158, a general canon governing all consecrations and blessings treated in the Third Book of the Code, orders that a record

[1] C. 1166, § 1.

[2] Tit. *De Coemeterii Benedictione*.

[3] Tit. VIII, c. 29.

[4] *Loc. cit.:* The Pontifical states that after the solemn blessing has been completed the bishop enters the church and prepares to say Mass, or a priest celebrates solemn Mass in his stead.

[5] Schulte, *Benedicenda*, pp. 53-55; Van der Stappen, *Sacra Liturgia*, IV, Q. 344.

be made and kept of every consecration and blessing. The reason is obvious. A place, once it is blessed, either solemnly or simply, is blessed for the duration of its existence,[6] or until by some act of ecclesiastical authority the blessing is withdrawn.[7] To rely on the memories of men is a dangerous expedient, for the passage of time often makes them inaccurate, uncertain and mistaken. Succeeding generations must depend in matters of importance on authenticated records or documents.

The document attesting to the fact of the blessing of a cemetery should contain the following details:

(1) The full legal title by which the cemetery is henceforth to be known.

(2) A clear, accurate and concise statement of the fact or facts which it purports to attest. It should be evident from the composition of the document that the cemetery was solemnly and not simply blessed, or *vice versa.*

(3) The exact location of the cemetery and a description of its boundaries. It has often happened, in days when the importance of exactness and completeness in documents was not as fully realized as it is today, that this detail was omitted. As a consequence years later, when the cemetery had become two or three times its original size, and no records of the various acquisitions could be found, no one knew just what part of the cemetery was and what part was not blessed. This is not, therefore, a useless detail.

(4) The name of the consecrating bishop, religious superior, or delegated priest; or in the case of a simple blessing, the name of the pastor or delegated priest when the cemetery is parochial, and the name of the priest delegated by the bishop when the cemetery is sectional rather than parochial. Any delegation or permission that was necessary and obtained in order that the minister of the blessing could act validly and licitly should be stated.

[6] Cf. cc. 1150, 1170. Consecration and blessing are of their nature perpetual.—Vermeersch-Creusen, *Epitome,* II, n. 473.

[7] Cf. c. 1187.

(5) The date of the blessing.

(6) The signature of the one making out the document. This person will usually be the same as the minister of the blessing. Therefore, cf. n. 4 above.

(7) The date on which the document is drawn up and signed. The record of the blessing should be made out immediately after the ceremony.

(8) The seal of the bishop, of the religious superior, or of the parish, as the case demands.

This document which attests to the blessing of a cemetery must be preserved. The Code (c. 1158) provides for the preservation of this document by requiring that it be kept in duplicate, one copy in the diocesan chancery, and the other in the parish whose cemetery has been blessed in either a solemn or simple manner. When the territory is not a diocese, or when the diocese is being governed by a vicar capitular or administrator, which condition makes it necessary for an outside bishop to perform the solemn blessing, then the record is to be kept not in the diocese of the ministering bishop, but in the archives of the territory in which the cemetery is located.[8]

The Code in canon 1158 makes no provision for several situations that commonly occur. Besides parishes (c. 1208, § 1), also exempt religious,[9] and other religious communities, and even private families,[10] have a right to have their own cemeteries which may be blessed either with a solemn or a simple blessing. As for the record of blessing, one record should be preserved in the archives of the church or of the religious community; the other, according to the Code which makes no distinction between religious and diocesan or parochial cemeteries, should be kept in the archives of the episcopal curia. Coronata does make an exception to canon 1158 in favor of the *blessing* (not the *solemn blessing*) of the cemeteries of exempt regulars. He says that one copy should be kept in the files of the religious house and the other in the curia of the religious ordinary.[11]

[8] Vermeersch-Creusen, *Epitome,* II, n. 472.

[9] C. 1208, § 2.

[10] C. 1208, § 3.

[11] *De Locis et Temporibus Sacris,* n. 6; *Institutiones,* n. 727.

Vermeersch-Creusen,[12] De Meester[13] and Cappello[14] are of the same opinion. They base their reasoning on the fact that, as far as the blessing of a cemetery is concerned, exempt regulars are authorized by law to act independently of the ordinary of the place.[15] The solemn blessing of a cemetery would present a different case, for that is an act which the bishop of the place ordinarily performs, and of which he should therefore preserve a record.[16]

But while the opinion of Coronata and the other eminent canonists mentioned may certainly be followed, it seems rather that the Code's primary purpose points to an official preservation of the documents. Since the blessed cemetery of the exempt clerics is located in a diocese, the record of its blessing should be filed with the ordinary of the place as well as with the religious ordinary. The latter may live many hundreds of miles from the diocese in which the religious cemetery is situated, and while such a superior should have some record of the blessing, it seems equally if not more important that the bishop of the place should possess a record of the blessing.

When cemeteries are meant for the use of several parishes or of a whole city, the record of the solemn or simple blessing is to be preserved in the episcopal curia. The Code does not expressly consider this case, but it seems that a copy of this record need not be kept in any other place. Very often a cemetery of this kind may not be in any one parish but may border on many parishes, and since it is not a parochial cemetery anyway, the only place where the record of the blessing can logically be preserved is the files of the chancery office. However, many regional or inter-parochial cemeteries are of such size that, in the cemetery itself, there is an office in which are kept many other important documents and papers, such as the record of the burials and of the cemetery lots, contracts for graves, etc. It would be fully in keeping with the purpose of canon 1158 to have a copy of the record of the blessing also in the files of such a cemetery office.

[12] *Epitome,* II, n. 472.
[13] *Compendium,* n. 1116.
[14] *Summa Iuris Canonici,* II, n. 664.
[15] C. 1156.
[16] C. 1155.

Private families may also have special burial plots apart from the common cemetery. Since the Code (c. 1208, § 3) permits these to be blessed like cemeteries, a record should be preserved of the blessing. The place where the record of such a blessing should be kept is the parish files, that is, the files of the parish within the limits of which the cemetery plot is located, and not of the parish to which the family belongs in the event that this parish is not identical with the parish in the territory of which the cemetery plot is located. The record, or an authentic copy of it, is naturally also to be preserved in the archives of the diocesan curia.

Article III. The Proof of the Blessing

The best proof of the blessing of a cemetery is a truly authentic document. A public ecclesiastical document constitutes such a document, for it is a written instrument which relates an act executed by a properly appointed ecclesiastical public person in pursuance of his official duty, and which is committed to writing by the same official or, if recorded by another, at least signed by him.[17] A document of this nature constitutes full proof of the fact which it attests.[18]

When a public document is lacking, the blessing may be proved through the testimony of the minister of the blessing, or by some one who in an official capacity witnessed the ceremony. No other proof is needed, for the minister (bishop or priest) testifies to an act performed by himself in virtue of the office he held at the time of the blessing.[19] Needless to say, when such is the case a document should be immediately drawn up to remedy this defect.

The Code (c. 1159, § 1) also admits as proof of the blessing of a cemetery the testimony of one reliable and unprejudiced witness as long as his testimony does not occasion the suffering of damage or injury by a third party. This witness need not be an eye-witness,[20] but he himself must be certain and must base his certainty on indisputable sources. The testimony of such a witness, however, could

[17] C. 1813.

[18] C. 1816.

[19] Cf. c. 1791, § 1.

[20] Coronata, *Institutiones*, n. 727.

not be considered as furnishing full proof if another party—a non-Catholic, for example, who has a family plot in the cemetery, and is trying to prove his right to bury his non-Catholic relatives in it—claims that it is not blessed. Injury might be done to this third party if no more proof than that given by the one witness were required.

Lacking all witnesses, recourse may be had to presumptions.[21] Presumptions do not directly prove the fact, but they can often be had in such quality or quantity that they point unmistakably to the fact. In a solemn blessing, for instance, five crosses are erected at specific points in the cemetery. In a cemetery that is simply blessed, one cross should stand in the center. If these crosses were found in a cemetery, there is strong presumption that the ground in that place has been made sacred by blessing. It would be a just presumption to assume that a cemetery had been blessed, especially if other supporting presumptions were present, if for years Catholics had been buried in it with all the rites of the Church, and non-Catholics had been excluded from it, and if during these many years no one ever questioned its sacred character.

Article IV. Invalid Blessing

Should it happen that, because of the lack of episcopal orders or of apostolic delegation, the solemn blessing of a cemetery is invalid or that, because of the lack of priestly orders, the simple blessing of a cemetery is not valid, the cemetery is either to be reblessed [22] or a sanation is to be obtained from the Roman Pontiff. A sanation is possible because such blessings are sacramentals of ecclesiastical institution over which the Roman Pontiff has full power.[23]

Article V. The Repetition of the Blessing

Since both the solemn and the simple blessing render a cemetery for all time a sacred place,[24] a cemetery once blessed never needs to

[21] Coronata, *De Locis et Temporibus Sacris*, n. 7.

[22] Cf. *infra, The Repetition of the Blessing*, pp. 124-127.

[23] Wernz, *Ius Decretalium*, III, n. 437; Gasparri, *De SS. Eucharistia*, I, n. 156; Coronata, *De Locis et Temporibus Sacris*, n. 5.

[24] Vermeersch-Creusen, *Epitome*, II, 473.

be reblessed. However, the fact of blessing at times becomes doubtful, when, for example, there is no record of the blessing, or when there is no one living who remembers the blessing or even the purchase of the cemetery, or when there is a lack of signs or presumptions pointing to the fact of blessing. In such a case what is to be done?

The general principle is that when there is a really positive doubt concerning the blessing of a cemetery, there should be no hesitation about blessing the cemetery in order to dispel all doubt and to make certain that the ground in which Catholics are to be buried is sacred ground.[25] A merely negative doubt does not suffice to warrant a reblessing.[26] The simple lack of proof does not constitute doubt, and unless there is some good reason to believe that the cemetery has not yet been rendered sacred, there should be no new blessing. If a cemetery, for instance, was considered solemnly blessed inasmuch as there were situated in it five wooden crosses which were thought to be the crosses set up for the solemn blessing of the cemetery, and later it became known that these crosses were placed in the cemetery by lay people merely to mark the bounds of the cemetery, then that cemetery must be blessed because there now exists more than just a negative doubt concerning the blessing even though Catholics had been buried there for years. The very foundation on which the blessing was based has proved to be groundless.

Another situation that seems to demand a reblessing of the cemetery is the case in which a cemetery has undergone many additions since it was first used as a burial place, and in which it is known for certain that the original cemetery was blessed, but it is also known or reasonably suspected that the newer parts, now indistinguishable from the old, have never been blessed. Inasmuch as records are not available to show what was the original section and what were the later acquisitions, the present augmented cemetery, notwithstanding the blessing of the original part, must be blessed anew. Elsewhere it has been shown that additions to blessed cemeteries do not become *ipso facto* blessed by joining them to blessed cemeteries.[27] It must

[25] C. 1159, § 2.

[26] Coronata, *Institutiones*, n. 727.

[27] Cf. *supra*, pp. 109-118.

be added, however, that if the dimensions of the present cemetery are but slightly greater than the original cemetery, it will rest with the prudence of the ordinary to judge whether the cemetery is to be reblessed.

In blessing a cemetery whose original blessing is at best extremely dubious, the blessing should be given *absolutely* and not conditionally. It has always been the tradition of the Church to reconsecrate or rebless sacred places about the consecration or blessing of which there existed positive doubt.[28] Like the sacrament of baptism, the consecration and blessing of a place are never to be repeated. Unlike baptism, however, when there is genuine doubt as to the fact of consecration or blessing, the rite is to be performed not *sub conditione* but *absolute*. This Pope Benedict XIV taught in his apostolic letter *Iam inde* of May 12, 1756,[29] thus confirming what had long been the known practice in the Church since the time of Pope Gregory the Great (590-604).[30] The Code incorporates this procedure in canon 1159, § 2, where it states: " . . . . in dubio autem, peragatur (consecratio vel benedictio) ad cautelam." Vermeersch-Creusen, commenting on this canon, point out the distinction between a *benedictio conditionalis* and a *benedictio ad cautelam*. One must observe, they say, that the conditional repetition of a blessing is one thing, and the repetition *ad cautelam* is another; for the latter is equivalent to an absolute and unconditional blessing, whereas the former is not.[31]

The blessing of a sacred place has been compared to baptism.[32] The two are very similar, in fact, just as similar as sacraments and sacramentals can be. In many details sacramentals resemble the sacraments, upon which, after all, they have been modeled, but in many essential respects sacramentals differ from the sacraments.

[28] Cf. *supra*, p. 38.

[29] *Fontes*, n. 440.

[30] *Epistolarum Liber IV, Epistola XVII ad Felicem—MPL*, LXXVII, 1325-1326.

[31] *Epitome*, II, n. 473: "Observes aliud per se significari iteratione *conditionata*, aliud iteratione *ad cautelam* simpliciter concessa: haec est absoluta, sed propter iustam rationem permissa." Cf. also: Augustine, *Commentary*, VI, 8-9; De Meester, *Compendium*, n. 1117; Coronata, *Institutiones*, n. 727.

[32] Benedictus XIV, *loc. cit.*

One of the important distinctions between the two is that the sacraments were immediately instituted by Christ, whereas the sacramentals have been instituted by the Church.[33] This has one important meaning: the Church has much more freedom in legislating concerning the sacramentals than concerning the sacraments. The Church, in the matter of baptism, has made it one of her laws that this sacrament is not to be repeated unless the fact of baptism in a particular case is doubtful; and then it is to be administered conditionally.[34] The Church was not free to make that law any other way; not free, in other words, to say that baptism could be given absolutely, as long as there was some probability that it had already been conferred. With regard to the blessing of a sacred place the Church also states in her law[35] that such a blessing, once conferred, is never to be repeated. But while it is true that once a place is blessed it is never to be reblessed, it is equally true that at times the fact of blessing is dubious. In this case the place is to be blessed as though it had never been blessed before, that is to say absolutely. Thus the Church, having full authority to legislate concerning sacramentals, authorizes the bishop to bless a cemetery concerning the blessing of which there exists a positive doubt, not conditionally as in the administration of baptism, but absolutely.

Article VI. The Loss of the Blessing

There is no mention in the Code of Canon Law of the loss of blessing *(exsecratio)* of cemeteries, although this subject is treated explicitly with regard to churches.[36] Before the Code, too, the Church provided considerable legislation concerning the ways in which churches and altars might lose their blessing, but issued no legislation to state what constituted the *exsecratio* of cemeteries.[37] But since

[33] Tanquerey, *Synopsis Theologiae Dogmaticae* (23. ed., 3 vols., Parisiis: Desclée et Socii, 1934), III, nn. 447-449.

[34] C. 732.

[35] C. 1159, § 2.

[36] C. 1170.

[37] C. 20, D. I, *de cons.*, together with the glossa ordinaria ad v. "exustae;" C. 24, D. I, *de cons.*, and the glossa ordinaria ad v. "instauranda."

every article that has received the blessing of the Church is capable of losing that blessing at least when the article is utterly destroyed, it has always seemed reasonable to hold that cemeteries were capable of losing their blessing. The pre-Code authors who considered the subject of the loss of a cemetery's blessing were agreed that cemeteries could lose their blessing in ways analogous to those in which churches lost theirs. Authors writing after the Code also agree that there is possible an *exsecratio* of cemeteries as well as of churches.

All canonists will be found to say that the only ways by which a cemetery can lose its blessing are ways analogous to the *exsecratio* of churches. Canon 1170 gives three ways by which churches may lose their consecration or blessing: (1) by the complete destruction of the church; (2) by the collapse or removal of the major portion of its walls; and (3) by the reduction of the church to profane uses by the ordinary of the place.

First of all it can be stated that the second of these three ways cannot apply to cemeteries. Even the walls that may surround a cemetery are not analogous to the walls of a church, because they are not an essential part of the cemetery. They can disintegrate and collapse or be removed entirely, and the cemetery exists as it was before. Its blessing is not bound up in the preservation of the walls, whereas in churches the walls are an essential part of the church building, and they participate in a very real manner in the blessing or consecration.

One of the two ways, therefore, by which a cemetery may lose its blessing is by the destruction of that cemetery. Moulart (1832-1904) [38] following Reclusius (+ after 1775) [39] held that the destruction of the crosses blessed by the bishop or by the priest delegated by the bishop in the rite of the solemn or simple blessing constituted the loss of the blessing of the cemetery. Many [40] held that this was no cause for the loss of the blessing, for while the blessing of the crosses is an important part of the ceremony of blessing, it does not strictly constitute the essence of the rite. After the ceremony of

[38] *De Sepultura et Coemeteriis*, p. 117.

[39] *Tractatus de Re Parochiali* (Romae, 1773), pars 2, tit. 8, n. 71.

[40] *De Locis Sacris*, n. 145.

blessing is over, the ground in the cemetery is no longer what it was before the ceremony; now it is sacred, whereas before it was no different from the ground outside its borders. The removal or destruction of the crosses, then, would hardly bring about a loss of that blessing or effect the consequent return of the cemetery to its former profane and non-sacred character.

Utter destruction of the cemetery is hardly conceivable. Moreover it is not necessary as a condition from which the loss of the blessing will follow. Using the analogy of the consecrated church,[41] one may state that cemeteries will lose their blessing when destruction in some form so destroys the cemetery as to render it useless as a cemetery. Earthquakes, even moderate ones, have been known to cut a pattern of deep crevices throughout the area. Violent floods frequently remove two or three or more feet of topsoil from land in their path. Aerial bombings and artillery bombardment can, during the time of war, lay waste whatever happens to come within its range. As can clearly be seen, these forms of destruction can devastate a cemetery to such an extent that not only are further burials impossible, but many of the existing graves will have to be moved to another place. Such destruction, in the opinion of all authors, constitutes the *exsecratio* or loss of blessing with reference to cemeteries.[42] Even though the cemetery was not so utterly destroyed as to make repairs impossible, Wernz-Vidal state that, if and when the cemetery is restored to its original condition, it must be blessed just as though it were an altogether new cemetery.[43]

The second way for a cemetery to lose its blessing is for the ordinary of the place to decree the return of the cemetery to profane uses. By this decree the blessing is withdrawn. However, before

[41] C. 1170.

[42] Many, *De Locis Sacris,* n. 145; Coronata, *De Locis et Temporibus Sacris,* n. 147; De Meester, *Compendium,* n. 1178; Wernz-Vidal, *Ius Canonicum,* IV, n. 568; Naz, "Cimetière," *Dictionnaire de Droit Canonique,* III, 738. Naz is the only author to mention aerial bombings.

[43] "Porro ex natura rei, si coemeterium omnino ita destruitur, ut non amplius fini ad quem destinatur inservire possit; si deinde ad pristinum finem factis debitis reparationibus iterum destinaretur, videtur nova benedictio impertienda perinde ac in erectione novi coemeterii: sed iudicium de totali destructione pendet ex variis loci circumstantiis."—*Ius Canonicum,* IV, n. 568.

the local ordinary issues such a decree he should see to it that there is a just if not a grave cause for it, and that the remains of all the bodies buried in the cemetery have been completely and reverently removed to another cemetery.[44] This type of *exsecratio* is known as a *profanatio coemeterii,* from the fact that it entails a conversion or reduction of the blessed cemetery to profane purposes. Although the rule of law *(regula iuris)* held that a place once dedicated to God ought never to be turned over again to merely human purposes,[45] it has always been necessary from time to time to withdraw the blessing of a cemetery, in order to release the cemetery for other uses.

The Council of Trent dealt with this problem as far as churches were concerned, but not in relation to cemeteries. By its authority churches, parish churches as well as others, which through lack of funds or because of their unavoidable and irreparable dilapidated condition, and for other reasonable causes, could not be properly cared for, could be reduced to profane, though not sordid use by the bishop.[46] Gallemart (+1625), in his commentary on the decree of the Council of Trent,[47] was of the opinion that what was said by the Council of churches could be said also of cemeteries, and in support of his view he cited a declaration of the Sacred Congregation of the Council.[48]

[44] Cappello, *Summa Iuris Canonici,* II, n. 716; Coronata, *De Locis et Temporibus Sacris,* n. 147; De Meester, *Compendium,* n. 1178; Wernz-Vidal, *Ius Canonicum,* IV, n. 568.

[45] Reg. 51, R. J., in VI°: "Semel Deo dicatum non est ad usus humanos ulterius transferendum."

[46] Sess. XXI, *de ref.,* c. 7.

[47] *Sacrosanctum Oecumenicum Concilium Tridentinum, additis Declarationibus Cardinalium Concilii Interpretum, ex Ultima Recognitione* (editio reformata, Tridenti, 1737), sess. 21, c. 7, decl. 7, p. 164.

[48] "Ecclesia diruta parvorum reddituum potest, ex sententia Congregationis, in usus profanos non tamen sordidos converti, et transferri ad matricem seu viciniorem ecclesiam, ubi erigendum est altare sub eadem invocatione, imposito onere titulari: ut nimirum episcopus curet ibi celebrari singulis hebdomadibus per sacerdotem idoneum. Coemeterium item profanandum, et deinde ossa transferenda sunt ad novum coemeterium, quod a titulari constituatur in eo loco, quo magis placuerit populo construendum."—*Loc. cit.*

Both Moulart[49] and Many[50] held that a bishop could reduce a blessed cemetery to profane uses in virtue of the authorization given by the Council of Trent. They argued that there existed no blessed cemetery which did not belong to some church, or which was not connected in some intimate way with some parish church or churches. If the Council of Trent allowed the bishop to withdraw the blessing of the church, it was also thereby granting him the power to take away the blessing of the cemetery which served that church, for without the church the cemetery could not exist for long. This was especially true of a churchyard cemetery, but none the less substantially true also of a cemetery which was situated at some little distance from the church. The fate of the church decided also the fate of the cemetery: *"accessorium naturam sequi congruit principalis."*[51]

Reclusius held the opposite opinion. A cemetery, according to him, was something altogether apart and separate from the church it served. Even if the bishop could remove the blessing of the church, he could not reduce the cemetery of that church to profane uses without obtaining special faculties from the Holy See.[52]

The Code does not solve the difficulties associated with this kind of *exsecratio,* for it mentions nothing about the *profanatio* of cemeteries. However, post-Code authors (who have already been mentioned in this section) are of one mind in maintaining that the ordinary of the place may, if the case warrants it, withdraw the blessing of a cemetery and reduce it to its original state. In the lack of any definite pronouncement from the Holy See, it seems that such a view is a very reasonable solution for an extremely practical problem. For if the Church allows the local ordinary to remove the consecration (not to mention the blessing) of a church and to reduce it to profane but not sordid uses, as she most certainly does in canons 1170 and 1187, then she most certainly should be understood to permit the *profanatio* of cemeteries to be effected in a like manner.

Local ordinaries not infrequently face the problem of having to

[49] *De Sepultura et Coemeteriis,* pp. 115-116.

[50] *De Locis Sacris,* n. 146.

[51] Reg. 42, R. J., in VI°.

[52] *Tractatus de Re Parochiali,* pars 2, tit. 3, nn. 65-68.

vacate a blessed cemetery for one reason or another. Sometimes the ordinary finds that, because of the shift of the Catholic population, the blessed cemetery in the locality has become a deserted place, and that a new Catholic cemetery is needed elsewhere. He knows that the Catholics of the vicinity cannot maintain two cemeteries. The only practical solution for him may be to remove to a new location the remains of the Catholics buried in the blessed cemetery, and then by a decree (c. 1187) to reduce the cemetery to its former unblessed condition, and sell it to another cemetery corporation for non-Catholic burials, or divide it into lots to be sold as other real estate.

At other times the blessed cemetery may have to be moved because of its present unhappy location. When the cemetery was first established and blessed it may have been outside the city but easily accessible to it. Then when the city grew and its borders extended far beyond the cemetery, the latter with reference to the new city became situated in very inappropriate environs, unfortunate both for the cemetery and for the city. Or perhaps the city or the State may use its police powers or its legislative prerogative to declare that the cemetery is a public nuisance and accordingly orders its abatement or removal.[53] The civil authority also by invoking the power of eminent domain may leave a bishop no alternative but to move his blessed cemetery.[54] In all these cases, especially when the civil authorities are involved, the ordinary must act and act quickly.

[53] Zollman, *American Church Law*, n. 612.

[54] Zollman (*American Church Law*, n. 615) basing his statements on decisions handed down in United States courts states: "The police power and the strong arm of equity are not the only instrumentalities by which cemeteries are removed from the path of progress. The power of eminent domain may be and sometimes has been effective in accomplishing the same purpose. A cemetery may be directly in the path of a proposed public improvement. It may be necessary to widen a street and for this purpose condemn a strip of land used as a burying ground. In such a case the imperative needs of the living must take precedence over the deference due to the dead. Cemeteries under such circumstances will not fare better than other private property. Their land may be condemned under such circumstances just like other property. The remains buried there will have to be disinterred and monuments erected over them taken down."

He may, therefore, safely follow the unanimous opinions of present-day authors,[55] and consider himself to have the power to withdraw the blessing from Catholic cemeteries and from Catholic sections of non-Catholic or municipal cemeteries, and to return them to profane uses.

[55] Cf. *supra*, pp. 129-130.

CHAPTER X

THE IMMUNITY OF BLESSED CEMETERIES

THE matter which will be treated in this chapter is one that has many problems. The question will come up presently as to whether or not the cemeteries of the Church enjoy immunities today as before the Code. Some authors will say that they do; others will say that they do not. It is at first a bewildering situation; one knows not who is right and who is wrong. But strange to say, in spite of all the apparent contradictions, most all of the authors are in complete agreement on the question of immunities. The answer is to be found, as in so many cases of this nature, in the lack of uniform terminology. Authors use the same words, but often with different meanings, and without making the necessary distinctions. The two words involved mainly are the terms "immunity" or "immunities" and "exemption." Every immunity is an exemption; but not every exemption in an immunity. For example, a church or cemetery is exempt from the civil jurisdiction of the State in which it is situated, but this exemption is not strictly speaking an immunity, although in a less technical sense, as shall be seen, it can be considered an immunity. There, precisely, is where the difficulty lies. One author will use the word "immunity" to include the exemption of sacred places from the civil power; another author, not understanding the term in such a broad sense, will limit "immunity" to a much narrower meaning. The statements and conclusions of such authors naturally will be different one from the other.

Ecclesiastical persons, places and things have the capacity of enjoying immunities. Since, however, this is a treatise on blessed cemeteries the term "immunity" here will be used with reference to sacred places *(loca sacra)* in general, and blessed cemeteries in particular. According to canon 1154, a blessed cemetery is a sacred place: and since there is no specification in that canon as to who owns the place, it will be immaterial in this chapter who owns the cemetery, as long as it is blessed.[1]

ARTICLE I. THE NOTION OF IMMUNITY

The ecclesiastical immunity which sacred places have the capacity of enjoying may be defined as the right by which such places are free and immune from secular burdens, and from acts that are unbecoming to their sacred character.[2] One of the best expositions of the accurate meaning of ecclesiastical immunity is to be found in Coronata's volume on public ecclesiastical law.[3] Pointing out that authors, not only before the Code but even after 1918, have disagreed concerning many of the immunities of the Church, Coronata explains that the great reason for the many discrepancies is the lack of a clear definition of terms. Thereupon, with circumspect judgment and with a careful use of words, he discloses what ecclesiastical immunity is, and what it is not.

First, Coronata begins with an explanation of what immunity is not. Ecclesiastical immunity does not embrace the naturally inherent

[1] What Coronata says of exemption of sacred places from civil jurisdiction (c. 1160) can be extended to include ecclesiastical immunities also, for both exemption from civil authority and immunities are due to sacred places, not so much because they are owned by the Church (since the Church may at times not own them (c. 1206, § 2) as because they have received the special liturgical blessing of the Church. Hence, the ecclesiastical exemption and immunity of sacred places "valet non solum de locis sacris in dominio Ecclesiae universae aut particularis personae iuridicae ecclesiasticae positis, sed etiam de locis sacris quae forte in dominio alicuius personae privatae sint aut etiam in dominio personae moralis non ecclesiasticae, e. g., in dominio ipsius Status civilis aut municipii; tales enim personae morales locum sacrum possident ut personae physicae privatae et qua tales legibus ecclesiasticis tum in acquisitione, tum in retentione, dominio, possessione et alienatione ligantur."—*Institutiones*, n. 728.

[2] The above definition has been narrowed down from the more inclusive definition of Reiffenstuel, so as to be applicable only to sacred places. Reiffenstuel's definition is as follows: "Ius quo ecclesia, et alia loca sacra, necnon personae ecclesiasticae, ac res ipsorum libera ac immunia sunt a muneribus et oneribus saecularibus, atque ab actibus earum sanctitati et reverentiae debitae repugnantibus."—*Ius Canonicum Universum*, lib. III, tit. 49, n. 4.

[3] *Ius Publicum Ecclesiasticum* (2. ed., Taurini: Marietti, 1934), nn. 143-169.

rights *("iura nativa")* of the Church. The *iura nativa* are all those rights which the Church possesses because of the very nature of the Church, a perfect society and completely independent of the civil power, and because of the work she has been divinely assigned to do. All that is necessary and useful for the attainment of the purpose of her existence, and without which she could not subsist as Christ founded her, the Church has a divine and inalienable right to possess. These innate or naturally inherent rights—to name only those which have a bearing on the subject of cemeteries—are: the right to acquire, administer and dispose of temporal goods independent of the State; the right of possessing her sacred places (churches, oratories, altars and cemeteries—c. 1154) and of exercising her jurisdiction over them in a manner which is unhampered by, and in a way for which the Church is not made answerable to any temporal authority.[4] And thus the *iura nativa* are not to be considered as concessions made to the Church by the State, or as immunities which the Church has arrogated to herself, but rights which are rooted in the very nature of the Church, and flow directly from the institution of the Church by Christ Himself, and therefore derive from the divine law.[5]

Having explained, therefore, what immunity is not, Coronata[6] proceeds to discuss what ecclesiastical immunity is. Besides these innate and naturally inherent rights which belong to the Church as something which derives from the divine law itself, there are others which, considered solely in their nature, are not strictly due to the Church, even though they are extremely helpful and fitting, and at times even necessary. A few examples of these latter will suffice. There is nothing repugnant in removing a malefactor from a sacred place for the sake of punishing him; as a matter of fact such a procedure is a virtuous act of justice and does not necessarily entail any irreverence to the sacred place. However, the removal of such

[4] C. 1160.

[5] Coronata, *Ius Publicum Ecclesiasticum*, n. 151. Cf. Cavagnis, *Institutiones Iuris Publici Ecclesiastici* (4. ed., Romae, 1906), IV, n. 224; Cappello, *Summa Iuris Publici Ecclesiastici* (2. ed., Romae: Apud Aedes Universitatis Gregorianae, 1928), nn. 371, 372.

[6] *Loc. cit.*

a one could be disorderly, could lead to bloodshed, and could eventuate at a time when divine services are in progress; accordingly, it is very proper that some limitation or even prohibition be placed on such a seizure, or some precautions taken, in order to guarantee respect for the sacred place.[7]

Again, it is not altogether improper for well-meaning citizens, wishing to avail themselves of the facilities of a church or a cemetery, to hold meetings in a sacred place. But since such non-religious meetings are somewhat incongruous and at times perhaps irreconcilable with the decorum and sanctity of sacred places, it is meet that all secular assemblages be excluded from sacred places. Exemptions of this kind are properly known as immunities. It is plain that immunities differ from the innate and naturally inherent rights of the Church (1) in that the latter derive directly from divine natural or positive law, and the former as a rule indirectly, and (2) in that the Church requires the *iura nativa* for her very existence, whereas immunities are a helpful but not indispensable complement to the *iura nativa.*

The importance of the distinction between the innate rights of the Church and the immunities of the Church is seen particularly when an examination is made of canon 1160, which reads as follows: "*Loca sacra exempta sunt a iurisdictione auctoritatis civilis et in eis legitima Ecclesiae auctoritas iurisdictionem suam libere exercet.*" This is a statement of the *innate right* of the Church to exercise full and unchallenged jurisdiction over her sacred places, and is not a statement of the *immunity* of the Church from civil authority. For the significance of ecclesiastical immunity is that in entails exemption from certain secular burdens or from legitimate laws of the civil power to which strictly speaking all places both secular and sacred are bound. To speak, therefore, of the exemption of sacred places from civil jurisdiction as an immunity, is to speak inaccurately; at least it is to use the term "immunity" in its broader and less technical meaning. Augustine[8] and De Meester,[9] for example, refer to the

[7] Cf. Reiffenstuel, lib. III, tit. 49, n. 23; Wernz, *Ius Decretalium,* III, n. 446.

[8] *Commentary,* VI, 9.

[9] *Compendium,* n. 1118.

exemption expressed in canon 1160 as *localis immunitas,* although in their commentary of the canon they show clearly that the *immunitas* of which they speak is the God-given right *(ius nativum)* of the Church to the free jurisdiction of her sacred places.

Article II. Innate and Naturally Inherent Rights

All authors who treat of canon 1160, even though they do not all use the same precise meaning for the terms they use, agree as to the substance of the canon. They are in perfect harmony in declaring that the *loca sacra* are under the very special authority of the Church, more so than any other *loca ecclesiastica,* and that this authority or jurisdiction is a right that derives directly from the divine law, and in no way at all, not even indirectly, from the civil law. Moreover, the jurisdiction of the Church over her sacred places is a jurisdiction that operates independently of all civil authority. The civil power must recognize that the *loca sacra* are entirely outside of its jurisdiction, just as the government of one country is absolutely incompetent and without jurisdiction over the properties of another country. Any authority that civil governments or civil magistrates exercise over the *loca sacra,* if it has not been given to them by the Church, is an unjust and usurped authority.[10]

It is to be pointed out that not every piece of ecclesiastically owned property enjoys this absolute exemption from the jurisdiction of the State, but only the *loca sacra,* namely, according to canon 1154, those places which by consecration or blessing are appointed for divine worship or for the burial of the faithful. It is the blessing of the Church that puts these sacred places outside the pale of civil authority so completely. Likewise it is to be noted that canon 1160 takes for granted the other basic natural rights of the Church to acquire, administer and to dispose of property on which churches and cemeteries are established. The canon is concerned only with the special exclusive jurisdiction which the Church has in regard to

[10] Cf. Wernz, *Ius Decretalium,* III, nn. 143-153; Vecchiotti, *Institutiones Canonicae* (16. ed., 3 vols., Augustae Taurinorum, 1875-1876), II, 111; Cororata, *Ius Publicum Ecclesiasticum,* nn. 166-169.

her sacred places, a jurisdiction that exists over and above her fundamental right of possessing temporal goods in her own name.[11]

Sacred places serve an almost exclusively spiritual end. It is unthinkable that churches should be under any other jurisdiction than that of the Church, because they are so intimately bound up in the worship of God. Cemeteries, too, have a very spiritual end, one that is inferior to churches it is true, but one that is none the less real. From the very beginning cemeteries, historically, juridically and liturgically, have been inseparable from churches.[12] While living the faithful knelt side by side in churches to worship God; when dead they were reverently laid to rest side by side in the sacred ground of the Church's cemeteries. Through the sacred places, the faithful

[11] Coronata, *Ius Publicum Ecclesiasticum,* n. 143, and especially, note on p. 194. The right to acquire, administer and dispose of temporal goods is a question for public ecclesiastical law, and does not fall within the province of this work. The concern of this dissertation is in seeing what the blessing of the Church gives to cemeteries by way of addition to what was already possessed previously. In other words, the question may be put in this fashion: what does a blessed cemetery possess as a right which an unblessed but ecclesiastically owned cemetery does not possess? The basis of comparison, of course, is with reference to innate rights, principally the right of separate ecclesiastical jurisdiction (c. 1160).

[12] Wernz-Vidal (*Ius Canonicum,* IV, p. 674, note 16) sum it up thus: "Nullo modo oblivioni dandum est coemeteria in quibus corpora fidelium digna ratione et adhibitis sacris ritibus sepelienda sunt, intimam habere connexionem cum cultu divino. Quare sepultura christiana, non est solum officium humanitatis et pietatis naturalis, sed est officium stricte religiosum, exclusive pertinens ad Ecclesiam quoad omnes suas partes, sicut alia officia religiosa in templis peragenda. Coemeteria proinde non sunt aliqua *materia mixta,* sicut non sunt materia mixta templa ad alia officia religiosa destinata; sunt enim loca sacra; mixta materia dici non possunt nisi in *sensu lato,* in quantum statui interest, ut coemeteria non ita habeantur et custodiantur, ut inde aliquod nocumentum temporale subsequatur. Cum Ecclesia aliquos sepeliri non permittit ritu sacro quoad hos (v. gr. quoad infideles) subintrat officium humanitatis et pietatis naturalis de competentia status: sed Ecclesia iam de hac re curam habet, reservando in suis coemeteriis partem non benedictam pro ipsorum sepultura. Quodsi agatur de sepultura baptizatorum, verum ius circa ipsam habet Ecclesia, tametsi eos excludat a *sacra* sepultura; nihilominus facile tolerat ut pro acatholicis baptizatis Status coemeterium civile constituat, sicut agnoscit Status ius pro nonbaptizatis v. gr. pro hebraeis, infidelibus."

on earth, both in life and in death, have always been kept in close association with one another and with their God. Thus it is to preserve and to guarantee man's religious or spiritual freedom, that the Church demands by ecclesiastical law (c. 1160) what she already has by divine law: the absolute jurisdiction over her sacred places.[13]

In many recent concordats between the Holy See and various countries, for example, Latvia,[14] Poland[15] and Lithuania,[16] the Church made every effort to secure her freedom of jurisdiction over sacred places. In her Lateran Pact with Italy, however, the Holy See was not successful in getting a guarantee of unmolested jurisdiction.[17] In many States the Church is denied even her basic right to have her own blessed cemeteries; and therefore she cannot hope to have the further right of exclusive jurisdiction over them.[18] The curtailment or outright denial of either right is an injustice to the Church and a violation of the divine natural law and also of the direct precepts of canon law.[19]

The main force of the jurisdiction of the Church over her blessed cemeteries is to be found in her undisputed right to exclude from

[13] Cf. Vecchiotti, *Institutiones Canonicae,* II, 111-112; and particularly: Cocchi, *Commentarium in Codicem Iuris Canonici,* V, nn. 5, 49.

[14] "XIV. Les églises, chapelles, cimetières Catholiques sont considérés comme propriété de l'Eglise Catholique en Lettonie; ils sont librement administrés par l'autorité ecclésiastique, ne peuvent être aliénés ou confisqués par que ce soit, ni destinés a d'autres usages contra la volonté de l'autorité ecclésiastique.

"XV. L'immunité des églises, chapelles et cimetières sera observée selon les normes du Droit Canon.

"XVI. Les propriétés de l'Eglise pourront être soumises aux impôts, comme les biens des autres citoyens, excepté les édifices destinés au culte divin, ainsi que le Séminaire, le évêchés et les presbytères."—May 30, 1922—*AAS,* XIV (1922), 579.

[15] Feb. 10, 1925, art. VI, and art. XIV—*AAS,* XVII (1925), 275, 278.

[16] Sept. 27, 1927, art. VI—*AAS,* XIX (1927), 427.

[17] Concordato fra la Santa Sede e l'Italia, Feb. 11, 1929, art. 9—*AAS,* XXI (1929), 279.

[18] Cf. *supra,* p. 95 for France and Germany. As for Austria, cf. Pius IX, allocut. *Nunquam certe,* 22 iun. 1868—*Fontes,* n. 550; and Belgium, De Meester, *Compendium,* n. 1118.

[19] Cf. cc. 1206, §§ 1-2; 1160.

burial all whom she deems unfit and unworthy. From the very beginning of her existence the Church has made it a point to possess her own cemeteries, where she could provide blessed ground for the interment of all the faithful deceased. Traditionally the Church has exercised her native jurisdiction over cemeteries in such a manner as to exclude from burial in blessed ground all non-Catholics and all unworthy Catholics. This policy was established at least as early as the fifth century, when Pope St. Leo the Great laid down the principle that Catholics should not associate in death with those with whom they were not allowed to communicate in life: *"Quibus vivis non communicavimus, mortuis communicare non possumus."* [20] This principle was given further confirmation by Pope Innocent III in the year 1200, and still forms the basis for the legislation in the Code.[21]

The divine injunction expressed in the words of canon 1160 is entirely possible in every city and country, provided that the civil governments are willing to be just. The Church asks for the ownership and separate administration of her own cemeteries, and in this she is asking for no more than is her due.[22] But since some States are unwilling to allow the Church to possess her own burial ground, the Church asks that she be given a part of the communal cemetery for her exclusive use, that is, a part which she can bless and over which she can and should have complete jurisdiction. If even this is denied her, the Church can still manage to provide blessed ground for the burial of the faithful.[23] but she is suffering an unpardonable injustice.[24]

On the other hand, the Church may, and often does, permit civil laws and burdens to be enforced within the territory of her sacred

[20] *Epist.* CLXVII—*MPL,* LIV, 1205-1206.

[21] C. 12, X, *de sepulturis,* III, 28; cc. 1239 and 1240. For a detailed treatment of both the historical and the present legislation concerning the denial of Christian burial, cf. Kerin, *The Privation of Christian Burial.*

[22] C. 1206, § 1.

[23] C. 1206, §§ 2-3.

[24] Cf. Wernz-Vidal, *Ius Canonicum,* IV, n. 565; Coronata, *De Locis et Temporibus Sacris,* nn. 9, 149; Cocchi, *Commentarium in Codicem Iuris Canonici,* V, nn. 5, 49.

places, without thereby necessarily jeopardizing or compromising her own jurisdiction. For instance, the Church may allow the police powers of the State and the hygienic laws of the official department of health to be imposed on her blessed cemeteries. Such laws or ordinances have for their purpose the well-being of the citizenry, and it is not to be doubted that the whole community is benefited by them. Thus, the legislative body of a State may enact laws to the effect that all cemeteries be set up outside the limits of a city or a town, and that all interments be made in graves that are six feet below the surface of the ground. The civil authority may even suggest that a cemetery be moved to another site when, after first being established at a distance from populated centers, it later became enveloped in the very heart of the urban population.

From a study of civil court cases it can readily be seen that the civil power does not hesitate to consider itself competent to order the removal of a cemetery or to stop all interments, when it judges that an assured conservation of the public health or a relieved discomfort for the district community warrants such a decision.[25] However, as Wernz-Vidal point out, the Church has the first responsibility of keeping good order and of observing the norms of hygiene which reason dictates, and this she can do without any aid from the civil authority. But if she, for the sake of uniformity and convenience or out of charity, puts her cemeteries under the police and hygienic regulations of the States, it does not at all follow that she *must* do so or that she could not do otherwise. Nor is it true that because one finds the blessed cemeteries of the Church under certain laws of the State, the Church lacks competence in these matters. The Church in these cases merely uses the civil apparatus of law for the preservation of public safety and general health, instead of setting up a corresponding agency of her own for the same purposes.[26]

[25] Zollman, *American Church Law,* nn. 610-615.

[26] Wernz-Vidal, *Ius Canonicum,* IV, n. 564. Cf. also Cappello, *Summa Iuris Publici Ecclesiastici,* nn. 372, 5; 91; Cocchi, *Commentarium in Codicem Iuris Canonici,* V, n. 49. Many (*De Locis Sacris,* n. 226), writing before the Code, expressed his view that police powers and matters of public health were within the jurisdiction of the civil authority even as to sacred places, and that therefore all cemeteries in these respects must be considered bound by the secu-

Because of the exemption from civil authority which the sacred places of the Church enjoy,[27] the Church may not be forced to exhume the remains of any of those buried in her cemeteries.[28] This does not mean or even imply that exhumation is impossible or difficult of realization. It means only that the Church has complete authority over her blessed cemeteries, and no one but the Church may licitly remove any of the bodies buried in them. It may happen that the State may for a good reason wish to have exhumed the body of some one buried in a Catholic cemetery. Thus, for example, if a man died a violent death by the hand of a criminal who has been apprehended and is now being tried by a criminal court on the charge of murder, it may at times be necessary, because the post-mortem examination was not thorough enough in view of new evidence, to obtain the body for further examination. This exhumation can be arranged, but the State must always obtain the consent of the proper ecclesiastical authority, for to the ecclesiastical authority alone belongs the right to allow a disinterment from the sacred ground of Catholic cemeteries.

Furthermore, merely civil authorities have no right to condemn a blessed cemetery because of its location, and order the removal of all the remains to another place. The civil power has a right to suggest such an action, and the Church may and perhaps ought, when such an action serves the common good, to comply with the suggestion. The important thing to remember is that the proper

lar power. He gave as his reason that the end of the civil society is to promote the public or common happiness and the temporal welfare of its citizens, and that it is by virtue of this purpose or end that the civil authority can establish any regulations it reasonably deems fit or necessary for the preservation of the common good. The Code and the authors after the Code are decidedly of a different mind on this question (cf. c. 1160 and the authors cited immediately above). While not minimizing the importance of the civil power in caring for the welfare of its citizens, the Church insists on her divine right to the possession of an undivided jurisdiction over her blessed cemeteries. Whatever powers the State has over blessed cemeteries come not from any innate right on the part of the State, but from the gratuitous concession or the involuntary toleration of the Church.

[27] C. 1160.

[28] C. 1214, § 1.

ecclesiastical authorities must be consulted and their permission must be obtained before any exhumation may take place, whenever there is a question of a blessed cemetery.[29]

The ecclesiastical authority competent to give the requisite permission for an exhumation is the ordinary.[30] This is to say that if the cemetery belongs to an exempt religious community the permission for exhumation must come from the major regular superior; if the cemetery belongs to any other religious community or to any parish or diocese the proper ecclesiastical authority is the ordinary of the place.[31] Coronata holds that in the case of an emergency, when the bishop or vicar general cannot be reached, the dean *(vicarius foraneus)* may give the permission, and that in extreme emergency the permission may be presumed.[32] Canon 1214, § 2, orders the ecclesiastical superior to make certain that the body or the remains to be exhumed can be known from all others buried in the cemetery. This canon applies to individual exhumations, and not to the removal of all the bodies from a cemetery which for some good reason must be abandoned as a burial ground. In this latter case all the remains, known and unknown, must be removed to the new cemetery.[33]

The permission of the ordinary must be obtained in all cases in which the remains rest in sacred ground, even if the cemetery belongs to the same civil power which desires to exhume the body.[34] In those cases, therefore, in which the whole municipal cemetery is blessed, or in which a special Catholic section is blessed,[35] any removal must be sanctioned by the competent ordinary. Should the body of a non-Catholic be buried in blessed ground but without any of the rites of the Church, ecclesiastical permission would be just as necessary to exhume such a body as to disinter the remains of a Catholic who had received all the rites of the Church. The basis for this is not so

[29] Cf. De Meester, *Compendium*, n. 1183; Cocchi, *Commentarium in Codicem Iuris Canonici*, V, n. 54; Wernz-Vidal, *Ius Canonicum*, IV, n. 569.

[30] C. 1214, § 1.

[31] Cf. 198; also c. 488, 8°.

[32] *De Locis et Temporibus Sacris*, n. 151.

[33] Cf. *supra*, p. 130, on the loss of the blessing of a cemetery.

[34] Coronata, *Institutiones*, n. 796.

[35] C. 1206, § 2.

much canon 1214, § 1, which very likely cannot be extended to include this case, but canon 1160, which gives the ecclesiastical authority the right to permit or refuse the exhumation of the bodies of Catholics and non-Catholics alike who have been buried in her blessed cemeteries.

On the other hand, the body of a Catholic which is buried in a non-Catholic cemetery cannot be exhumed without the permission of the ordinary, but not for the same reason that governed the exhumation of the body of a non-Catholic in a Catholic cemetery. In the present case canon 1160 does not directly apply; canon 1214, § 1, however, does have a bearing. For the body of a Catholic which is interred with all the funeral rites of the Church in ground which strictly considered is not sacred ground, but rather blessed ground, having received only the "*benedictio tumuli,*" [36] has been accorded the benefit of a permanent Christian burial ("*perpetuae sepulturae ecclesiasticae*") in the sense of canon 1214, § 1.[37]

It need hardly be pointed out that when the Church wishes to effect an exhumation from her own blessed cemeteries, she will do well to consult the civil law on the matter of exhumation. Civil law seldom makes a distinction between municipal or secularly owned cemeteries and the blessed cemeteries of the Church, and will insist on certain formalities and precautions that must be observed. Failure to comply could very easily be the occasion of civil prosecution.[38]

Article III. Immunities Properly So Called

Before the Code the blessed cemeteries of the Church enjoyed by ecclesiastical law all of the immunities of consecrated and blessed churches: the immunity from profane and unbecoming acts, and the right of asylum.[39] The Code, however, even though explicity re-

[36] Cf. *supra*, p. 107.

[37] For the meaning of Christian burial (*sepultura ecclesiastica*) cf. c. 1204. See also the excellent treatment of this question in Kerin, *The Privation of Christian Burial*, pp. 97-125.

[38] Cf. Wernz-Vidal, *Ius Canonicum*, IV, n. 569. Cf. also *The Jurist* (3 vols., Washington, D. C., 1941—), I, 173.

[39] Cf. *supra*, pp. 39-45.

asserting the immunities as far as churches are concerned,[40] fails to extend by positive legislation these same immunities to cemeteries. Is this omission on the part of the Code to be taken to mean that churches alone are to enjoy ecclesiastical immunities, and cemeteries are no longer to enjoy them, or do cemeteries in some way still enjoy the immunities they had before the Code?

First of all, there is the fact. The Code does not positively accord the strict ecclesiastical immunities to cemeteries, whereas before the Code cemeteries as well as churches enjoyed these immunities. This failure on the part of the Code to include reference to immunities in its section on cemeteries can mean one of two things: either the Church wishes that the law of the Code (cc. 1178-1179) which grants immunities to churches be applied (as in pre-Code times) also to cemeteries; or the Church desires in her canon law to uphold her claim for the immunities of churches, but in her positive law to waive her claim for the immunities of cemeteries.

It does not seem probable that the two canons (1178-1179) which define the immunities of churches can be extended to cemeteries. Before the Code the laws which applied to churches, wherever they could, applied also to cemeteries, *mutatis mutandis*. This close association cannot be understood to continue after 1918 in the manner in which it existed before that time. In the pre-Code era the Church at one time or other made laws concerning the blessing, the violation and the reconciliation of churches, and having made them, let it be understood that these same laws were to govern cemeteries. The canonists and liturgists, in like manner, devoted many pages to the law on churches, and in a brief page or two explained that the same applied also to cemeteries.

But the Code has changed all this. The Code has initiated a new era in the law on cemeteries. For the first time in the history of canon law, the Church has made a truly separate set of laws to govern cemeteries. It is true that in many details the legislation on churches and the legislation on cemeteries parallel each other, and in some cases the law regarding both remains the same. But if the law on cemeteries is the same as the law on churches, it is because the

[40] Cc. 1178-1179.

Code specifies that it is the same for both. For example, the seven introductory canons (1154-1160) to the respective laws on churches and cemeteries are common to both; in the special section of the Code on cemeteries (cc. 1205-1214) one canon in particular, canon 1207, refers to the law on churches, making that law applicable also to cemeteries. It is in canon 1207 that one would expect to find that the ecclesiastical immunities of churches were extended to cemeteries, for in this canon the Code distinctly states that what is said of the interdict, the violation and the reconciliation of churches is to be the law likewise for cemeteries. But there is no mention of immunities there or elsewhere with reference to cemeteries.[41] Therefore, in view of what has been said, it seems altogether intentional on the part of the Church to have omitted all reference to immunities in its section on cemeteries.

In the opinion of Coronata the reason for the Code's non-inclusion of any mention of ecclesiastical immunities in the chapter on cemeteries is that these immunities had already fallen into a state of practical non-existence before the Code.[42] Wernz (1842-1914),[43] at the turn of the century, declared that one immunity, the *ius asyli*, was no longer recognized in civil law with regard to churches, and if churches were not so honored, it is not to be expected that cemeteries received any greater consideration. Thus, many years before the Code, a criminal who took refuge in a church or cemetery was just as liable to apprehension there as in any other public place. Because of the disregard of civil law toward immunities established by ecclesiastical law, the Church found it difficult and often even impossible to enforce her long-standing immunities. Accordingly, in 1918 when the Church was eliminating and restating some of her laws, adding

[41] It is to be remembered that by the term *immunities* there are included only those which are immunities in the strict sense, namely, the immunities from profane acts and the right of asylum. There are other immunities which are such only in the broader sense, namely, exemption from civil jurisdiction (c. 1160), which all sacred places should enjoy (*supra*, pp. 138-145), and immunity from the things which are mentioned in canon 1211 and which offend against the reverence which befits cemeteries.

[42] *De Locis et Temporibus Sacris*, nn. 42, 44.

[43] *Ius Decretalium*, III, n. 448.

new ones, and reorganizing all her legislation, she separated churches and cemeteries on the matter of immunities, retaining the immunities as far as churches were concerned, the disregard of the civil law notwithstanding, but relinquishing them with reference to cemeteries.

While it is perfectly true that one of the reasons for the Church's withdrawal of the ecclesiastical immunities of cemeteries is because of the failure of the civil law to recognize them, it is by no means the main reason. The real reason is that the immunities as expressed in the ecclesiastical law of pre-Code times are no longer as necessary for cemeteries as they once were. In pre-Code law the Church found it necessary to insist that profane acts in cemeteries as well as in churches violated the reverence and decorum that by divine law belonged to such sacred places.

Though it was of the very nature of these sacred places to be set aside as immune from acts that were, if not unholy and sacrilegious, at least worldly and mercenary, the situation was serious enough for the Church to have to specify that certain things outraged the holiness of a sacred place. Thus, for example, it was found necessary to prohibit by positive ecclesiastical law within the bounds of a church or a cemetery such acts as the buying and selling and the every-day business transactions of the market-place, public meetings of a purely secular or political nature, and the establishment of secular courts to try civil and criminal cases. The Church also had to enact legislation on the right of asylum which sacred places traditionally afforded to criminals or to those who were suspected of crime. In the earlier days the establishment of a just and detailed penal code and of a well-regulated and efficient law enforcement body was not as well organized as in later times, and the *ius asyli* was a protection against the violation of a sacred place, and also a caution to civil officers and magistrates who often through haste and sheer cruelty offended against justice.[44]

But at the time of the Code most of the acts which earlier had made ecclesiastical laws on the immunities of cemeteries necessary were no longer a threat to the holiness of cemeteries. To keep these ecclesiastical laws when there was little use for them would have

[44] Cf. *supra*, pp. 39-45.

served no purpose. In many countries all cemeteries were civil or municipal, and were therefore governed and protected by civil law.[45] In other countries the civil law amply protected cemeteries from acts foreign to the obvious purpose of a cemetery.[46]

It is hardly necessary to point out that, even during the times when the ecclesiastical legislation on immunities was so imperative, the legislation was more vital to the protection of churches than to the safeguarding of cemeteries. Public meetings, buying and selling, civil court proceedings, all these were much more likely to take place in churches than in cemeteries. There is little likelihood that such things would happen in cemeteries today, and if now and then there is an isolated case of the perpetration of one or the other of the profane acts mentioned in earlier ecclesiastical law, it would be so rare that there would be no need to make provision against it in the common law of the Church. Any abuse could very easily be repressed by some appropriate act of intervention on the part of the local ordinary.

Although the Church has omitted from her present legislation all reference to the immunities of cemeteries, it is not to be concluded that she leaves them without any protection whatsoever. Cemeteries in a sense still enjoy immunities, not any longer by virtue of ecclesiastical law, but surely still in virtue of the divine law. The cemeteries of the Church have from the very beginning enjoyed the protection of divine law. Up to the time when the Church initiated her legislation on immunities, divine law had already provided for the fitting protection of ecclesiastical cemeteries. Now that the troublous times are over and the Church has withdrawn her laws on the immunities of cemeteries, the divine law again takes care of the situation without the aid of ecclesiastical sanctions.[47]

Since the promulgation of the Code of Canon Law, therefore, ecclesiastical immunities as such are a thing of the past with regard to cemeteries. But if understood in the proper meaning of immunities it can be said that cemeteries after 1918 do enjoy immunities, that

[45] Cf. *supra*, p. 95.

[46] Cf. Zollman, *American Church Law*, Chap. XVII.

[47] Coronata, *De Locis et Temporibus Sacris*, nn. 149, 42, 44.

is, immunities which are vindicated by the divine law. The term "divine law immunities" must be correctly understood. While it is not exactly true to say that all ecclesiastical immunities are derived directly from the divine natural or positive law, it is true to say that most ecclesiastical immunities have their foundation or their basis in the divine law. Immunities of ecclesiastical law (which cemeteries no longer enjoy) far outnumber the immunities which come formally *(formaliter seu immediate)* from the divine law. The natural and positive divine law demands only a minimum of immunities; the civil and ecclesiastical laws have both fortified and added to the number of immunities deriving from the divine law.

If one were to strip the notion of immunities of all trace of canonical and civil legislation, leaving only the substructure of the divine law, one would have the meaning of "divine law immunities" as the term is used in this dissertation. The term thus includes not only those immunities which derive directly *(immediate)* from the divine law, but also that part of every ecclesiastical immunity which strikes its native root unalterably in the divine law.[48] The best manner of studying the divine law immunities is to measure them against the already familiar ecclesiastical immunities. Therefore the only practical way to answer the question: What are the divine law immunities which blessed cemeteries enjoy today? is to take the immunities which cemeteries before the Code enjoyed by ecclesiastical law, and to see if and how far they have been based on divine law.

[48] Coronata in his *Ius Publicum Ecclesiasticum* (nn. 150-151) gives four opinions on the juridic origin of immunities: the first, that the immunities derive solely from the civil law; the second, that they derive from the divine natural or positive law; the third, that they have their origin in canon law; the fourth, that they have their foundation in the divine law and were only later on stated in canon law. He rejects the first three theories and accepts the fourth, after making it clear that *some* immunities do have their origin in civil law, and that *some* do come directly from divine law. Cf. also: Concilium Tridentinum, sess. XXV, *de ref.*, c. 20; De Angelis, *Praelectiones Iuris Canonici ad methodum Decretalium Gregorii IX exactae* (4 vols., Romae, 1877-1887), lib. III, tit. 49, n. 2; Cappello, *Summa Iuris Publici Ecclesiastici,* nn. 354-355; Ottaviani, *Institutiones Iuris Publici Ecclesiastici* (2. ed., 2 vols., Romae: Typis Polyglottis Vaticani, 1935-1936), I, nn. 193-196.

The ecclesiastical immunities of the old law were divided traditionally into two classes: immunities from profane and unbecoming acts; and the right of asylum. Ecclesiastical law [49] from time to time, as the necessity for it arose, specified that certain acts were to be prohibited within the sacred precincts of blessed cemeteries. These acts were forbidden because of their evident impropriety and irreverence. Practically all of these acts which the Church by positive law forbade were already prohibited at least radically by the divine natural law. There are other acts, too, which have never been proscribed expressly in ecclesiastical law, but which are barred by the divine law. For the divine law proscribes any and all things which are repugnant to the sanctity of blessed cemeteries.

A cemetery is a sacred place, and all acts in it should be in keeping with the profound reverence and dignity which belongs to a cemetery, both because of the high purpose which it serves, and because of the ecclesiastical blessing which it has received. Accordingly, all immoral acts *(actus turpes)* are forbidden because they directly violate the immunity of a sacred place required by the divine natural law. Worldly or profane acts are likewise prohibited by divine law: certainly theatrical performances, public dancing, seditious gatherings and discussions, criminal trials conducted by secular tribunals; very probably also public and group meetings of secular organizations, civil trials by secular courts, and other acts which in the common estimation of men should not take place in a cemetery. More remotely disallowed by the natural law are such acts as the planting and harvesting of crops, gardening, or the use of cemeteries as a pasturage for cattle or sheep.[50] Cemeteries enjoy immunity from the acts mentioned above in virtue of the divine law; churches possess this immunity not only from the divine law but also by canon law (c. 1178, which applies only to churches).[51]

Likewise, the Code stipulates that churches enjoy a further

[49] Cf. *supra*, pp. 39-42.

[50] Cf. Moulart, *De Sepultura et Coemeteriis*, pp. 109-110; Many, *De Locis Sacris*, n. 150; Coronata, *De Locis et Temporibus Sacris*, nn. 40-41; Cocchi, *Commentarium in Codicem Iuris Canonici*, V, n. 54; Wernz-Vidal, *Ius Canonicum*, IV, n. 569.

[51] Cf. Coronata, *Institutiones*, nn. 795, 751.

immunity, namely, the right of asylum, an immunity which before 1918 both churches and cemeteries enjoyed.[52] The *ius asyli* is an immunity which cemeteries at the present time do not possess, because it had its origin, not in the divine natural or positive law, but in civil law.[53]

Roman law, holding its temples as sacred because they were dedicated to the Roman gods and goddesses, recognized that criminals who took refuge in the temples were not to be forcibly extracted, but enjoyed in them a *ius asyli,* a right of asylum. This did not mean that the criminal was not to be punished for his misdeeds; it meant rather that the civil law was suspended in the pursuit of a criminal at the door of the temple. Inside the temple the criminal was assured some protection from his sometimes angry pursuers, the temple's precincts were not violated, and the criminal was not released until there was a guarantee that he would receive a just sentence. This right of asylum was extended to Catholic churches some time after their restoration in the early fourth century. It is difficult to say just when cemeteries began to enjoy the privilege, but it was probably during the fifth or sixth century. And even then it was not granted to them for the reason that they were cemeteries, but because of their close proximity to a church which, together with its environs, enjoyed this immunity from the civil law.[54]

By the time of the II General Council of the Lateran (1139) cemeteries possessed this *ius asyli* in their own right.[55] From that time on, right up to the time of the Code, cemeteries as well as churches were by ecclesiastical law considered to enjoy the right of asylum. Civil law, however, mainly by refusing to recognize this immunity of churches and cemeteries, made it difficult for the Church to retain the *ius asyli.* But as the Church lost the recognition of the civil law, the need for the right of asylum as a protection to the criminal and to the sanctity of the sacred place diminished. The

[52] C. 1179.

[53] Coronata, *De Locis et Temporibus Sacris,* nn. 42-44; Cocchi, *Commentarium in Codicem Iuris Canonici,* V, n. 54; Wernz-Vidal, *Ius Canonicum,* IV, n. 569.

[54] Cf. *supra,* pp. 42-43.

[55] Mansi, XXI, 530. Cf. *supra,* p. 42.

Code (c. 1179) reasserts the Church's policy of demanding the respect of the civil law in the matter of the right of asylum of churches, but no longer with regard to cemeteries.

The immunity of the *ius asyli*, although it had its origin in the civil law and was taken over and developed by canon law, is not without its basis in the divine law. As Wernz points out,[56] there is nothing intrinsically evil in removing a malefactor from a sacred place even by means of physical force, provided that it is done at a proper time and in a fitting manner. Divine law demands that justice be done to one who is guilty of a crime even when he has taken refuge in a blessed cemetery; but it demands also that the sacredness of blessed cemeteries be protected from violation. Anything, therefore, that would work an injustice to the criminal or that would expose the cemetery to violation is forbidden by the natural law, and accordingly is prohibited just as truly since the Code as before the Code, when ecclesiastical law added its sanctions to the divine natural law.

Thus criminals have no longer the right of asylum in the cemeteries of the Church. But this does not mean that, should a criminal take refuge in a cemetery, the law-enforcement officers may use any means whatsoever to apprehend and remove him. For even apart from the immunity of the right of asylum, the correct and decent thing for such officers to do, when the circumstances do not make it impossible, is to inform the proper ecclesiastical authorities of the situation. The latter will make it their duty to co-operate in every way, and at the same time they will provide the proper safeguards for the preservation of the fitting reverence which is due to the sacred place.

[56] *Ius Decretalium*, III, n. 446.

CHAPTER XI

THE DISPOSAL OF LOTS IN A BLESSED CEMETERY

CANON 1209, § 1, although it does not directly touch the subject, raises the question as to the possibility of selling the consecrated ground of cemeteries. This canon gives local ordinaries and religious superiors authorization to permit the faithful to build vaults in a blessed cemetery, and to allow them to dispose of them if they so desire. The Code, therefore, clearly allows private persons to build, own and sell—with certain restrictions specified in canon 1209, § 1—their own personal or family tombs in the blessed cemeteries of the Church. Nothing is said of the ground on which these tombs or vaults are built, that is, whether it can really be owned and alienated by private individuals. In the canonical legislation before the Code it was forbidden to make the sacred ground of the Church's cemeteries the object of sale.

This is a problem that goes back almost to the earliest Christian cemeteries. There were many martyrs in the early Church, and all the faithful out of devotion to them wanted to be buried near their sepulchres. The faithful had always been well taken care of in the matter of burial, the poorest as well as the wealthiest. But the poor and the rich, both from the same noble motives, vied with one another for interment, either for themselves or for their relatives, next to the body of a martyr.[1] Usually this privilege of burial near a martyr was accorded first to bishops and other Church dignitaries, to emperors and other notable laymen.

There were to be distinguished, therefore, in those early days of Christianity, what might be called the common burial place, and the more honorable one, the latter being near the graves of the martyrs. An abuse was not slow to make its appearance. Some clerics, seeing a chance of enlarging the sources of revenue of the church to which they were attached, or out of personal avarice, would set a price on

[1] H. Leclercq, "Ad Sanctos," *DACL*, I, 488-491.

the more coveted graves. This, of course, had no ecclesiastical sanction, and was roundly condemned by emperors, popes and councils.

The Emperor Anastasius (491-518), for example,—and Justinian (527-565) later reissued the decree, an act which showed that the abuse was not entirely curbed by the former decree [2]—ordered a sum of money to be paid to the churches of Constantinople in order that there would be no need for the clerics or *fossores* to exact any "charge" for the services they rendered at the time of the burial.[3] The exequies were to be conducted *gratis*, and violators of this decree were to pay a substantial fine.[4] The provision of the Emperors Anastasius and Justinian was all-embracing; it included, therefore, in its order, that the grave itself was to be given free to all, to the rich as well as to the poor.[5]

About this same time the attitude of the Church itself was expressed in a letter of Pope St. Gregory the Great (590-604). In terms that had unmistakably only one meaning the pontiff condemned the practice of asking a price for burial ground. He said that such a thing was a shameful abuse, prompted by the detestable vice of avarice. He did not, however, put his objection on the basis of simony. St. Gregory argued rather that it was not in keeping with Christianity, or with the priesthood, or with the episcopate, for a Christian, or a priest, or a bishop, to exact a price for a place of burial. The pontiff pointed out that if the pagans refused to accept money from Abraham for the grave of Sara and actually took the money only because Abraham insisted on it, certainly priests should show no less a charity. St. Gregory made it plain that there should be no price asked for the grave; but he did allow spontaneous free-will offerings of parents or relatives to be received as a means of defraying other incidental expenses connected with the act of burial.[6]

[2] N. (praefatio) 59.

[3] Bingham, *The Antiquities of the Christian Church,* I, 118; Catalanus, *Pontificale Romanum,* pars 2, tit. 6, nn. 21-24.

[4] C. (1,2) 18.

[5] Bingham, *loc. cit.*

[6] ". . . Grave nimis et procul est a sacerdotis officio pretium de terra concessa putredini quaerere, et de alieno velle facere luctu compendium. . . . Hoc autem vitium et nos postquam, Deo auctore, ad episcopatus honorem accessimus,

The letters of St. Gregory the Great served as the basis for the legislation of many councils. Little by little conciliar legislation allowed the faithful to make spontaneous offerings even for the place of burial itself. But each time the law made two points very clear: first, nothing was to be exacted, no such thing as a price was to be put on graves; secondly, if anything was to be received at all, it had to come unsolicited, and from the free and spontaneous choice of the donor. All abuses were condemned without reservation.[7]

Notwithstanding the clearly defined teaching of the Church on the matter, it became necessary for Pope Innocent III (1198-1216) to condemn what was evidently a somewhat widespread abuse in his day. It seems that it had been the policy of some priests to ask for and even demand that a certain required payment be made before they would permit any grave to be opened. The Pontiff decreed that this should be abolished at once. He ordered that clerics should be positively restrained from exacting any price for ground used for

de Ecclesia nostra omnino vetuimus, et pravam denuo consuetudinem nequaquam usurpari permisimus; memores quia dum Abraham a filiis Emor, hoc est Ephron filio Seor, sepulcrum pretio ad humandum corpus coniugis postularet, pretium accipere renuit, ne commodum videretur de cadavere consecutus (Genesis, xxiii). Si ergo tantae considerationis paganus vir fuit, quanto magis nos, qui sacerdotes dicimur, hoc facere non debemus? Unde ne hoc avaritiae vitium, ne vel in alienis denuo tentari praesumatur admoneo. Sed si quando aliquem in Ecclesia vestra sepeliri conceditis, siquidem parentes ipsius, proximi, vel haeredes pro luminaribus sponte quid offerre voluerint, accipere non vetamus. Peti vero aut aliquid exigi omnino prohibemus; quod valde irreligiosum est, ne aut venalis fortasse, quod absit, dicatur Ecclesia, aut vos de humanis videamini mortibus gratulari, si ex eorum cadaveribus studeatis quaerere quolibet modo compendium." *Epistola III* (ad Ianuarium), lib. IX Epistolarum—*MPL,* LXXVII, 940-941. In another letter (ad Donum Episcopum Messanensem) St. Gregory made it equally clear that the place of burial was not to be sold: "Quamvis nostrum institutum noveris, nos antiquam consuetudinem nostram a nostra Ecclesia omnino vetuisse, nec cuiquam assensum praebere ut loca humandi corporis pretio possint adipisci."—*Epistola III,* lib. VIII Epistolarum—*MPL,* LXXVII, 908.

[7] The Council of Meaux (845), c. 72—Hardouin, IV, 1496; the Council of Tribur (895), c. 16—Mansi, XVIII, 140-141; the Council of Ravenna (997), c. 3—Mansi, XIX, 221; the Council of Bourges (1031), c. 12—Mansi, XIX, 504-505.

burial.[8] The gloss [9] stated that a sepulchre which was a *locus sacer* was not to be sold; on the other hand, one that was not sacred or religious could be sold. Pope Alexander III (1159-1181) had earlier condemned the *sale of graves* as an act of simony, although voluntary offerings on the occasion of a burial were not forbidden.[10]

Barbosa explained that a grave in a blessed cemetery could not pass into the hands of any private person. The Church kept the *dominium,* the ownership, over all *loca sacra* and neither the whole blessed cemetery nor any part of it could be sold. However, a person could be given the use of a grave in blessed ground, and even the exclusive use for himself and for his family. Any offering that was received could be understood, in fact had to be understood, as compensating the ecclesiastical cemetery corporation for the perpetual and exclusive use of a grave or cemetery plot, and not as a transfer of ownership.[11]

From the time of St. Gregory the Great (590-604), therefore, it was conceded that, while nothing was to be exacted, offerings that were given spontaneously by the relatives or friends of the deceased could be accepted. Practically every council, too, which from the seventh to the fourteenth century mentioned the abuse, granted, as has been seen,[12] that unsolicited offerings were not condemned.[13] Accordingly, the practice grew up whereby the faithful as a rule made some donation at the time of arranging for a grave. The Popes insisted regularly, however, that the poor were to be given not only graves but also all the prayers and services of burial absolutely without any cost to them or to their families.[14] The Church left it to local custom, which sooner or later found its way into diocesan statutes and decrees of provincial councils, to determine what would

[8] C. 13, X, *de sepulturis,* III, 28.

[9] At the word "sepultura."

[10] C. 8 (and c. 9), X, *de simonia,* V, 3.

[11] *Iuris Ecclesiastici Universi,* Lib. II, c. 10, nn. 11, 12, 16.

[12] Cf. *supra,* p. 156.

[13] Cf. Samuellius, *De Sepulturis Ecclesiasticis,* tract. 2, disp. 1, controv. 13, concl. 4, n. 9.

[14] Alexander VII, const. *Sacrosancti,* 18 ian. 1658, § 2, n. 19—*Fontes,* n. 235; Gregorius XVI, ep. encycl. *Inter gravissimas,* 3 febr. 1832, § 9—*Fontes,* n. 483. Cf. S. C. Ep. et Reg., *Theanen.,* 5 febr. 1591—*Fontes,* n. 1439.

be an equitable offering for a grave in a blessed cemetery, and also who were to be considered *pauperes*.[15]

The law before the Code, therefore, was very emphatic in prohibiting the sale of graves in a blessed cemetery. It was not that the natural law or the divine positive law forbade such a transaction, for there was nothing inherently wrong in selling blessed ground as long as the price was not increased because of the blessing. Unblessed land has an intrinsic value which the blessing of the Church in no way changes. In the same way a chalice that is worth $100.00 before it is consecrated is worth just as much after the consecration. There would be simony if something more than the material value was demanded for no other reason than that the chalice had been consecrated or the ground blessed. But in the matter of the sacred ground used for burials, the Church declared by positive legislation that to receive money *tamquam pretium* for graves was a custom that was wrong *(prava)*, perverse *(perversa)* and to be abolished *(abolenda)*. And authors were generally agreed that such a sale involved an act of simony in contravention of the ecclesiastical law.[16]

If the sacred ground of Catholic cemeteries could not be the object of sale, was it possible that some money could be received or that some charge could be levied even under some other heading, authors asked. For three things were very clear: first, cemetery property cost the Church considerable expense in regard both to the initial purchase and also to the current upkeep; secondly, many could afford to pay something to help defray the expenses entailed

[15] Cf. S. C. C., *Nullius Montis Cassini*, 26 ian. 1726, ad 11—*Fontes*, n. 3309.

[16] Cf. *supra*, p. 157. "De iure quidem naturali, nihil obstare videtur quin aliquid recipiatur; sicut enim calix consecratus vendi potest, modo nihil addatur ratione consecrationis, sic et terra benedicta, aut aliqua eius pars, in dominium aut usum tradi posse videtur, modo pretium non augeatur ratione benedictionis; tunc enim non spirituale, sed temporale venditur.—*Sed quidquid hoc est, iure canonico, nihil percipi potest tanquam pretium*."—Many, *De Locis Sacris*, n. 152. "Quamquam disputari possit utrum iure divino et naturali prohibita sit sepulcri benedicti venditio, ubi ratione benedictionis pretium non augetur; *ex iure tamen ecclesiastico, aliquid tamquam pretium pro sepultura in loco communi recipere aut exigere apud omnes simoniacum est*."—Moulart, *De Sepultura et Coemeteriis*, pp. 112-113. (The *italics* in both citations are not those of the original authors.)

in keeping a cemetery; and thirdly, a great many made offerings at the time of arranging for a burial.

Pre-Code canonists were unanimous in asserting that something could be expected from the relatives of the deceased who could afford it, but that this "charge" was in no way to be construed as giving them ownership (*dominium, proprietas*) over any part of the blessed cemetery. They insisted, too, that all the faithful without exception had a right to ecclesiastical sepulture, and that the money they paid was in no way connected with this right, for with or without the stipend they could have all the funeral rites of the Church including the ground for burial. The money they paid (if they were in a position to give anything at all) was to go towards the maintenance of the cemetery, the wages of the workmen, etc.[17]

Apart from the blessed ground itself which was not to be sold, apart also from the expenses which were necessarily involved in the upkeep of a cemetery and to which a monetary value *(pretium aestimabile)* could be attached, there were also two other considerations which made the asking of some payment at the time of burial justifiable. The first of these was what authors called the *pretium pro nobiliori seu honorabiliori sepulchro*; the second, the *pretium pro usu exclusivo seu privativo sepulchri determinati.*

Every Catholic had a right to *a grave* in the sacred ground of the cemeteries of the Church, but no one had a right to be allowed a preference or a choice of one grave over another. Therefore, if one requested that a plot in a particular location of the cemetery be set aside for himself and his family, he could justly be asked to make some payment for the favor. Furthermore, hand in hand with the privilege of the selection of a *special plot* went the right of the *exclusive use* of the plot. This right of the "owner" of the plot to exclude all others from his reserved section, and the obligation imposed on the Church to protect the "owner's" rights, were things to which some extrinsic value could be attached. The funds thus collected by the cemetery authorities from those who wished special services over and beyond their strict due enabled them to purchase the ground for the cemetery and to provide decent and perpetual care,

[17] Many, *De Locis Sacris*, n. 152.

not only for those who could make an offering, but also for those who were really poor.[18]

Since the promulgation of the Code of Canon Law there is no longer unanimous agreement on the question of the sale of graves or lots in a blessed cemetery. Some hold the pre-Code teaching that ground before it is blessed can be sold, but once it has been rendered sacred by the blessing of the Church it cannot any longer be bought or sold. There is, on the other hand, what might be considered a new school of thought, on this question since the Code. This latter group maintains that since blessed ground retains the intrinsic value which it had before being blessed it can be sold, provided, of course, that there is no additional price appended to the original value because of the blessing of the Church.

Most of the discussion of this question centers around the interpretation of canon 1209, § 1. The canon reads as follows:

> "§ 1. Tum in coemeteriis paroecialibus, ex licentia scripta Ordinarii loci eiusve delegati, tum in coemeterio proprio alius personae moralis, ex licentia scripta Superioris, fideles sibi suisque exstruere possunt sepulcra particularia; quae, de consensu eiusdem Ordinarii aut Superioris, possunt quoque alienare."

Augustine offers the following free translation and commentary on this canon:

> "Paragraph 1 of canon 1209 permits *lots or vaults (sepulchra particularia)* to be constructed with the written consent of the local ordinary or his delegate on the parish cemetery. The same written consent may be given by the superior, either local or major, of the corporation on whose cemetery such a private sepulchre is chosen by the faithful. These private sepulchres, or graves, or lots may, with the consent of the ordinary or superior,

[18] Cf. Reiffenstuel, lib. III, tit. 28, nn. 66-69; Schmalzgrueber, lib. III, tit. 28, nn. 80-81; Giraldi, *Expositio Iuris Pontificii*, pars I, sect. 755 (vol. I, p. 563); Bargilliat, *Praelections Iuris Canonici* (1895 ed.), n. 1325; Moulart, *De Sepultura et Coemeteriis*, pp. 113-115; Wernz, *Ius Decretalium*, III, n. 785; Many, *De Locis Sacris*, n. 152, *Concilii Plenarii Baltimorensis II, Acta et Decreta*, n. 393; *Rituale Romanum*, tit. VI, c. 1, n. 8.

be alienated. Alienation is, of course, here to be understood of a conveyance for burial purposes. If suspicion of simony should arise from the term *alienation,* it may be observed that this is only an apparent difficulty, easily removed. If a certain sum would be charged for the grave itself, by reason of its being consecrated ground, there would indeed be simony. However, here there is question only of the exclusive right of usufruct, which is reserved to a determined person or family with regard to a specified lot. The cemetery itself or any part thereof is not sold or leased. But the exclusive right to a determined and honorable place has a material value and its sale, therefore, does not imply simony." [19]

In this brief citation from Augustine is epitomized the long-standing problem of the sale of blessed ground in Catholic cemeteries, together with the traditional or pre-Code solution of the problem. No one among the post-Code authors puts the case for the non-sale of blessed ground in Catholic cemetries in such plain and uncompromising language. Perhaps the unequivocal and positive expression of his view is due in large measure to the fact that he wrote so soon after the promulgation of the Code (1920, with a revision in 1923), and he had his eye turned mainly toward pre-Code legislation. His commentary does not give any indication of any other possible interpretation of the terminology of the Code (especially canon 1209, § 1). The latest editions of Wernz-Vidal, too, following the earlier editions of Wernz, seem to take but the one pre-Code view of the question.[20] But other authors who are on the same side as Augustine and Wernz-Vidal on the prohibited sale of ground in blessed cemeteries take cognizance of the other position, namely, that of the authors who hold that lots in blessed cemeteries can be sold. Beste very plainly admits two schools of thought; [21] De Meester hints that others may differ from his opinion.[22]

Wernz-Vidal explain first that cemeteries which have been blessed by the Church cannot be bought or sold without the permission of

[19] *Commentary,* VI, 110-111. The *italics* are the author's.

[20] *Ius Canonicum,* IV, n. 570.

[21] *Introductio in Codicem,* p. 587.

[22] *Compendium,* n. 1177.

the Holy See since they are sacred places, and as such are *extra humanum commercium.* Then they go on to consider the question of the sale of graves: "*. . . num possit pro pretio concedi locus ad sepulturam in coemeterio.*" Wernz-Vidal divide their answer into five steps or stages.

(a) If the cemetery is not blessed, the owners of the cemetery, whoever they are, may sell the graves for a stated price or they may merely sell the use of the ground, keeping the ownership. It is profane ground and therefore there is no difficulty from the point of view of ecclesiastical legal complications.

(b) The authors point out an abuse with regard to the cemeteries of the Church, wherein the poor suffer an injustice if they are required to pay a stipulated price for the ground in which they are to be buried. The poor have both the right to the sacred rites of burial, as well as the right to the sacred place of sepulture.[23]

(c) If the poor be excepted, there is nothing amiss in the practice of charging those who can pay it a certain funeral tax *for the use of a specific grave in a blessed cemetery,* for such a tax is not the price of the grave as such, but is levied only to maintain the cemetery or church to which the cemetery is attached. Futhermore, the tax is justified because of long-standing custom.[24]

(d) More justified still is the asking of a price for a family plot, from which all can be excluded except those for whose *use* it is intended. This *exclusive use* can be estimated in terms of money, and as a matter of fact men are wont to put a price on it.[25]

[23] *Ius Canonicum,* IV, n. 570. On these two points, needless to say, there is entire agreement between both schools of thought.

[24] "(c) Quod si non agatur de pauperibus, sed de fidelibus bonis temporalibus praeditis, nihil obstat quominus pro usu sepulcri determinati in coemeterio benedicto taxam quamdam funerariam solvant; cum haec taxa rationem non habeat pretii, sed ad eam exigendam potest adesse titulus conservandi aut reparandi coemeterii vel ecclesiae cum titulo ministrorum sustentandorum, accedente consuetudine hac occasione exigendi praedictam taxam."—*Loc cit.*

[25] "(d) Multo magis pretio soluto comparari potest *usus exclusivus* certi loci coemeterii ecclesiastici pro aliqua familia, ita ut ipsa invita extraneus ibidem sepeliri non possit; qui usus privativus, pretio temporali aestimari potest et inter homines aestimari solet."—*Loc. cit.*

(e) This is all the more justified since the Code in canon 1209, § 1, allows private individuals, who have obtained the competent ecclesiastical permission, to erect family and hereditary tombs or vaults with their own funds, and to sell or alienate them, again with the proper permission, even after they have been blessed. The fact that these ancestral tombs have been blessed does not put them forevermore beyond the possibility of being sold. The original owner may sell his family tomb to another who then becomes the owner. There must be no raising of the sale-price because of the blessing it has received. This would be simony.[26]

As can be readily seen from the above, Wernz-Vidal do not admit of the sale of the sacred ground in a blessed cemetery, even though there can be no danger of an increase in the price because of the blessing. They do allow for a price which can be required of those who can afford it. This price, however, is not for the ground itself, but for the *exclusive use* of the grave or plot. The only thing which they allow to be sold is the structure of the tomb or vault which is separate from the ground itself (c. 1209, § 1). They speak always in this connection of a *sepulcrum aedificatum:* ". . . propriis sumptibus aedificatum sepulcrum deinde benedictum;" and ". . . sepulcrum . . . propriis sumptibus aedificatum et postea benedictum."

Wernz-Vidal and Augustine are supported in this the traditional view of the question of the sale of sacred ground by at least De Meester, Beste, Vermeersch-Creusen and Prümmer. Beste distinctly states that the ownership of a grave never passes to private persons, but is retained by the ecclesiastical cemetery corporation, and that the object of the contract and of the price is the exclusive

[26] "(e) Haec item firmantur canone 1209, § 1, ex quo propriis sumptibus aedificatum sepulcrum deinde benedictum, sive familiare sit sive haereditarium, potest quis alienare seu vendere, dummodo venditio fiat de consensu Ordinarii loci, vel Superioris, prout agatur vel de coemeterio paroeciali vel de coemeterio personae moralis. Per se patet non posse augeri pretium propter benedictionem, sicut calicis consecrati pretium ratione consecrationis augeri non potest. Benedictio non efficit, ut sepulcrum quoddam *gentilitium* propriis sumptibus aedificatum et postea benedictum non amplius sit in *ullius privati dominio;* . . . sed illud solum efficit, ut dominus non amplius habeat *liberam* rei dispositionem *ad usus profanos* contra canonicas sanctiones."—*Loc. cit.*

use of the grave, and not the grave itself.[27] De Meester likewise makes it plain that it can hardly be admitted that something can be asked as a price for a grave.[28] He readily agrees that some price can be exacted from those who are not too poor to pay it, but the price is not for the ground as such, but only for the maintenance of the cemetery, of the church and of the ministers who may depend on this *taxa,* and for the particular location *(pro nobiliori et honoratiori sepultura)* and exclusive use *(pro usu privativo)* of the grave selected.[29]

Vermeersch-Creusen, in interpreting the provisions of canon 1209, § 1, point out that the vaults and tombs which a man may get permission to build in a blessed cemetery can be alienated or sold. In explaining the reason for this, they demonstrate that they are of the school which believes that the ground in blessed cemeteries cannot be sold.[30] Prümmer has the same thing to say, namely that it is not the sacred place that is alienated, but the *locus honorabilior aut commodior.*[31]

The second school of thought on the question at hand is represented by such authors as Coronata, Cappello and Cocchi.[32] Their

[27] "Vix dubitari licet, quin obiectum eiusmodi contractus non sit dominium seu ipsa proprietas tumuli vel areolae funeralis, contra ac nonnulli pauci affirmant, sed potius usus privativus loci ad sepulturam in perpetuum vel saltem donec cadavera tumulandorum corrupta fuerint, uti alii communius opinantur." —*Introductio in Codicem,* p. 587.

[28] "Pro simplici fossa in proprio coemeterio [i. e., in the cemetery of one's own parish] ex iure communi facienda aliquid per modum pretii exigere difficilius admitti potest."—*Compendium,* n. 1177.

[29] *Loc. cit.*

[30] "Hoc pacto non alienatur dominium terrae sanctae, sed eius usus qui privative ab emptore acquiritur; obiectum contractus non est facultas sepeliendi in loco sacro, sed locus sepulturae honorabilior et commodior; quae duo sane sunt pretio temporali aestimabilia nec quicquam sacri continent."—*Epitome,* II, 519.

[31] *Manuale Iuris Canonici,* n. 374. Cf. also Eichmann, *Lehrbuch des kirchenrechts* (Paderborn: Schöningh, 1923), p. 398; O'Reilly, *Ecclesiastical Sepulture in the New Code of Canon Law,* pp. 37-38.

[32] Coronata, *De Locis et Temporibus Sacris,* n. 139; Cappello, *Summa Iuris Canonici,* II, n. 711; Cocchi, *Commentarium in Codicem Iuris Canonici,* V, n. 51.

argument is simple and straight-forward: There is nothing in the natural or positive divine law to prevent graves, lots or sections in a blessed cemetery from being sold. There is nothing in the present Code. It is not against right reason to sell cemetery plots; in fact, it is quite reasonable, for the grave has a sale-value entirely independent of the blessing, and independent, too, of the use to which the ground is put. The pre-Code legislation on the matter of the sale of cemetery lots does not seem to be applicable to post-Code times, for direct reference to it is entirely omitted in the Code. The argument is as simple and brief as that.

Although the problem under the present law regarding the possibility of the sale of the sacred ground of blessed cemeteries is not discussed by any author—the above-mentioned canonists of both schools do hardly more than take one side or the other without any further comment on the merits of their own or the opposite opinion—it is a subject that deserves recognition as a question to be discussed. The question itself is not whether the Church actually *does* sell the graves in her blessed cemeteries, but whether in the new law she *can* sell them. In the old law it was seen [33] that the Church prohibited the sale of such ground. In the new law there is no mention of this prohibition. And yet numerous authors since the Code (those of the first school) [34] still retain the pre-Code view that the sacred ground of Catholic cemeteries cannot be sold.

As a matter of fact it may not be an advisable practice for the Church to sell cemetery plots, certainly not unless she takes very careful precautions especially in the wording of the contract. For an outright sale of the grave or lot without any restrictions whatsoever, or without the proper safeguards, could entail an endless train of unpleasant disputes and civil court cases. In the United States the interpretation of the civil courts with regard to cemeteries owned by religious corporations is that, even though cemetery lots be conveyed by deed of sale, the owner has really only a grant to the use of the lot as a place of burial subject to the regulations of the cemetery

[33] Cf. *supra*, pp. 157-158.

[34] Cf. *supra*, pp. 161, 163.

corporation.[35] In other countries the Church cannot sell the sacred ground of the cemeteries where she buries her deceased because she does not own the cemeteries.[36]

But there appears to be no solid reason intrinsically why the sacred ground of Catholic cemeteries *cannot* be sold. There certainly can be no question of simony, either in contravention of the divine or of the ecclesiastical law. The blessing of the cemetery is not the object of the sale. Just as a chalice can be sold for its intrinsic worth even though it is consecrated, so, too, ground can be sold even after it is blessed.[37] It is true that the Church at one time did prohibit the sale of graves in a blessed cemetery.[38] But the very authors who tell of this prohibition explain that there is no compelling reason in the nature of things that it be so.[39]

The law had its origin at a time when persons might untruthfully

[35] "A cemetery association holds the fee of lands purchased for the purposes of the association. The persons to whom lots are conveyed for burial purposes take only an easement—the right to use their lots for such purposes." —Bouvier, *Bouvier's Law Dictionary and Concise Encyclopedia* (8. ed., 2 vols., St. Paul, Minn.: West Publishing Co., 1914), I, 438-439. Zollman (*American Church Law,* n. 622) makes the following deductions from an extensive study of cases that have been adjudged in United States civil courts: "The universal holding [i. e., view] therefore is that the 'certificate' or 'receipt' which the purchaser of a lot generally receives, creates only a mere license or easement or usufructuary right or privilege of interment or right to possess, care for, and maintain the lot until such right is lawfully terminated . . . ; which [receipt] otherwise entitles the holder only to have bodies interred in such ground 'remain undisturbed so long as the cemetery shall continue to be used as such, and so long also, if its use continue, as such remains shall require for entire decomposition; and also the right, in case the cemetery shall be sold for secular purposes, to have such remains removed and properly deposited in a new place of sepulture. . . .' A cemetery deed absolute in form has therefore been declared to be a grant of the use of the lot as a place of burial in subordination to the right of the corporation in the soil or freehold. This privilege or easement or license is neither unlimited on the part of the usufructuary nor arbitrary on the part of the cemetery owner."

[36] Cf. *supra,* p. 95, and c. 1206, § 2.

[37] Cf. cc. 727; 730.

[38] Cf. *supra,* pp. 155-158.

[39] E. g., Moulart, *De Sepultura et Coemeteriis,* pp. 112-113; Many, *De Locis Sacris,* n. 152.

and maliciously accuse the Church of simony, and it was the part of wisdom for the Church to forbid the exaction of a price for graves in her blessed cemeteries. Even as the Church forbade the sale of cemetery lots it sanctioned the receiving of an offering at the time of burial, a fact which can be taken as an indication that the purpose of the Church's law was to preclude any suspicion of simony. And canonists almost immediately explained that not only was an offering permissible, but a charge was allowable because of titles other than ownership (v. g., maintenance of cemetery and church, the *ius exclusivum* and the *locus honorabiliori.* Of course, though abuses were to be found, the poor were always given fitting sepulture in sacred ground.[40]

At the time of the Code people were long since accustomed to some manner of charge on the occasion of arranging for a lot in a cemetery. There were many cemeteries owned by non-Catholics for the use of non-Catholics, and every Catholic knew that there was a sizable payment made for every grave. Those Catholics who lived in predominantly non-Catholic sections and who were forced to use the non-Catholic cemetery for burial purposes knew that they would have to pay for their grave. Catholics, therefore, came to expect their own cemetery corporations as well as any other cemetery corporation to charge some fee for their place of burial. Whether they thought they were buying the ground or merely the use of the ground is not of great importance. The important fact is that there was no longer any danger of suspected simony on the part of the Church when she did ask for some payment to be made. And because there was not that danger the law, which the possible suspicion of simony made necessary hundreds of years ago, was not repeated in the Code of Canon Law, and inasmuch as it was not repeated it does not exist today.[41]

[40] Cf. *supra,* pp. 157-158; 159-160.

[41] Cf. c. 6, 6°. Cicognani (*Canon Law,* pp. 507-508) in his commentary on canon 6, says: ". . . number 6 of this canon prescribes that *all other disciplinary laws of the old law* which were in force until now, and which are neither explicitly nor implicitly contained in the Code, *have lost all force of law,* with the exception of the laws contained in the approved liturgical books and laws derived from the natural and the positive divine law. Another sweeping

The only canon which comes close to the question at all is canon 1209, § 1. This canon states, it will be recalled, that private persons with their own funds may be allowed with the proper ecclesiastical permission to construct their own special burial places, which they may, again with ecclesiastical approbation, alienate. It is very obvious that the Code has in mind some sort of structure above and in addition to the ordinary earth graves, such as vaults, or crypts, or mausoleums. For the Code speaks in this canon of private individuals building these special tombs *("exstruere sepulcra particularia")* at their own expense. It is in this sense that authors interpret this canon. And therefore, while saying that the structural sepulchres can be bought and sold, the Code says nothing about the sale of the sacred ground itself, not even to forbid it.

abrogation of pre-Code legislation! not only the old disciplinary laws, whether universal or particular, which are *opposed to the Code;* not only penal laws which are omitted, are abrogated, but also those *universal laws which exist outside the legislation* promulgated in the Code, namely, those other disciplinary laws which are not explicitly found in the Code. . . . Laws are said to be implicitly contained in the Code, when from the prescript of one or several canons they are deduced as a necessary conclusion therefrom, or without which the force of the canons cannot be accounted for. Laws contained implicitly in the Code are . . . those laws only which are directly deducible from the Code, because they are included in the law therein expressed, as the conclusion in the premise, the species in the genus, or as the part is contained in the whole, or that which is less is contained in that which is greater. . . . *Such laws* [i. e., those disciplinary laws that are not contained explicitly or implicitly in the Code] *must be regarded as having been deliberately omitted and purposely discarded by the legislator; hence they have lost all their force through the promulgation of the Code."* (Italics inserted.) The law forbidding the sale of graves in a blessed cemetery is not to be found either explicitly or implicitly in the Code, and must therefore be considered to have lost all force of law.

CHAPTER XII

THE VIOLATION, THE RECONCILIATION AND THE INTERDICT OF BLESSED CEMETERIES

Canon 1207: Quae de interdicto, violatione, reconciliatione ecclesiarum canones praescribunt, etiam coemeteriis applicentur.

THE matter about to be treated in this chapter is not one that should receive its fullest study with reference to cemeteries. The Code, in its section on cemeteries, does not consider it necessary to treat specifically of the violation, the reconciliation and the interdict of cemeteries, except to say that what is prescribed elsewhere concerning the violation, the reconciliation and the interdict of churches applies also to cemeteries. It is logical, therefore, that these topics should be handled principally with regard to churches, where they will be treated in full detail. It should not be necessary to duplicate the treatment when dealing with cemeteries. Hence, it is the purpose of this chapter to give only a brief review of violation, reconciliation and interdict, putting the emphasis rather on the adaptation of the law on churches to make it applicable to cemeteries.[1]

ARTICLE I. THE VIOLATION OF BLESSED CEMETERIES

1. *The Notion of Violation*

Not all Catholic cemeteries are subject to violation, for it is not mere ownership that is the basis for violation. As a matter of fact, cemeteries that are owned by the municipal authority may be violated just as well as those which belong to some local ecclesiastical cemetery corporation. Ownership, therefore, plays no part. A cemetery in order to be the subject of violation must be a sacred place in the sense of canon 1154.

By the blessing of a church a place becomes a sacred place *(locus sacer)*. A cemetery is changed from a *locus profanus* to a *locus sacer* by one of two constitutive blessings *(benedictio constitutiva)*; by the solemn blessing of cemeteries, the formula of which

[1] For a treatment of the law on churches cf. Gulczynski, *The Desecration and Violation of Churches* (The Catholic University of America Canon Law Studies, n. 159, Washington, D. C.: The Catholic University of America Press, 1942), pp. 49 ff.

is found in the Pontifical,[2] or by the simple blessing of cemeteries, the formula of which is in the Ritual.[3] The blessing of a grave *(benedictio tumuli)*,[4] being only an invocative blessing *(benedictio invocativa)*, does not render either the grave or the cemetery within which the grave is located a sacred place.[5] Even if there are many graves so blessed the cemetery is not a *locus sacer* within the meaning of canon 1154. Hence, violation is possible only in those cases in which the cemetery is a *locus sacer*, that is, a cemetery which has received a constitutive and not merely an invocative blessing.[6]

The violation does not entail the loss of blessing; in fact it does not essentially affect the sacred character of the cemetery at all. It does, however, bring about a certain moral defilement, which until it is removed by the rite of reconciliation makes the cemetery unfit for Christian burial and the sacred rites of the Church at the grave. Coronata describes the violation of a cemetery as a contamination of the sacredness of a blessed cemetery, leaving the blessing intact while suspending the effects of the blessing.[7] A cemetery is violated by definite base acts specified by the Code in canon 1172, where it is also insisted that the acts, before they violate a cemetery, must be certain, notorious and committed within the cemetery itself.[8]

The Code mentions four ways by which a cemetery may be violated:

(1) Criminal homicide;
(2) Sinful and copious shedding of blood;
(3) Impious and sordid uses;
(4) Burial of an infidel or of a person excommunicated upon a declaratory or condemnatory sentence.

[2] Tit. *De Coemeterii Benedictione.*

[3] Tit. VIII, c. 29.

[4] C. 1206, 3; *Rituale Romanum*, tit. VI, c. 3, n. 12.

[5] Cf. *supra*, p. 107.

[6] Coronata, *De Locis et Temporibus Sacris*, n. 146; Cocchi, *Commentarium in Codicem Iuris Canonici*, V, n. 50; Beste, *Introductio in Codicem*, p. 586.

[7] Cf. *De Locis et Temporibus Sacris*, n. 27.

[8] C. 1172 deals with the violation of a church, and therefore there is no mention in this canon of the violation of a cemetery. However, as above indicated, canon 1207 makes canon 1172 along with others applicable to cemeteries. Accordingly, when reference is made to these canons it will be just as though they referred explicitly to cemeteries, *mutatis mutandis*.

Before the Code the factors of the violation of a cemetery presented a somewhat larger list:

(1) Violation of a contiguous church;
(2) Homicide;
(3) Sinful and copious shedding of blood;
(4) *Seminis humani effusio;*
(5) Burial of the unbaptized; of the *excommunicati vitandi;* of those who were interdicted *nominatim,* because they were also *vitandi.*

The Code in the second paragraph of canon 1172 expressly eliminates the first cause in the pre-Code list when it states that the violation of a church does not automatically cause the violation of an adjoining cemetery, and *vice versa.*[9] There is no mention in the new law of the *seminis humani effusio,* and therefore this factor ceases to exist as a potential cause of the violation of a cemetery. But the Code adds a new one of its own, namely, impious and sordid uses to which a cemetery is subjected. As for the conditions necessary for the violation of a cemetery, practically the same conditions exist in the new law as were required in the old.[10]

2. *The Conditions for Violation*

The various acts enumerated in canon 1172 are acts which cause a violation only when the following three conditions are present: the acts must be certain, notorious and perpetrated inside the cemetery.

(1) The acts must be certain. A probable doubt, therefore, which cannot be solved eliminates the act as a cause of violation.[11] The doubt may be one of law or of fact. A doubt of law, for example, may exist as to the interpretation of "a copious flow of blood." As to a doubt of fact, one can imagine many cases. For instance, it may

[9] § 2. Violata ecclesia, non ideo coemeterium, etsi contiguum, violatum censetur, et viceversa.

[10] For the pre-Code legislation on the violation of cemeteries, see *supra*, pp. 46-54.

[11] Vermeersch-Creusen, *Epitome,* II, n. 489.

be doubted whether it was a murder or whether it was a killing in self-defense; or whether the uses to which the cemetery was subjected were really sordid or impious; or whether the person buried was certainly unbaptized; or whether there was some probability that he was baptized. In all cases there will perhaps be some doubts, but all or most of them can eventually be dispelled. It is only when the act is certainly one mentioned in canon 1172, and one that is certainly notorious and perpetrated within the boundaries of the blessed cemetery that a violation ensues.[12]

(2) The acts must be notorious. Acts that are known only to the agent or to two or three discreet persons are not notorious; rather they are *occult*. Acts which have already been divulged, or which were done in such circumstances of place and persons that they will be divulged or can easily be known, are said to be *public* acts. In order to be *notorious*, acts must be publicly known and committed in such circumstances that they cannot under any pretext be concealed or excused on any legal grounds. In other words, an act is notorious (*notorium notorietate facti*) when the external act is known together with the criminal imputability or guilt. "It is the element of inexcusability or of knowledge of the criminal character of the deed that appears to distinguish a public from a notorious crime," says Augustine.[13] An act is also notorious *notorietate iuris* subsequent to a judicial sentence which has become irrevocable *(res iudicata)*, or subsequent to a judicial confession of the delinquent made in court after the manner of canon 1750.[14] A man, e. g., who kills another in a blessed cemetery does not have to intend or even know of the consequent violation, for the violation follows the criminal, notorious act, and does not depend for its existence on the knowledge of the malefactor that his act entails a violation.[15]

(3) The acts must be committed in the blessed cemetery. There

[12] Cf. Coronata, *Institutiones*, n. 748.

[13] *Commentary*, VIII, 17.

[14] Cf. c. 2197; Ayrinhac-Lydon, *Penal Legislation in the New Code of Canon Law*, n. 6; Coronata, *Institutiones*, nn. 1646-1647.

[15] "Cum violatio nullatenus poenae rationem habeat, ignoratio talis violationis pollutionem minime impedit. Non requiritur ut actus ponatur formaliter tamquam loco sacro iniuriosus."—Vermeersch-Creusen, *Epitome*, II, n. 489.

is not the problem with cemeteries that there is with churches in defining just what comprises the cemetery. With churches there is the question of whether the church is violated if the act which otherwise is sufficient for effecting the violation of a church took place in the sacristy or the vestibule, or in the crypt or in the basement or on the roof. But the boundaries of cemeteries are as a rule well defined, and an act which takes place on any part of that cemetery will defile it. Excluded, of course, is that section of the cemetery which may have been left unblessed and is reserved for the burial of non-Catholics and unworthy Catholics. Even a cemetery which is not owned by the Church, if it is blessed, is subject to being violated. Canon 1206, § 2, provides for the blessing of the entire municipal cemetery when Catholic burials are in excess of the non-Catholic, or for the blessing of a specially reserved section of the public cemetery. In both these cases the cemetery in its entirety or in a special section has received the constitutive blessing which has made it a sacred place and therefore susceptible along with the strictly Catholic cemeteries to violation. There is one difference, however. Civil cemeteries which are blessed by the Church and in which the majority of burials are of the bodies of Catholics are not violated by the burial of an infidel or of a heretic. As was pointed out earlier,[16] canon 1206, § 2, is understood by authors to contain an implied dispensation from the law on violation, but only with regard to the burial of infidels and the judicially sentenced excommunicates, the reason being that blessed civil cemeteries would constantly be in need of reconciliation from the violation caused by such burials. For all persons indiscriminately are buried in these cemeteries, no other cemetery being provided. It must be borne in mind, however, that the dispensation implied in canon 1206, § 2, is not a blanket dispensation from all manner of violation; these cemeteries can be violated by a criminal homicide, by a sinful and copious shedding of blood and by impious or sordid uses.[17]

A difficulty can arise when, for example, the perpetrator of the act happens to be inside the cemetery and the victim of the per-

[16] Cf. *supra*, pp. 105-106.

[17] Cf. Coronata, *De Locis et Temporibus Sacris*, n. 146.

petrated act is outside the cemetery, and *vice versa.* This will be found especially true when there is question of homicide or of some serious injury which results in a considerable shedding of blood. But authors generally solve these cases in this wise:

(1) Man inside the cemetery is killed by a man outside—violation.
(2) Man outside the cemetery is killed by a man inside—no violation.
(3) Man mortally wounded outside, dies inside—no violation.
(4) Man mortally wounded inside, dies outside—violation.
(5) Man wounded inside, bleeds profusely outside—no violation.
(6) Man wounded outside, bleeds profusely inside—no violation.
(7) Fight starts inside, ends in death or copious bleeding outside —no violation.
(8) Fight starts outside, ends in death or copious bleeding inside —violation.

Many of these cases were extensively discussed by authors in the old law, especially by the decretalists,[18] and still constitute the accepted interpretation of the present law.[19]

3. *The Causes of Violation*

(1) *The crime of homicide.*[20] There are three important notions under this heading: it must be a crime; it must entail death; and it must be the death of a human being. In order to be a crime homicide supposes serious guilt, and serious guilt means the presence of an intention to kill and the absence of a proportionate reason. Hence it would not be criminal homicide in the sense of canon 1172 if the killing of a man resulted from an accidental shooting, or from some other accidental cause, namely, when the one who brought about the death of another had no idea that his act would cause death, or

[18] Cf. *supra*, p. 49.

[19] See: Augustine, *Commentary*, VI, 40; Coronata, *De Locis et Temporibus Sacris*, n. 28; De Meester, *Compendium*, n. 1132; O'Reilly, *Ecclesiastical Sepulture in the New Code of Canon Law*, pp. 23-25; Cocchi, *Commentarium in Codicem Iuris Canonici*, V, n. 17; Vermeersch-Creusen, *Epitome*, II, n. 489. Cf. also the excellent treatment of this matter in Gasparri, *De SS. Eucharistia*, I, nn. 245-250; Many, *De Locis Sacris*, n. 147.

[20] C. 1172, § 1, 1°.

when at least, if some hurt were intended, death was not foreseen. Even if a man, for example, were seriously culpable for his drunken condition and in this state were to cause the death of another within the boundaries of a blessed cemetery, there would be no violation unless the man, in getting intoxicated, foresaw or intended murder. Likewise death at the hands of one who is not capable of a moral act, such as an infant or a person who is out of his mind does not entail violation. In such cases there can be no question of a crime. Also a man who kills another in self-defense, even if he intends to kill brings about the death of the aggressor only for the reason that such an act proved to be the exclusive means of saving his own life. Such a man is not criminally guilty, and there is no ***crime of homicide,*** and therefore the cemetery is not violated.

Suicide, provided it is perpetrated with the knowledge and intention necessary to make it a crime, causes the violation of a cemetery. Technically considered it is not homicide, since the latter is the taking of one man's life by another, but all authors agree that suicide is a cause of violation in the new law as well as in the old law. Abortion, also, is the taking of human life, and if criminally procured inside a blessed cemetery causes violation. Lynching, because of its nature, is a cause of violation.

In effecting a criminal homicide it is immaterial what means are used. It may be by means of a gun or any other lethal weapon, or by poison, by strangulation, but cutting the arteries, or in any other way by which death may be induced.[21]

(2) *Sinful and copious shedding of blood.* There are three important notions to be pointed out relative to this cause of violation: the act must be gravely sinful; there must be a considerable shedding of blood; the blood must be human blood. Any one incapable of committing grave sin cannot by his act cause the violation of a blessed cemetery. Any one not intending serious sin cannot bring about the defilement of a cemetery. Thus, were a person to sustain

[21] Cf. Augustine, *Commentary,* VI, 36-37; Vermeersch-Creusen, *Epitome,* II, n. 489; Coronata, *Institutiones,* n. 748; Ciprotti, "De Consummatione Delictorum Attento Eorum Elemento Obiectivo," *Apollinaris* (Romae, 1928—), VIII (1935), 390; Woywod, "Violation of Corpses and Graves," *The Homiletic and Pastoral Review,* XXXVII (1937), 1174-1175.

a nosebleed which was caused by high-blood pressure, or (especially in children) by running, coughing, or blowing the nose, there would be no question of violation. Should bleeding be caused by other accidental means, or even as a result of a scuffle or fight which, however, is not gravely sinful (as can readily happen among boys), the cemetery would not be considered violated. It is very possible that workmen in digging a grave or cutting the grass might suffer serious bleeding. This, of course, does not entail violation, because there is presumably no moral guilt on any one's part.

The *"iniuriosa effusio"* of canon 1172 is interpreted by post-Code authors to mean what pre-Code authors understood it to mean, namely, an act that was both gravely sinful and unjustly inflicted.[22] Thus a man who attempted suicide, and in the attempt caused himself to lose a great quantity of blood but not so much as to endanger his life, is considered not to have been the victim of an injustice. Likewise, were a capital sentence carried out in a cemetery in a way that caused a great flow of blood (e. g., by decapitation), since the act is not unjust to the sentenced man, there would be no violation of the cemetery.[23]

There must be a copious flow of human blood. Therefore, to cause an animal to bleed profusely even without any justification or good reason for doing so, would never bring about the violation of a cemetery. The wound may be serious or trivial, it may have come within an inch of taking one's life, or it may have been no more serious than a persistent nosebleed (caused, however, by a gravely sinful act). A wound such as would break a bone (v. g., of a leg or arm) or cause concussion of the brain does not bring with it the violation of the cemetery, unless there was also serious bleeding. It is not necessary that the blood come in direct contact with some part of the blessed cemetery. The hemorrhage may be internal, or the wound may be also external, but the bleeding may remain in contact solely with the clothing or the bandages which absorb the blood. It is not required that all of the bleeding take place in the cemetery; the wound may have been caused in the cemetery and only

[22] Cf. *supra*, p. 50.

[23] Coronata, *Institutiones*, n. 748.

some of the bleeding have taken place there. Very often the victim will be removed even before all bleeding has been checked.[24]

(3) *Impious and sordid uses.* This is an altogether new cause of violation. Thus one cannot go to pre-Code authors for an interpretation of the meaning which this cause may have in law, as is possible in the case of the other causes. While new in law itself, it is not new in the practice of the Sacred Congregation of Rites. For this Sacred Congregation handed down two decisions in the first half of the last century ordering that churches which had been used as a barracks for soldiers over a considerable period of time (in one case for only two days) were to be reconciled because the Sacred Congregation considered them very likely violated.[25]

It is to be noted that the Code uses the term *"usus"* instead of the word *"actus."* This it did for a very obvious intention. The Code is saying in effect that one sordid or impious act (not otherwise mentioned in canon 1172, § 1) is not sufficient for effecting the violation of a cemetery. There must be a series of acts joined in a moral unity such as would be necessary to constitute the *use* of a cemetery for the particular unholy purpose which those acts entail. Or a continuation in the one act may eventually establish a *use.* Setting cattle to graze in a cemetery might well be an example of the first (i. e., a series of acts that would become a use); making of a cemetery a place to quarter soldiers would be an example of the second (an act continued over some period of time). Individual acts of impiety or isolated acts of irreverence, even though the same act is done repeatedly, cannot be considered as implying a *use* of a cemetery for these purposes, and therefore there is no violation. The old law included in the number of causes of violation (or *pollutio* as it was called in the old law) the *effusio seminis humani.*[26] It is

[24] Cf. Coronata, *De Locis et Temporibus Sacris,* n. 28; O'Reilly, *Ecclesiastical Sepulture in the New Code of Canon Law,* p. 25; De Meester, *Compendium,* n. 1132; Ciprotti, "De Consummatione Delictorum Attento Eorum Elemento Obiectivo," *Apollinaris,* VIII (1935), 390-391. Cf. also Gasparri, *De SS. Eucharistia,* I, n. 251.

[25] S. R. C., *Carpen.,* 3 mart. 1821—*Fontes,* n. 5840; S. R. C., *Tolentina,* 27 febr. 1847—*Fontes,* n. 5946.

[26] Cf. *supra,* pp. 50-51.

true to say that this cause as such is dropped from the new law. But in a sense it can be the cause of violation even today, provided, however, that as an act it happens more than once or twice. In the old law one such sinful act was enough to cause the cemetery's *pollutio.* Today the same immoral act must certainly be included under the term *"impius,"* but to be a cause of violation it must not only be an *"actus impius,"* but become an *"usus impius."*

Impious uses are those which are opposed to the virtue of religion. Thus for atheistic or anti-religious societies to use a cemetery for a regular place of meeting, where they plot and plan their nefarious activities, would be to cause the violation of the cemetery. For godless organizations to abuse the cemetery with frequent acts of vandalism, such as removing or destroying the headstones, breaking the crosses that stand over the graves, digging up the bodies of the deceased, etc., would be to bring about the canonical defilement of the cemetery. Were heretical sects to use the cemetery as a place to carry out their religious services, especially if done out of contempt of the Catholic faith, violation of the cemetery would ensue.[27]

The cemeteries blessed in accordance with the ruling of canon 1206, § 2, constitute an exception to this rule of violation. In virtue of canon 1206, § 2, it will be recalled, the Church is allowed to bless the whole municipal cemetery in cases when she cannot have her own cemeteries, and when the number of burials is predominantly Catholic. It was said above in the treatment of this canon [28] that there is implied in canon 1206, § 2, a dispensation from canon 1172, § 1, 4°, namely, that when the Church blesses municipal cemeteries there is no violation caused by the burial of infidels and heretics. The reason was given that canon 1206, § 2, could have no practical meaning if every time an infidel or heretic was buried in a blessed municipal cemetery the cemetery became violated. For it is a foregone conclusion that in these civil cemeteries which are open to the public, to Catholics and non-Catholics alike, by their very nature, there will be almost daily burials of infidels and heretics. And if

[27] Cf. Coronata, *Institutiones,* n. 748; also De Meester, *Compendium,* n. 1132.

[28] Cf. *supra,* pp. 105-107.

such non-Catholics are buried in blessed ground, the Church, in the case, not being able to prevent it, it stands to reason that in many instances there will be a non-Catholic burial service at the grave. It is the custom nowadays even for infidels to have some sort of religious service at the time of burial, although the person when living was not affiliated with any religious sect. Heretical funeral services conducted in a blessed cemetery certainly constitute a repulsive practice. But in the circumstances described in canon 1206, § 2, the Church is recognized to have no right to prevent the burial of non-Catholics in the municipal cemeteries which she has blessed, and therefore she will not be able to prevent heretical burial services at the graves of non-Catholics. Accordingly, it seems necessary to hold that if canon 1206, § 2, contains a dispensation from the violation that would otherwise follow the burial of infidels and certain excommunicated persons, it also must imply a dispensation from another cause of violation, namely, from the custom of heretical burial services conducted in the blessed cemetery on the occasion of the burial of non-Catholics.

Impious uses will also include those things which are manifestly irreverent and repugnant to the sanctity of the place. Accordingly, cemeteries which are used as a place for lewd or immoral dances, performances or games, and for other sinful and base purposes, are to be considered defiled.

Sordid uses will include such things as have a physical or material baseness or uncleanness about them. To make of a cemetery, for instance, a camp or barracks for quartering soldiers, or a corral for horses, or a pasture for cattle, would be to turn the cemetery to sordid uses, and would therefore violate the cemetery.[29]

(4) *The burial of the unbaptized or of a judicially sentenced excommunicate.* First of all it is plain that the term *burial* means one thing: interment. The Code does not speak of *"sepultura ecclesiastica,"* but simply of *"sepultura."* Therefore the other elements of Christian burial as found in canon 1204 *("translatio ad ecclesiam et exsequiae in eadem")* do not enter into the interpretation

[29] Cf. Augustine, *Commentary,* VI, 38; Vermeersch-Creusen, *Epitome,* n. 489; Beste, *Introductio in Codicem,* p. 565.

of canon 1172, § 1, 4°. That actual burial is meant can be seen from a response of the Sacred Congregation of Rites on April 23, 1875.[80]

An *infidelis* is one who has not received baptism. The Code states it simply that the burial of an unbaptized person in a blessed cemetery violates that cemetery.[81] Before the Code there was a great discussion concerning the extent of the term *infidelis*. Authors were generally agreed that catechumens should be exempted; but most of the discussion centered around unbaptized infants. Unanimously they held that the interment of the unbaptized infants of infidels caused violation; the great difference of opinion was concerning the unbaptized infants of Catholic parents. Some held that infants of Catholic parents who died without baptism could be said to be destined by their parents to be baptized and therefore were not to be considered as violating the sacred place where they were buried. Others held the opposite view.[32]

Since the Code authors again are found to be in agreement concerning catechumens, because the Code has solved all doubts. Canon 1239, § 2, states that catechumens who through no fault of their own die without baptism are to be given Christian burial; which means that catechumens are not only to receive burial in sacred ground, but that they are to be given all the other funeral rites of the Church, even the exequies in the church.[33] Post-Code authors, however, are divided on the question of the burial of unbaptized infants of Catholic parents, just as authors were before the Code. A goodly number of authors interpreting canon 1172, § 1, 4°, maintain that unbaptized infants, no matter who their parents may be, are infidels and are included along with all other unbaptized persons with reference to the ensuing violation of the cemetery in which they are interred. These authors argue that if the Code wanted to exempt them it could have done so in canon 1239, where it does explicitly exempt catechumens. That same canon (c. 1239) asserts that all

[80] This response uses the words: "... ex tumulatione cadaverum."—*Fontes*, n. 6073.

[81] Cc. 1207; 1172, § 1, 4°.

[32] For a review of this discussion, cf. *supra*, pp. 51-52.

[33] Cc. 1239, §§ 2-3; 1204; 1205.

unbaptized persons are to be excluded from Christian burial. Numbered among the canonists holding this opinion are: Augustine,[34] Wernz-Vidal,[35] Ciprotti[36] and Woywod.[37]

Other authors exempt the unbaptized infants of Catholic parents from inclusion in the term *infidelis* employed in canon 1172. They point out that, since there is question of a *res odiosa,* such children ought not to be classed as *infideles*. Some of those who follow this opinion are: Coronata,[38] De Meester,[39] Cance,[40] Cappello,[41] Vermeersch-Creusen,[42] Beste[43] and Naz.[44] Some of these authors go so far as to say that even the unbaptized infants of infidel parents are not to be included in the term *infidelis* employed in canon 1172. Coronata, De Meester, Vermeersch-Creusen, and Naz understand the "infidel" of canon 1172 to be one who voluntarily lives in infidelity and who is guilty of grave fault. But this restrictive interpretation of who is an infidel seems hardly to be justified by the clear and unqualified language of the Code. Furthermore, it was not a position held in any general way even by pre-Code authors.[45] However, as for the children of Catholic parents who die before they have been baptized, it seems that the burial of such children in blessed ground will not violate that ground. This is at least a probable opinion, perhaps even the more common one, and thus creates a *dubium iuris.* And since thus it is doubtful in law that the burial of the unbaptized infants of Catholic parents is a cause for the violation of a cemetery, it is to be considered certain that such burials do not defile a cemetery.[46]

[34] *Commentary,* VI, 38.

[35] *Ius Canonicum,* IV, n. 366, note 48.

[36] "De Consummatione Delictorum Attento Eorum Elemento Obiectivo," *Apollinaris,* VIII (1935), 391.

[37] *A Practical Commentary,* n. 1211.

[38] *De Locis et Temporibus Sacris,* n. 28; *Institutiones,* n. 748.

[39] *Compendium,* n. 1132.

[40] *Le Code de Droit Canonique,* III, n. 11.

[41] *Summa Iuris Canonici,* II, n. 672.

[42] *Epitome,* II, n. 489.

[43] *Introductio in Codicem,* p. 565.

[44] "Cimetière," *Dictionnaire de Droit Canonique,* III, 739.

[45] Cf. *supra,* pp. 51-52.

[46] Cf. c. 15.

By canon 1240, § 1, 2°, those who are excommunicated upon a declaratory or a condemnatory sentence by a competent ecclesiastical court may not be given Christian burial; and by canon 1172, § 1, 4°, the burial of these persons in a blessed cemetery *ipso facto* brings about the violation of that cemetery. This is different from the old law which required that the excommunicate be an *excommunicatus vitandus* before his burial would violate the blessed cemetery.[47] Coronata in his earlier work *De Locis et Temporibus Sacris*[48] advanced the opinion that only the *excommunicati vitandi* were included in canon 1172, § 1, 4°. He was led to this pre-Code view by canon 1242, which directs that the body of an *excommunicatus vitandus* which had been laid to rest in sacred ground unlawfully was to be exhumed and reinterred in the unblessed section of the cemetery. In his later work he adopts the common opinion that the burial of anyone who has been excommunicated by an ecclesiastical court violates the cemetery in which the burial is made.[49] Wernz-Vidal point out that all misunderstanding will disappear if one remembers that the notions of penal law have been considerably changed by the Code of Canon Law. One should consider those who are excommunicated upon a declaratory or condemnatory sentence since the Code as equivalent to the *excommunicati vitandi* of pre-Code days.[50] Vermeersch-Creusen pose the question: What of the *excommunicati vitandi* who are such without any formal sentence of an ecclesiastical court? There is only one such case in the Code, namely, the case of one who lays violent hands on the person of the Roman Pontiff. The penalty is incurred *ipso facto*.[51] Vermeersch-Creusen answer the question by saying that the mind of the Legislator must be studied rather than the wording of the law. Their opinion in the matter is that the burial of one excommunicated by the very law itself as a *vitandus* (c. 2343, § 1) is to be considered as violating the cemetery.[52]

[47] Cf. *supra*, pp. 53-54.

[48] N. 28. Cf. also De Meester, *Compendium*, n. 1132.

[49] *Institutiones*, n. 748. Cf. Beste, *Introductio in Codicem*, p. 565.

[50] *Ius Canonicum*, IV, n. 366, note 48. Cf. Ciprotti, "De Consummatione Delictorum Attento Eorum Elemento Obiectivo," *Apollinaris*, VIII (1935), 391.

[51] C. 2343, § 1.

[52] *Epitome*, II, n. 489. Cf. Cappello, *Summa Iuris Canonici*, II, n. 672.

The burial of all apostates, heretics, schismatics, and members of forbidden societies in blessed ground is explicitly prohibited by the Code.[53] But it does not follow that, because they are not to be buried in blessed ground, their interment in blessed ground entails a violation of the cemetery. For the average apostate, heretic, schismatic, mason, etc., has not been condemned or declared an excommunicate by judicial sentence. Thus the burial of bad Catholics, of non-Catholics or Protestants, and of members of forbidden lodges and organizations is not *ipso facto* to be taken as entailing the violation of a blessed cemetery.

In many countries, as previously indicated,[54] the Church—and the same is true of other non-civil organizations or corporations—cannot own cemetery property. The cemeteries are State owned and administered. The Church, even in those cases when she has a special section for her faithful or when she blesses the whole municipal cemetery,[55] has by and large little or no control over these civil cemeteries. Wherever she can prevent it, the Church is to use every means to keep out of the blessed cemetery those whom canon law excludes from Christian burial. But if in the circumstances specified in canon 1206, § 2, the State insists on burying infidels and judicially sentenced excommunicates in the blessed ground of its civil cemeteries there is no violation of the cemetery. For according to the more common opinion canon 1206, § 2, implies a dispensation from the violation caused by the burial of infidels, and of heretics, schismatics, apostates and members of masonic and like societies.[56]

4. *The Consequence of Violation*

The violation of cemeteries does not have the effect of taking away or diminishing the blessing which the cemeteries received, but it has been traditionally a law of the Church that no burial may be made in a violated cemetery. The defilement brought about by the violation must first be removed by a rite which is known as the rite

[53] C. 1240, § 1, 1°.
[54] Cf. *supra*, p. 95.
[55] C. 1206, § 2.
[56] Cf. *supra*, pp. 105-107.

of reconciliation. Once the cemetery is purged of the violation, and only then, may interment and all the burial rites of the Church be allowed in it. In the new law, in contrast to the somewhat more strict pre-Code law, everything is predisposed for a prompt and speedy reconciliation of the violated cemetery. There is no need, therefore, for a cemetery to remain long under the stigma of violation, for it is plainly evident in law that the mind of the Church is that the important function of the blessed cemetery in Catholic life and death should be suspended as little as possible (c. 1172, § 1) and for as short a time as possible.[57]

5. *The Penalties for Violators of Cemeteries*

Canon 2329 decrees penalties for those who violate a blessed cemetery by any of the acts mentioned in canon 1172, § 1. The acts themselves do not automatically involve the penalties, for the Code orders that they are to be imposed by the ordinary *(ferendae sententiae poenae)*. But some penalties must be inflicted on the guilty persons, and the ordinary should take into account the gravity of the act and the culpability of the malefactor. One punishment in particular is mentioned in canon 2329, that of the *interdictum ab ingressu ecclesiae*. This specific type of interdict forbids the person under interdict to take part in any of the divine offices in any church, and prohibits all the sacred rites of Christian burial which take place in the church should the guilty one die still encumbered with the interdict. An interdicted person may not receive burial in a church or oratory.[58]

Article II. The Reconciliation of a Violated Cemetery

The violation of a cemetery is not and never was meant to be a penalty for the faithful. The Church is mindful of this and orders that the reconciliation of a violated cemetery be performed as quickly as possible.[59] There is no relaxation in the Code making the recon-

[57] Cf. cc. 1207; 1173-1177.

[58] Cf. c. 2277. Cf. Ciprotti, "De Consummatione Delictorum Attento Eorum Elemento Obiectivo," *Apollinaris*, VIII (1935), 389-391.

[59] Cc. 1207; 1174.

ciliation of a violated cemetery less necessary than in pre-Code law,[60] but one can see in the present law of the Code that the Church is most solicitous that the violation and reconciliation of cemeteries should throw no needless burden on those of the faithful who may be waiting to bury their loved ones in blessed ground and with all of the consoling rites of the Church. The Code names the ordinary ministers of the reconciliation of cemeteries, and then adds a provision to take care of an emergency when the ordinary ministers cannot act promptly enough to take care of some grave and urgent necessity.[61]

If the cause of the violation has been the burial of an infidel or of a judicially sentenced excommunicate (1172, § 1, 4°), the Code requires that the body of such a one be removed from the violated cemetery before the proper minister is to proceed to the reconciliation of that cemetery. But the Code quickly adds that if this will cause grave inconvenience, the reconciliation may proceed without the exhumation and transfer of the body to another place.[62]

Thus the reconciliation of a violated cemetery is necessary, but the Church in effect signifies by her legislation that it be done as promptly as possible in order that the innocent may not be made to suffer too great an inconvenience. If one or several bodies of the faithful departed were awaiting burial at the time of the violation, and the removal of the body of the infidel or excommunicate would not at all be assured or would at least entail a delay of several days, grave inconvenience would be involved, and the cemetery could then be reconciled without the previous exhumation of the body whose burial occasioned the violation. Civil authorities, for example, may demand some sort of investigation to see if and why the exhumation is necessary, and the Code would not requre that the reconciliation be put off until the inquiry is completed and the body transferred.[63]

60 Cf. c. 1173.

61 C. 1176.

62 Cc. 1207; 1142; 1175.

63 Cf. c. 1175. When the Church has blessed the whole municipal cemetery under the conditions of canon 1206, § 2, no exhumation will be necessary, both because it may be presumed to be impossible in the circumstances, and because the canon mentioned contains an implied dispensation.—Cf. *supra*, pp. 105-107.

The Code makes possible a *reconciliatio ad cautelam.* The Church evidently realizes that in the matter of violation there is much room in practical cases for doubt, both of the law and of fact. For while the conditions and causes of violation are generally clear, in a great many instances it will be difficult after a thorough study of both law and facts to know *for certain* whether violation has taken place. A doubtful violation is to be considered as no violation,[64] and yet the only practical solution at times is to have recourse to the reconciliation of the cemetery. This will put an end to all doubts; the cemetery after the provisional reconciliation will be certainly enjoying the full effects of its original blessing, and all concerned will have peace of mind.[65]

1. *The Rites of Reconciliation*

There are four rites by which a violated cemetery may become reconciled: two in the *Pontificale Romanum* and two in the *Rituale Romanum.* In relation to a violated cemetery there are four possibilities, and thus there are four rites of reconciliation. A cemetery has been either (1) solemnly blessed or (2) simply blessed; it is either (3) adjacent to a church or (4) it is distant from it. If a solemnly blessed cemetery together with the consecrated church adjoining it needs reconciliation, the rite in the Pontifical is to be used: *De Ecclesiae et Coemeterii Reconciliatione.* The rite for reconciling a solemnly blessed cemetery when there is no need for the reconciliation of a church [66] or when the cemetery and church are separated from each other is again in the Pontifical: *De Reconciliatione Coemeterii sine Ecclesiae Reconciliatione.* The Ritual provides a rite for the reconciling of a simply blessed cemetery when the

[64] Coronata, *De Locis et Temporibus Sacris,* n. 30; Vermeersch-Creusen, *Epitome,* II, n. 490; Wernz-Vidal, *Ius Canonicum,* IV, n. 369.

[65] The Sacred Congregation of Rites on February 27, 1847, decided in favor of a *reconciliatio ad cautelam* in a practical case which it was called upon to review. A church had been used for two days as a camp for soldiers.—*Fontes,* n. 5946.

[66] The violation of a church does not necessarily cause the violation of an adjacent cemetery; the violation of a cemetery does not automatically violate an adjoining church.—C. 1172, § 2.

adjoining church is to be reconciled at the same time: *Ritus Reconciliandi Ecclesiam Violatam.*[67]

The Ritual also provides a rite for reconciling a violated blessed cemetery when the adjacent church does not need reconciliation or when the cemetery is separated from the church. *Ritus Reconciliandi Coemeterium Violatum.*[68] In the reconciliation of a cemetery one of these four rites must be used; there is no other way of effecting the reconciliation.[69] For the one other situation that may arise, namely, when both the cemetery and the church are violated and only one of them is solemnly blessed, the rite—if a single rite is to be used—is the one in the Pontifical: *De Eccelsiae et Coemeterii Reconciliatione.* In this case, however, the cemetery and the church may be reconciled separately even when they are contiguous, the special rite of reconciliation conforming to the original consecration or blessing, but the dual ceremony is not necessary.[70]

Ordinary holy water is used in the reconciliation of a cemetery that has been simply blessed.[71] In the reconciliation of cemeteries that have been solemnly blessed water specially blessed for the purpose is to be used. The blessing of this water, if it has not already been blessed by the bishop, may be executed by the priest-minister of the rite of reconciliation. If the priest blesses the water he is to use the formula found in the *Pontificale Romanum* under the title

[67] Tit. VIII, c. 28. The rubric reads in part: "Violata ecclesia, non ideo coemeterium, etsi contiguum, violatum censetur, et viceversa. Si vero coemeterium ecclesiae pollutae contiguum violatum fuerit, illud una cum ecclesia reconciliatur." It was pointed out in the historical section (*supra*, pp. 56-57) that it is a mistake to think that when a church and its churchyard cemetery are both violated the reconciliation of the church only is necessary. It is true that by one rite both are reconciled, but it is not a rite which reconciles the church directly and the cemetery indirectly, or which reconciles the church so that the reconciliation of the cemetery follows because of the principle: *Accessorium naturam sequi congruit principalis* (Reg. 42, R. J. in VI°). It should rather be looked upon as a rite which takes the place of two distinct rites: it reconciles the church directly, and it reconciles the cemetery directly.

[68] Tit. VIII, c. 30.

[69] Cf. c. 1174, § 1.

[70] Coronata, *De Locis et Temporibus Sacris*, n. 148; O'Reilly, *Ecclesiastical Sepulture in the New Code of Canon Law*, p. 32.

[71] Cf. *Rituale Romanum*, tit. VIII, cc. 28 and 30; c. 1177.

De Benedictione et Impositione Primarii Lapidis pro Ecclesia Aedificanda.[72] He should be vested in amice, alb, cincture, stole and cope of white color.[73]

2. *The Minister of Reconciliation*

(1) *The Minister of the reconciliation of a cemetery that has been solemnly blessed.* In the old law the reconciliation of a solemnly blessed cemetery was considered to be an act of episcopal orders, and hence like the consecration or solemn blessing of a sacred place, could not be performed by non-bishops. A bishop could not even delegate one of his priests to act as minister of this rite without an apostolic indult permitting him to do so.[74]

The Code, however, has made some very radical changes, making it evident now that this rite is no longer reserved to those in episcopal orders.[75] The general rule governing the minister of the rite of reconciliation of solemnly blessed cemeteries is that they are competent to perform this rite who are the ordinary ministers of the blessing of sacred places (c. 1156).[76] Further provision is made in the Code [77] for a grave and urgent necessity, when, for example, it is important that the cemetery be reconciled and there is no time to approach the ordinary.

Hence the ministers will be as follows:

1. The ordinary of the place for all cemeteries in his territory except the cemeteries of exempt religious.
2. The priest delegated by the local ordinary for all cemeteries which the latter has a right to reconcile.[78]
3. The major superior of clerical exempt religious for cemeteries of his order.

[72] Cf. c. 1177; *Rituale Romanum*, tit. VIII, c. 28, n. 8; Augustine, *Commentary*, VI, 45.

[73] *Rituale Romanum, loc. cit.*

[74] *Supra*, p. 57.

[75] Coronata, *De Locis et Temporibus Sacris*, n. 148; *Institutiones*, n. 749.

[76] C. 1176, § 2.

[77] C. 1176, § 3.

[78] Cc. 1176, § 2; 1156; 198, § 1.

4. The priest delegated by the regular superior for cemeteries of the order.[79]

5. The rector or pastor of the church to which the cemetery belongs provided that there is a case of grave and urgent necessity when time does not allow the ordinary to be approached. He has the obligation of notifying the ordinary that he used the faculty given him by canon 1176, § 3, to reconcile the cemetery.

6. The chaplain of the cemetery if the cemetery is provided with one. The chaplain can act only in a case of emergency when he cannot approach the ordinary to obtain delegation for this act. If, however, the ordinary has given him delegation once and for all, he may consider himself the ordinary minister of the reconciliation of the cemetery over which he is appointed as chaplain. He is with this general delegation not restricted to emergencies only, and by virtue solely of Code law he need send no notification to the ordinary. A notice will be due the ordinary in virtue of his office. Whenever a chaplain acts with the power given him by canon 1176, § 3, he is obliged to make a report of his action to the ordinary.[80]

7. Any rector or pastor in the event that the cemetery is an interparochial cemetery. When cemeteries serve several parishes it may be that the bishop has appointed for them a chaplain, to whom he has given the special delegation of reconciling the cemeteries under his care in cases when they have become violated. But if the bishop has not otherwise provided for the situation, then in a grave and urgent emergency when the bishop cannot be reached any pastor may reconcile the violated cemetery according to canon 1176, § 3. As soon as one pastor, however, has undertaken to perform the rite of reconciliation, he alone has the right to continue, all others being excluded, unless for some legitimate reason he cannot proceed to the reconciliation which he started.[81]

In all the above cases, whether the minister be a bishop, a religious superior or a simple priest, the rite to be used is one of the two found

[79] Cc. 1176, § 2; 1156; 198, § 1.

[80] Although the Code does not mention the chaplain of a cemetery, Coronata (*De Locis et Temporibus Sacris,* n. 148; *Institutiones,* n. 749), Cappello (*Summa Iuris Canonici,* II, n. 716), and Vermeersch-Creusen (*Epitome,* II, n. 490) include him along with the rector of the church to which the cemetery is attached.

[81] Coronata, *De Locis et Temporibus Sacris,* n. 148; Cappello, *Summa Iuris Canonici,* II, n. 716..

in the *Pontificale Romanum.* The determining factor will be whether or not there is an adjoining church to be reconciled at the same time.[82]

(2) *The Minister of the reconciliation of a cemetery that has been simply blessed.* Before the Code there were many authors who maintained that before a priest could reconcile a cemetery which had been simply blessed he needed the explicit delegation of the bishop. Many more held that such a delegation was not necessary.[83] The Code now settles the question by making it clear that a delegation from the bishop is not required in the minister of reconciliation. The general rule is expressed in canon 1176, § 1.[84]

According to the law of the Code, therefore, the ministers will be the following:

1. The rector of the church to which the cemetery is attached, or the pastor, as the case may be.
2. The chaplain or director of the cemetery. It is frequently the case, especially in the United States, that burials from all the parishes in a given area are made in an interparochial cemetery. To take charge of this cemetery the bishop appoints a chaplain or director. This priest because of his office and appointment by the bishop is the logical agent for reconciling the cemetery under his charge.[85]
3. Any priest, appointed (not delegated) by the rector or chaplain, or at least having the presumed consent of the rector or the chaplain. The consent may be lawfully presumed if the rector or chaplain is not available and at the same time it is necessary that the cemetery be reconciled, for example because of a scheduled burial.[86]

Article III. The Interdict of a Blessed Cemetery

1. *The Notion of Interdict*

A cemetery, once it has received the solemn or simple blessing of the Church, can lose its blessing *(exsecratio)* or suffer its removal

[82] Coronata, *loc. cit.*

[83] Cf. *supra*, pp. 59-61.

[84] Cf. c. 1207.

[85] Cf. Coronata, *De Locis et Temporibus Sacris*, n. 148; Cappello, *Summa Iuris Canonici*, II, n. 716; Vermeersch-Creusen, *Epitome*, II, n. 490.

[86] Coronata, *Institutiones*, n. 749.

(profanatio);[87] it can suffer a temporary curtailment of some of the effects of the blessing *(violatio)*;[88] and it can be shut off from the faithful to the extent that all burials in it are stripped of every vestige of liturgical funeral rites *(interdictum)*. A cemetery that has lost its blessing can regain it only through a reblessing; a cemetery that has been violated must be reconciled before any burials can take place; a cemetery that has been interdicted must have the interdict removed either through the natural lapse of the allotted time or by means of a dispensation before the ecclesiastical burial rites can be resumed.

Canon 1207 states that cemeteries are subject to interdict, and that the laws governing the interdict of cemeteries will be found elsewhere in the Code. Interdict is a penalty and therefore it is found treated in the Fifth Book of the Code. The Code defines interdict as "censura qua fideles, in communione Ecclesiae permanentes, prohibentur sacris quae in canonibus, qui sequuntur, enumerantur." [89]

An interdict is called a censure, that is, a medicinal penalty; but it can also be a vindictive penalty. An interdict would be a censure in cases when it is imposed only for as long as the guilty person, or parish, or city, or diocese, or State, remains unrepentant and contumacious.[90] There would be question of a vindictive penalty if the interdict were imposed for a determined period of time, or forever, or until the ecclesiastical superior was satisfied that adequate atonement had been made.[91]

[87] Cf. *supra*, pp. 127-133.

[88] *Supra*, pp. 169-170.

[89] C. 2268, § 1.

[90] Canon 2241, § 1. Censura est poena qua homo baptizatus, delinquens et contumax, quibusdam bonis spiritualibus vel spiritualibus adnexis privatur, donec, a contumacia recedens, absolvatur.

[91] Canon 2286. Poenae vindicativae illae sunt, quae directe ad delicti expiationem tendunt ita ut earum remissio e cessatione contumaciae delinquentis non pendeat.

Canon 2291. Poenae vindicativae quae omnes fideles pro delictorum gravitate afficere possunt, in Ecclesia praesertim sunt: 1°. Interdictum locale et interdictum in communitatem seu collegium in perpetuum vel ad tempus praefinitum vel ad beneplacitum Superioris; . . .

Interdicts may be personal, that is, they may be inflicted directly on the persons of a given locality; interdicts may be local, directly affecting the place and only indirectly concerning the persons in the place. Local interdicts are general when they are imposed on a certain region or territory; particular when they affect only a determined place, such as a church, oratory, altar or cemetery, that is a *locus sacer*.[92]

One may very well ask: can a local interdict (such as that laid upon a cemetery) ever be a censure? The answer must be in the affirmative, because the Code calls the interdict in general a censure,[93] and lists the article on the interdict in the chapter entitled: *De censuris in specie*. Local interdicts, however, are not censures in the strict interpretation of the term, for censures imply guilt and contumacity (c. 2241, § 1), and it will be a rare occurrence to find that the persons who suffer from a local interdict are all guilty and contumacious. On the other hand, personal interdicts, namely, those which are put upon certain persons because of their crimes, are censures in the true meaning of the term.

However, every local interdict entails a censure, and in this sense local interdicts are censures. No ecclesiastical superior will impose a local interdict unless some crime or crimes have been committed to make the interdict necessary. The Code expressly states[94] that every time a local interdict is imposed, automatically those who were guilty of causing the interdict incur the censure of personal interdict. Thus, when a cemetery is interdicted, it is a local interdict which *is not a censure on the cemetery,* because cemeteries or other places are not passive subjects of censures; *it is not a censure on those who are innocent* of the act which occasioned the interdict, even though the innocent suffer on account of the local interdict; but *it is a true censure for those who are guilty* of the act which caused the interdict, because they are fit subjects of a censure, and are declared by the Code to be personally interdicted.

[92] Cc. 2268 § 2; 2269. Cf. De Meester, *Compendium,* n. 1769.

[93] C. 2268, § 1.

[94] C. 2338, § 4.

2. *The Effect of Interdict*

It should be evident that the interdict of a cemetery as such is a local particular interdict. When, therefore, a cemetery is interdicted, the immediate effect is that all ecclesiastical funeral rites are forbidden within the bounds of that cemetery. The fundamental right of the faithful to burial in blessed ground, however, is not prohibited.[95] One can see that it is not the faithful directly that are affected. It is the cemetery that is directly touched by the interdict. But the faithful in the locality are affected inasmuch as they may not be able to be buried in any other blessed cemetery, and in the interdicted cemetery they cannot receive the final burial rites of the Church.

The burial rites that are prohibited are those which are contained in approved liturgical books: the *Rituale Romanum* or other corresponding Rituals.[96] Since only the cemetery is interdicted the sacred rites connected with the transfer of the body to the church and the funeral services in church are not in the least to be interfered with or curtailed. Their solemnity does not have to be curtailed, because the interdict is confined to the cemetery and not to any other place not mentioned in the decree ordering the interdict.[97]

Augustine holds that after the interdict is lifted the rites that were omitted in the cemetery because of the interdict may be supplied.[98] This same view is shared by Coronata, Conran and Naz.[99]

3. *The Extent of the Interdict*

The local particular interdict of a cemetery does not involve an adjoining church; nor does the interdict placed upon a church carry

[95] Canon *2272*, § 2. [In interdicto locali particulari . . .,] si interdictum fuerit coemeterium, fidelium quidem cadavera sepeliri ibidem possunt, sed sine ullo ecclesiastico ritu.

[96] *Rituale Romanum*, tit. VI, c. 3, nn. 11-16; c. 1231, § 1.

[97] Coronata, *Institutiones*, n. 1791. Cf. also c. 2272, § 3, 2°.

[98] *Commentary*, VIII, 207.

[99] Coronata, *Institutiones*, n. 1791; Conran, *The Interdict* (The Catholic University of America Canon Law Studies, n. 56, Washington, D. C.: The Catholic University of America, 1930), pp. 75-76; Naz, "Cimetière," *Dictionnaire de Droit Canonique*, III, 740.

with it the interdict of a contiguous cemetery.[100] That a cemetery and its adjoining church are two distinct juridical entities is clear both from canon 2273 and from canon 1172, § 2. Oratories, however, or chapels in an interdicted cemetery suffer the same fate as the cemetery. This follows quite naturally from the principle *"in toto partem non est dubium contineri."* [101] Sole applies this principle in the following manner: ". . . in *toto,* idest in coemeterio interdicto, *partem,* idest oratoria in coemeterio erecta, *non est dubium contineri,* et consequenter interdictum latum in coemeterium extenditur ad omnia oratoria in coemeterio erecta." [102]

The interdict of a cemetery, since it is local, is circumscribed by the boundaries of the cemetery; but within the interdicted cemetery everyone is bound to observe the interdict. This means to include besides the natives of the place, strangers, visitors, newcomers, and even those who are otherwise exempt. The Code makes this very explicit when it says: "Interdictum . . . locale non urget extra locum interdictum, sed in loco interdicto omnes etiam exteri aut exempti, excluso speciali privilegio, illud servare debent." [103] The "exteri" are those who have no domicile in the locality, in the sense that they are not permanent residents of the place. The term is much wider than *peregrini,* for it includes, according to Cappello, *advenae* (those who have a quasi-domicile), *peregrini* (travellers and visitors), and *vagi* (those who have no domicile or quasi-domicile).[104]

Newcomers to a locality will also be affected by the interdict of a cemetery just as much as anyone else, even though it might be

[100] ". . . interdicta ecclesia, interdicta sunt sacella contigua, non vero coemeterium; interdicto sacello, non est interdicta integra ecclesia nec, interdicto coemeterio, interdicta est ecclesia ipsi contigua, sed interdicta sunt omnia oratoria in coemeterio erecta."—C. 2273.

[101] Reg. 80, R. J., in VI°.

[102] *De Delictis et Poenis* (Romae: Pustet, 1920), n. 243. See also Conran, *The Interdict,* pp. 79-80.

[103] C. 2269, § 2.

[104] *Tractatus Canonico-Moralis De Censuris iuxta Codicem Iuris Canonici* (2. ed., Taurinorum Augustae: Marietti, 1925), n. 468, hereafter cited as *De Censuris.* Cf. c. 91.

thought that they would be exempt because of the fact that they in no way at all could have had any part in the cause of the interdict. The reason is, of course, that a local interdict has direct bearing on the place, but as far as particular local interdicts are concerned the persons in the locality are just as effectively deprived of certain spiritual benefits as though they were under personal interdict.

The "exempti" are all those who are not under the jurisdiction of the superior imposing the interdict. Thus, for example, regulars and other religious who enjoy the privilege of exemption from the jurisdiction of the local ordinary [105] are expressly not exempt in the matter of local interdicts. A special privilege is necessary to excuse anyone, religious or lay, from the effect of a local interdict.[106] The one who imposes the interdict, e.g., the Holy See or a local bishop, may determine the extent of the binding power and may therefore grant exemptions to certain groups. But unless there is evidence to the contrary all persons are bound to observe the local interdict within the terms of the law (esp. cc. 2269, § 2, to 2273).[107]

On certain feasts the interdict which is placed upon a cemetery *(interdictum locale particulare)* is suspended. On these feasts the cemetery enjoys a status as though no interdict had ever been placed upon it. The full liturgical burial rite of the Church is allowed. The feasts specified by the Code are: Christmas, Easter, Pentecost, Corpus Christi and the Assumption of the Blessed Virgin.[108] The first paragraph of canon 2270 speaks of both general and particular local interdicts. The second paragraph which deals with the feast day suspensions of interdicts speaks of local interdicts in general. Authors have rightly concluded that the interdict of cemeteries which is a

[105] Cf. cc. 615; 618.

[106] C. 2269, § 2.

[107] "Effectus interdicti localis non sunt omnes et singuli a iure expresse statuti ac determinati, sed arbitrio Praelati interdictum ferentis relinquitur eorumdem extensio vel restrictio ita tamen ut principia disciplinae ecclesiasticae rite serventur simulque animarum saluti probe consulatur. Hoc sensu profecto intelligenda sunt verba 'si . . . interdicti decreto aliud non caveatur expresse,' quae leguntur initio canonis 2271."—Cappello, *loc. cit.*

[108] C. 2270, § 2.

particular local interdict comes under the feast day privilege.[109] This imports a decided change from the old law when these feast day exemptions were applicable only to general local interdicts and not to particular local interdicts.[110]

4. *The Cause of the Interdict*

A local particular interdict, such as that placed upon a cemetery, must never be imposed unless there is present a very grave wrong to be punished. Interdict is a privation of certain spiritual benefits and is inflicted, whether as a local or as a personal interdict, because of some gravely sinful act or acts. A personal interdict is put upon persons who have been guilty of personal misdeeds; a local interdict, since it has the effect of a local punishment, can be imposed only for the notorious wrong-doing of a community. It may never be imposed because of some one's private sin, and therefore a local particular interdict demands a greater guilt than would be necessary for the imposition of a special personal interdict. It may be that the wrongful act was committed by one person, but if it was maliciously abetted by the majority of the community or by those who may be said to represent the community, then a local particular interdict can be perfectly justifiable.[111]

5. *Those Who Can Impose an Interdict on a Cemetery*

Canon 2269, § 1, contains the law which determines who is the competent superior in imposing interdicts. The canon states the following: "Generale interdictum tam locale in territorium dioecesis,

[109] ". . . animadvertendum est quod exceptio de qua in can. 2270, § 2, valet *quoque pro interdicto locali particulari.* Legitur enim in cit. can. 2270, § 2: 'In die Nativitatis Domini, etc. . . . *interdictum locale suspenditur.* . . .' *Ergo etiam interdictum locale particulare suspenditur,* quia lex non distinguit, et hinc neque nos distinguere debemus. Eapropter si interdictum fuerit coemeterium, in die Nativitatis Domini, Paschatis, etc., fidelium cadavera sepeliri ibidem possunt cum ecclesiastico ritu, perinde ac nullum adesset interdictum."—Sole, *De Delictis et Poenis,* n. 241. Cf. also Conran, *The Interdict,* pp. 75-76; Coronata, *Institutiones,* n. 1789.

[110] D'Annibale, *Summula Theologiae Moralis* (3. ed., 3 vols., Romae, 1888), I, n. 375; Wernz, *Ius Decretalium,* VI, n. 227.

[111] Cf. Cappello, *De Censuris,* n. 474.

reipublicae, quam personale in populum dioecesis, reipublicae, ferri tantum potest a Sede Apostolica vel de eius mandato; interdictum vero generale in paroeciam vel paroeciae populum, et particulare sive locale sive personale, etiam Episcopus ferre potest." The general rule, therefore, governing the interdict of a cemetery *(interdictum locale particulare)* is that the bishop is the competent superior. It is understood, of course, that the Holy See also has the power and the right to impose particular local interdicts, although it will seldom use this prerogative. The Apostolic See will more often concern itself with general local interdicts.

An interdict is a punishment in the external forum, and cannot be imposed by one who is without ordinary jurisdiction in the external forum. The vicar general is, it would seem from the canon cited above, implicitly and definitely eliminated. The canon does not use the term *"ordinarius loci"* but *"episcopus."* This interpretation is also borne out by a previous canon which states that the vicar general does not have the power of inflicting penalties, unless this power is expressly given to him through a special mandate of the bishop.[112] On the other hand, the term *"episcopus"* in canon 2269, § 1, is unanimously interpreted by authors to include the vicar capitular or administrator of a vacant see, the apostolic administrator, the vicar and prefect apostolic, and the abbot and prelate *nullius.*[113]

Authors are likewise in full agreement in maintaining that religious ordinaries have no power to impose local interdicts. The jurisdiction they enjoy over their subjects is a personal jurisdiction and not a territorial one, and thus the only interdict they are able to inflict on their subjects is a personal interdict. At one time religious ordinaries did exercise the power of imposing local interdicts, but they have long been without it, mainly because of the nature of their jurisdiction. If religious superiors should lay a local interdict upon their churches and cemeteries, it would have an effect which extends

[112] C. 2220, § 2: Vicarius Generalis sine mandato speciali non habet potestatem infligendi poenas.

[113] Rossi, *La "Sepultura Ecclesiastica" e l' "Ius Funerum" nel Diritto Canonico,* n. 33; Augustine, *Commentary,* VIII, 199; De Meester, *Compendium,* n. 1770; Cappello, *De Censuris,* nn. 468, 466; Coronata, *Institutiones,* n. 1785; Ayrinhac-Lydon, *Penal Legislation in the New Code of Canon Law,* n. 132.

beyond their jurisdiction, because it would hold not only for their subjects but for all others besides.[114]

The bishop in imposing an interdict on a cemetery should observe certain formalities. In the old law he was required to have the consent of his chapter or consultors, but in the new law he is not bound to obtain their consent or even to consult them.[115] However, circumstances may be such that it will be the part of prudence for the bishop at least to hear the opinions of others before making the serious decision of imposing a local interdict.

When the bishop has decided to take the important step, he should prepare an edict or decree. In this decree he should state (1) the cause that made the interdict necessary, using his own good judgment as to how much of the cause and guilt he will include. The cause and guilt will already be a public matter—otherwise there would be no necessity of a local interdict[116]—and so there is no difficulty here arising from a possible divulging of private or secret sins. The decree will contain next (2) the name and the boundaries of the cemetery to be interdicted. Then there should follow (3) a clear and concise description of the effects of the interdict, that is to say, the bishop should point out distinctly just how the interdict will affect the persons in the locality. This will be especially important if the bishop does not intend to apply the interdict in its full rigor. The decree should state also (4) just who are and who are not bound by the interdict; (5) the date when the interdict is to begin, and (6) the date when it is to cease, and (7) (if necessary) the conditions, either direct or indirect, which will bring about the cessation of the interdict.

These elements are necessary in a decree of this kind, for the decree is not one that is made only for the files of the chancery office, but one that should be publicly promulgated. The bishop should have the decree read from the pulpit of the church or churches which

[114] Cf. Schmalzgrueber, lib. IV, tit. 39, n. 341; Ferraris, *Bibliotheca*, v. "Interdictum," art. 1, n. 21; Wernz, *Ius Decretalium*, VI, n. 220, note 497; Sole, *De Delictis et Poenis*, n. 235; Conran, *The Interdict*, p. 60. See also all the authors in the preceding footnote, *locis citatis*.

[115] Augustine, *Commentary*, VIII, 199; Coronata, *Institutiones*, n. 1785.

[116] *Supra*, p. 196.

will be affected by the interdict. He should also order that the decree be put in a prominent place in the vestibule of the church (or churches) where everyone may see it for himself. It seems that the bishop is not bound in every case to have a copy of the decree at the actual site of the cemetery, for in many instances the decree would be seen by a very negligible number of Catholics, and by a considerable number of non-Catholics. Invariably some of the latter would not be able to allow the matter to end there, but would make the interdict the subject of common gossip and an occasion for the misunderstanding and ridicule of Catholics, of the Church and of her laws.

6. *The Cessation of Interdict*

The local interdict of a cemetery can be removed at the time and in the manner established by the ecclesiastical superior who imposed the interdict. By a decree the competent authority bars (interdicts) all ecclesiastical rites in a certain defined cemetery. He can determine that the interdict will last forever, or that it will last for a definite period of time, or that it will continue until he feels that enough satisfaction has been made *(ad beneplacitum superioris)*. Or he may place certain conditions to its removal or cessation. In some cases, therefore, the interdict will cease of itself, e. g., because the period of time has elapsed, or because the conditions have been fulfilled. At other times, the interdict will not cease until the ecclesiastical authority which imposed the interdict, or his superior, or his successor, or his delegate, determines that the interdict is relaxed or dispensed.[117]

This is the manner in which the local interdict of a cemetery, as far as it is local *(qua locale)*, ceases. But as has been seen above,[118] the local interdict may have entailed the censure of personal interdict for all or some of the persons affected by the local interdict (e. g., c. 2338, § 4). In that case the removal of the interdict from the place does not *ipso facto* remove the censures from the persons who may have incurred them. These censures must be removed by absolution.[119]

[117] C. 2236, § 1.

[118] Cf. *supra*, p. 192.

[119] Cc. 2236, § 1, and 2248.

CONCLUSIONS

1. Cemeteries are not strictly to be considered as consecrated; it is more correct to say that they are solemnly blessed.

2. From the testimony of St. Gregory of Tours (sixth century) the following deductions can be made:

(a) Cemeteries were blessed before the sixth century;
(b) It was necessary in his day for cemeteries to be solemnly blessed;
(c) This blessing was reserved to the bishop of the place, but could be licitly performed by an outside bishop for a just cause.

3. An elaborate rite of solemn blessing was developed by the eighth century.

4. The rite of the simple blessing of cemeteries probably developed along with the rite of the blessing of churches, sometime before the thirteenth century.

5. The Code did not take away the pre-Code privilege of religious ordinaries of calling in an outside bishop when the local bishop has unjustly refused solemnly to bless cemeteries of their Order. In practice this privilege will hardly be used because of the prescriptions of canons 1155, § 1, and 337, § 1.

6. Contrary to the opinion of Vermeersch-Creusen, the following is the order of the Church's preferences with regard to the blessing of cemeteries:

(a) The blessing of a cemetery owned by the Church;
(b) The blessing of a special section of a cemetery which the Church *can not* (because her legal right has been taken away by civil law) or *does not* (because of the small number or poverty of the Catholics in the community) possess;
(c) The blessing of the whole municipal cemetery when the Church is denied her right to have her own cemeteries and when most of the burials are those of Catholics.

7. Additions to blessed cemeteries must be blessed, no matter how small they may be.

8. Cemeteries no longer enjoy the immunities which by ecclesiastical law they had before the time of the present Code. Whatever of the former ecclesiastical immunities was determined in consequence of the divine law still remains.

9. Before the time of the present Code cemetery lots as such could not be sold. In the present law there is nothing to indicate that the earth graves of blessed cemeteries cannot be the object of sale. In practice, however, only the exclusive use *(ususfructus)* and not the full title *(dominium)* is transferred to the owner of the cemetery lot; the real ownership remains vested in the cemetery corporation.

10. Canon 1206, § 2, which prescribes that local ordinaries bless municipal cemeteries, must be understood as granting a dispensation from the violation which ordinarily would follow upon the burial in sacred ground of the unbaptized or of persons excommunicated by judicial sentence.

BIBLIOGRAPHY

Sources

Acta Apostolicae Sedis, Commentarium Officiale, Romae, 1909—

Acta et Decreta Sacrorum Conciliorum Recentiorum (Collectio Lacensis), 7 vols., Friburgi Brisgoviae, 1870-1890.

Bullarium Franciscanum, compiled by Ioannes Hyacinthus Sbaralea, 7 vols., Romae, 1759-1904. Vols. V-VII compiled by Conrad Eubel.

Canones et Decreta Sacrosancti Oecumenici Concilii Tridentini, Romae: Ex Typographia Polyglotta S. C. de Propaganda Fide, 1904.

Codex Iuris Canonici Pii X Pontificis Maximi iussu digestus Benedicti Papae XV auctoritate promulgatus, Praefatione, Fontium Annotatione et Indice Analytico-Alphabetico ab Emo. Petro Card. Gasparri Auctus, Romae: Typis Polyglottis Vaticanis, 1917.

Codex Theodosianus, ed. P. Krueger, T. Mommsen, 3 vols., Berolini, 1905.

Codicis Iuris Canonici Fontes cura Emi. Petri Card. Gasparri editi, 9 vols., Romae (postea Civitate Vaticana): Typis Polyglottis Vaticanis, 1923-1939. (Vols. VII-IX ed. cura et studio Emi. Iustiniani Serédi.)

Collectanea S. Congregationis de Propaganda Fide, 2 vols., Romae: Typographia Polyglotta S. C. de Propaganda Fide, 1907.

Concilii Plenarii Baltimorensis II., in Ecclesia Metropolitana Baltimorensi, a die VII. ad diem XXI. octobris A.D. MDCCCLXVI., Habiti et a Sede Apostolica recogniti, Acta et Decreta, Baltimorae: Murphy, 1875.

Corpus Iuris Canonici, ed. Lipsiensis 2. post Aemilii Ludovici Richteri curas instruxit Aemilius Friedberg, 2 vols., Lipsiae, 1879-1881. Editio anastatice repetita, Lipsiae: Tauchnitz, 1922.

Corpus Iuris Civilis, 3 vols., Berolini, 1928-1929. *Institutiones,* quas recognovit P. Krueger; *Digesta,* quae recognovit T. Mommsen et retractavit P. Krueger; *Codex Iustinianus,* quam recognovit et retractavit P. Krueger; *Novellae,* quas recognovit R. Schoell, et absolvit G. Kroll.

Corpus Scriptorum Ecclesiasticorum Latinorum, 68 vols., Vindobonae, 1866-1936.

Decreta Concilii Plenarii Baltimorensis Tertii, Baltimorae: Murphy, 1886.

Decretales D. Gregorii Papae IX una cum Glossis Restitutae, Romae, 1582.

Hardouin, Jean, *Acta Conciliorum et Epistolae Decretales ac Constitutiones Summorum Pontificum,* 12 vols., Parisiis, 1715.

Jaffé, Philippus, *Regesta Pontificum Romanorum ab condita Ecclesia ad annum post Christum natum MCXCVIII,* 2 vols. in 1, ed. secundam correctam et auctam auspiciis Gulielmi Wattenbach curaverunt F. Kaltenbrunner (ad annum 590), P. Ewald (anno 590-882), S. Löwenfeld (anno 882-1198), Lipsiae, 1885-1888.

Liber Sextus Decretalium, una cum Clementinis et Extravagantibus Earumque Glossis Restitutis, Romae, 1582.

Mansi, Ioannes, *Sacrorum Conciliorum Nova et Amplissima Collectio,* 53 vols. in 59, Parisiis, Arnhem et Leipzig, 1901-1927.

Monumenta Germaniae Historica: Scriptores Rerum Merovingicarum, Tom. I, Edd. W. Arndt et B. Krusch, Hannoverae, 1885.

———: *Legum Sectio III: Concilia Aevi Merovingici,* Tom. I, recensivit F. Maassen, Hannoverae et Lipsiae, 1893.

Pontificale Romanum Clementis VIII Pontificis maximi iussu restitutum atque editum, Antverpiae, 1627.

Pontificale Romanum Clementis VIII primum nunc denuo Urbani VIII auctoritate recognitum, ed. tertia, Parisiis, 1683.

Pontificale Romanum Summorum Pontificum iussu editum et a Benedicto XIV Pontifice Maximo recognitum et castigatum, Mechliniae, 1862.

Pontificale Romanum Summorum Pontificum iussu editum a Benedicto XIV et Leone XIII Pontificibus Maximis recognitum et castigatum, Mechliniae, 1895.

Privilegia Omnium Religiosorum, compiled by Augustinus a Virgine Maria, Lugduni, 1661.

Rituale Romanum Pauli V Pontificis Maximi iussu editum, Romae, 1652.

Rituale Romanum Pauli V Pontificis Maximi iussu editum et a Benedicto XIV auctum et castigatum, Turonibus, 1896.

Rituale Romanum Pauli V Pontificis Maximi iussu editum a Benedicto XIV et a Pio X castigatum et auctum, Romae, 1903.

Rituale Romanum Pauli V Pontificis Maximi iussu editum aliorumque Pontificum cura recognitum atque auctoritate Sanctissimi D. N. Pii Papae XI ad normam Codicis Iuris Canonici accommodatum, 6. ed., post typicam, Turonibus: Mame, 1936.

Reference Works

Allard, P., *Ten Lectures on the Martyrs,* translated by Luigi Cappadelta, New York, 1907.

Augustine (Bachofen), P. Charles, *A Commentary on the New Code of Canon Law,* 8 vols., St. Louis: Herder, 1925-1938. Vol. II, 6. ed., 1936; Vol. VI, 3. ed., 1931; Vol. VIII, 3. ed., 1931.

Ayrinhac, H. A.-Lydon, P. J., *Penal Legislation in the New Code of Canon Law,* New York: Benziger Bros., 1936.

Baier, David, *Catholic Liturgics,* translated and adapted from the German of Richard Stapper, Paterson, N. J.: St. Anthony Guild Press, 1935.

Barbosa, Augustinus, *Collectanea Doctorum tam Veterum quam Recentiorum in Ius Pontificium Universum,* 5 vols., Lugduni, 1656.

———, *De Officio et Potestate Episcopi,* Lugduni, 1656.

———, *Iuris Ecclesiastici Universi Libri Tres,* Lugduni, 1660.

Bargilliat, Michael, *Praelectiones Juris Canonici,* 2. ed., 2 vols., Parisiis, 1895; 37. ed., Parisiis: Apud Baston, Berche et Pagis, 1923.

Baruffaldus, Hieronymus, *Ad Rituale Romanum Commentaria,* 2 vols., Florentiae, 1847.

Bauwens, Is., *Inhumation et Crémation,* 2. ed., translated by A. De Mets from the original Flemish, Bruxelles, 1891.

Benedictus XIV, *De Synodo Dioecesana Libri Tredecim,* 4 vols., Lovanii, 1763.

Beste, Udalricus, *Introductio in Codicem,* Collegeville, Minn.: St. John's Abbey Press, 1938.

Bingham, Joseph, *The Antiquities of the Christian Church,* 2 vols., London, 1856.

Blat, Albertus, *Commentarium Textus Codicis Iuris Canonici,* 5 vols. in 7, Romae: Collegio "Angelico," 1921-1938. Vol. II, 2. ed., 1921; Vol. III, pars II, 2. ed., 1934.

Bondini, A., *De Privilegio Exemptionis seu de Regularium Immunitate ab Ordinariorum Locorum Iurisdictione prout in Novo Iuris Canonici Codice Sancitur,* Romae, 1919.

Bouvier, John, *Bouvier's Law Dictionary and Concise Encyclopedia,* 8. ed., 2 vols., St. Paul, Minn.: West Publishing Co., 1914.

Breasted, James H., *Development of Religion and Thought in Ancient Egypt,* New York, 1912.

Cabrol, F., Dom-Leclercq, H., Dom, *Dictionnaire d'Archéologie Chrétienne et de Liturgie,* 14 vols., Paris: Letouzey et Ane, 1924—.

Cance, Adrien, *Le Code de Droit Canonique, Commentaire Succinct et Pratique,* 5. ed., 3 vols., Paris: J. Gabalda et Fils, 1930.

Cappello, Felix, *Summa Iuris Canonici,* 3 vols., Romae: Universitas Gregoriana, 1936-1939. Vol. II, 3. ed., 1939.

———, *Summa Iuris Publici Ecclesiastici,* 2. ed., Romae: Apud Aedes Universitatis Gregorianae, 1928.

———, *Tractatus Canonico-Moralis de Censuris iuxta Codicem Iuris Canonici,* 2. ed., Taurinorum Augustae: Marietti, 1925.

———, *Tractatus Canonico-Moralis de Sacramentis,* 3 vols., in 6, Taurini: Marietti, 1932-1939. Vol. I, 3. ed., 1938.

Catalanus, Joseph, *Pontificale Romanum in Tres Partes Distributum Clementis VIII ac Urbani VIII auctoritate recognitum,* nova ed., 3 vols., Parisiis, 1850-1851.

———, *Rituale Romanum Benedicti XIV iussu editum et auctum,* 2 vols., Patavii, 1760.

Catholic Encyclopedia, The, 15 vols., New York, 1907-1912.

Cavagnis, Felix, *Institutiones Iuris Publici Ecclesiastici,* 4. ed., Romae, 1906.

Chelodi, Ioannes, *Ius de Personis iuxta Codicem Iuris Canonici,* 2. ed., Tridentini: Libr. Edit. Tridentum, 1927.

Cicognani, Amleto, *Canon Law,* 2. revised ed., authorized English version by J. O'Hara and F. Brennan, Philadelphia: The Dolphin Press, 1935.

Cocchi, Guidus, *Commentarium in Codicem Iuris Canonici,* 8 vols., Taurinorum Augustae: Marietti, 1931-1940. Vol. V, 3. ed., 1932.

Conran, Edward, *The Interdict*, The Catholic University of America Canon Law Studies, n. 56, Washington, D. C.: The Catholic University of America, 1930.

Coronata, Matthaeus Conte a, *De Locis et Temporibus Sacris*, Taurini: Marietti, 1922.

———, *Institutiones Iuris Canonici*, 5 vols., Taurini: Marietti, 1933-1939. Vols. I-II, 2. ed., 1939; Vol. III, 1933; Vol. IV, 1935; Vol. V, 1936.

———, *Ius Publicum Ecclesiasticum*, 2. ed., Taurini: Marietti, 1934.

D'Alès, Adhémar, *Dictionnaire Apologétique de la Foi Catholique*, 4 vols., Paris, 1911.

D'Annibale, Ios., *Summula Theologiae Moralis*, 3. ed., 3 vols., Romae, 1888.

De Angelis, P., *Praelectiones Iuris Canonici ad methodum Decretalium Gregorii IX exactae*, 4 vols., Romae, 1877-1887.

De Herdt, J. B., *Sacrae Liturgiae Praxis iuxta Ritum Romanum*, 10. ed., 3 vols., Lovanii, 1902-1903.

De Meester, A., *Iuris Canonici et Iuris Canonico-Civilis Compendium*, ed. nova, 3 vols. in 4, Brugis: Desclée, 1921-1928.

De Rossi, John Baptist, *La Roma Sotterranea Cristiana*, 3 vols., Romae, 1864-1877.

Devoti, Ioannes, *Institutionum Canonicarum Libri IV*, ed. prima Romana post quintam, 4 vols. in 3, Romae, 1825-1826.

Dictionnaire de Droit Canonique, ed. R. Naz, 3 vols., Paris: Letouzey et Ane, 1924—

Duchesne, Louis, *Christian Worship: Its Origin and Evolution*, translated from the 3. French ed. by M. J. McClure, London, 1903.

Duranti, Ioannes, *De Ritibus Ecclesiae Catholicae Libri Tres*, Lugduni, 1608.

Engel, Ludovicus, *Collegium Universi Iuris Canonici*, ed. nona, cui adiectae sunt annotationes Caspari Barthel, 3 vols., Beneventi, 1760.

Eichmann, E., *Lehrbuch des Kirchenrechts auf Grund des Codex Iuris Canonici*, Paderborn: Schöningh, 1923.

Fagnanus, Prosper, *Commentaria in Quinque Libros Decretalium*, 4 vols., Venetiis, 1696-1697.

Ferraris, F. L., *Prompta Bibliotheca, Canonica, Iuridica, Moralis, Theologica, necnon Ascetica, Polemica, Rubricistica, Historica*, 9 vols., Romae, 1885-1899.

Ferreres, I., *Institutiones Canonicae*, 2. ed., 2 vols., Barcinone: E. Subirana, 1920.

Funk, F. X., *Didascalia et Constitutiones Apostolorum*, 2 vols., Paderbornae, 1905.

Gallemart, I., *Sacrosanctum Oecumenicum Concilium Tridentinum, additis Declarationibus Cardinalium Concilii Interpretum, ex ultima Recognitione*, ed. reformata, Tridenti, 1737.

Gasparri, Petrus, *Tractatus Canonicus de Sanctissima Eucharistia*, 2 vols., Parisiis, 1897.

Giraldi, Ubaldus, *Expositio Iuris Pontificii iuxta Recentiorem Ecclesiae Disciplinam*, nova ed. Romana, 3 vols. in 2, Romae, 1829-1839.

Gonzalez-Tellez, Emmanuel, *Commentaria Perpetua in Singulos Textus Quinque Librorum Decretalium Gregorii IX*, 5 vols. in 4, Venetiis, 1699.

Goodwine, John A., *The Right of the Church to Acquire Temporal Goods*, The Catholic University of America Canon Law Studies, n. 131, Washington, D. C.: The Catholic University of America Press, 1941.

Gulczynski, *The Desecration and Violation of Churches*, The Catholic University of America Canon Law Studies, n. 159, Washington, D. C.: The Catholic University of America Press, 1942.

Hastings, James, *Encyclopedia of Religion and Ethics*, 13 vols., New York: Scribner's Sons, 1908-1927.

Hornstein, M. Edouard, *Les Sepultures*, Paris, 1868.

Hyland, Francis, *Excommunication, Its Nature, Historical Development and Effects*, The Catholic University of America Canon Law Studies, n. 49, Washington, D. C.: The Catholic University of America, 1928.

Kerin, Charles, *The Privation of Christian Burial*, The Catholic University of America Canon Law Studies, n. 136, Washington, D. C.: The Catholic University of America Press, 1941.

Leclercq, Henri, Dom, *Manuel d'Archéologie Chrétienne*, 2 vols., Paris, 1907.

Le Vavasseur, F., *Ceremonial Selon Le Rit Romain d'apres Baldeschi et Favrel*, 6. ed., 2 vols., Paris, 1882.

Many, S., *Praelectiones De Locis Sacris*, Parisiis, 1904.

Maringola, Aloysius, *Antiquitatum Christianarum Institutiones*, 2 vols. in 1, Neapoli, 1857.

———, *Institutiones Liturgicae*, 2 vols., Neapoli, 1864-1865.

Maroto, Philippus, *Institutiones Iuris Canonici ad normam Novi Codicis*, 2 vols., Romae, 1919-1921. Vol. I, 3. ed., Romae: Apud Commentarium pro Religiosis, 1921.

Martène, Edmund, *De Antiquis Ecclesiae Ritibus*, 3 vols., Rotomagi, 1700-1702.

Marucchi, O., *Éléments d'Archéologie Chrétienne*, 3 vols., Paris, 1902-1905. Vol. I, 2. ed., 1905; Vol. II, 2. ed., 1903; Vol. III, 1. ed., 1902.

Maskell, W., *Monumenta Ritualia Ecclesiae Anglicanae*, 3 vols., Oxford, 1882.

McDonough, Thomas J., *Apostolic Administrators*, The Catholic University of America Canon Law Studies, n. 139, Washington, D. C.: The Catholic University of America Press, 1941.

Melo, A., *De Exemptione Regularium*, The Catholic University of America Canon Law Studies, n. 12, Washington, D. C.: The Catholic University of America, 1921.

Michiels, G., *Normae Generales Iuris Canonici*, 2 vols., Lublin-Polonia: Universitas Catholica, 1929.

Migne, Iacques Paul, *Patrologiae Cursus Completus—Series Graeca*, 161 vols., Parisiis, 1857-1866.

———, *Patrologiae Cursus Completus—Series Latina,* 221 vols., Parisiis, 1844-1864.

———, *Theologiae Cursus Completus,* 28 vols., Parisiis, 1863-1866.

Moulart, F. J., *De Sepultura et Coemeteriis,* Lovanii, 1862.

Murga (De), Petrus, *Disquisitiones Morales et Canonicae de Sepulturis,* 2 vols., Lugduni, 1666.

Northcote, J. S., *Les Catacombes Romaines,* Rome, Paris, 1859.

Northcote, J. S.-Brownlow, W. R., *Roma Sotterranea,* London, 1869.

O'Reilly, John A., *Ecclesiastical Sepulture in the New Code of Canon Law,* The Catholic University of America Canon Law Studies, n. 18, Washington, D. C.: The Catholic University of America, 1923.

Orellius, J. C., *Inscriptionum Latinarum Selectarum Amplissima Collectio,* 3 vols., Turici, 1828-1856. Vol. III edited by G. Henzen.

Ottaviani, Alaphridus, *Institutiones Iuris Publici Ecclesiastici,* 2. ed., 2 vols., Romae: Typis Polyglottis Vaticani, 1935-1936.

Passerini, P., *De Ecclesiarum Reconciliatione,* Parmae, 1694.

Petra, Vincentius, *Commentaria in Constitutiones Apostolicas,* 5 vols. in 2, Venetiis, 1729.

Pirhing, Ernricus, *Ius Canonicum Nova Methodo Explicatum,* 5 vols. in 4, Dilingae, 1674-1678.

Prümmer, Dominicus, *Manuale Iuris Canonici,* 3. ed., Friburgi Brisgoviae: Herder, 1922.

Reclusius, F. A., *Tractatus de Re Parochiali,* Romae, 1773.

Reiffenstuel, A., *Ius Canonicum Universum,* 5 vols. in 7, Parisiis, 1864-1882.

Rivet, L., *Institutiones Iuris Canonici Privati,* Romae: Ex Typographia Pontificia in Instituto Pii IX, 1914.

Rohde, *Psyche, The Cult of Souls and Belief in Immortality among the Greeks,* translated from the 8. ed. by W. Hillis, London, 1925.

Rossi, Giuseppe, *La "Sepultura Ecclesiastica" e l' "Ius Funerum" nel Diritto Canonico,* Bergamo: Arnaldi, 1920.

Rush, A. C., *Death and Burial in Christian Antiquity,* The Catholic University of America Studies in Christian Antiquity, n. 1, Washington, D. C.: The Catholic University of America Press, 1941.

Samuellius, F., *De Sepulturis Ecclesiasticis,* Lucae, 1650.

Scaglia, S., *Manuel d'Archéologie Chrétienne,* Turin, 1916.

Schmalzgrueber, F., *Ius Ecclesiasticum Universum,* 5 vols. in 12, Romae, 1843-1845.

Schroeder, H. J., *Disciplinary Decrees of the General Councils, Text, Translation and Commentary,* London, St. Louis: B. Herder Book Co., 1937.

Schulte, A., *Benedicenda: Rites and Ceremonies to be Observed in some of the Principal Functions of the Roman Pontifical and the Roman Ritual,* New York: Benziger Brothers, 1907.

Smith, William-Cheetham, Samuel, *Dictionary of Christian Antiquities,* 2 vols., Hartford, 1880.

Sole, Iacobus, *De Delictis et Poenis,* Romae: Pustet, 1920.

Spence-Jones, H. D. M., *The Early Christians in Rome,* New York, 1911.

Suarez, Franciscus, *Commentaria ac Disputationes in Tertiam Partem Divi Thomae,* 5 vols., Lugduni, 1608-1628.

Tanquerey, A., *Synopsis Theologiae Dogmaticae,* 23. ed., 3 vols., Parisiis: Desclée et Socii, 1934.

Thomas Aquinas, St., *Praeclarissima Commentaria in Quatuor Libros Sententiarum Petri Lombardi,* 2 vols., Parisiis, 1659.

Toso, Albertus, *Ad Codicem Iuris Canonici Commentaria Minora,* 5 vols., Romae: Marietti, 1920-1934.

Van der Stappen, J. F., *Sacra Liturgia,* 3. ed., 5 vols., Mechliniae: H. Dessain, 1912.

Van Hove, A., *Commentarium Lovaniense in Codicem Iuris Canonici,* 1 vol. in 5 toms., Mechliniae: H. Dessain, 1928-1939. Tom. I, *Prolegomena,* 1928; Tom. II, *De Legibus Ecclesiasticis,* 1930.

Vecchiotti, Septimius, *Institutiones Canonicae,* 16. ed., 3 vols., Augustae Taurinorum, 1875-1876.

Vermeersch, A.-Creusen, J., *Epitome Iuris Canonici,* 3 vols., Mechliniae et Romae: H. Dessain, 1934-1937. Vol. I, 6. ed., 1937; Vol. II, 5. ed., 1934; Vol. III, 5. ed., 1936.

Wapelhorst, Innocentius, *Compendium Sacrae Liturgiae iuxta Ritum Romanum,* 11. ed., Neo-Eboraci: Benziger Fratres, 1931.

Wernz, Franciscus, *Ius Decretalium,* 6 vols., Romae, 1898-1905.

Wernz, F.-Vidal, P., *Ius Canonicum ad Codicis Normam Exactum,* 7 vols. in 8, Romae: apud Aedes Universitatis Gregorianiae, 1923-1938. Vol. IV, pars I, 1934.

Woywod, Stanislaus, *A Practical Commentary on the Code of Canon Law,* 6. printing, 2 vols., New York: Wagner, 1941.

Zollman, Carl, *American Church Law,* St. Paul, Minn.: West Publishing Co., 1933.

Periodicals

Apollinaris, Romae, 1928—

Ecclesiastical Review, The (originally, *The American Ecclesiastical Review*), Philadelphia, 1889—

Homiletic and Pastoral Review, The, New York, 1900—

Jurist, The, Washington, D. C., 1941—

L'Ami du Clergé, Paris, 1879—

Monitore Ecclesiastico, Il, Romae, 1876—

Periodica de Re Canonica et Morali utili Praesertim Religiosis et Missionariis, Brugis, 1905—; ab anno 1927: *Periodica de Re Morali, Canonica, Liturgica.*

Sal Terrae, Santander, 1912—

Articles

Cappello, Felix M., "De Consecratione Ecclesiarum"—*Periodica,* XIX (1930), 139 ff.

Ciprotti, Pius, "De Consummatione Delictorum Attento Eorum Elemento Obiectivo"—*Apollinaris,* VIII (1935), 389-391.

Murphy, James H., "Parish Priests and Christian Burial"—*The Ecclesiastical Review,* LXVII (1922), 12-25.

Regatillo, E., "Sepultura Materialis"—*Sal Terrae,* XVII (1928), 913-919.

———, "Sepultura Materialis: Exsecratio, Interdictum, Violatio et Immunitas" —*Sal Terrae,* XVII (1928), 998-1002.

Woywod, S., "Several Points on the Desecration of Cemeteries"—*The Homiletic and Pastoral Review,* XXV (1924-1925), 171-173.

———, "Enlarging of Cemeteries and Consecration"—*The Homiletic and Pastoral Review,* XXXVI (1936), 971-972.

———, "Burial of Catholics in Non-Catholic Cemeteries"—*The Homiletic and Pastoral Review,* XXXVII (1936-1937), 79-81.

———, "Violation of Corpses and Graves"—*The Homiletic and Pastoral Review,* XXXVII (1936-1937), 1174-1175.

The Benedictine author, "The Consecration of a Cemetery"—*The Homiletic and Pastoral Review,* XXX (1929-1930), 976-982.

Anonymous, "The Disposal of Lots in Consecrated Cemeteries"—*The Ecclesiastical Review,* LXXVIII (1928), 430-432.

LIST OF ABBREVIATIONS

AAS—*Acta Apostolicae Sedis.*
ASS—*Acta Sanctae Sedis.*
C—Codex Iustinianus.
C. or c.—canon; caput.
Cc.—canones; capita.
C Th—Codex Theodosianus.
D—Digestum Iustinianum.
DACL—Cabrol-Leclercq, *Dictionnaire d'Archéologie Chrétienne et de Liturgie.*
Fontes—*Codicis Iuris Canonici Fontes cura . . . Gasparri editi.*
Hardouin—Hardouin, Jean, *Acta Conciliorum*, etc.
G—Institutiones Gaii.
I—Institutiones Iustinianae.
Mansi—Mansi, J. D., *Sacrorum Conciliorum Nova et Amplissima Collectio.*
MGH—*Monumenta Germaniae Historica.*
MPG—Migne, J., *Patrologia, Series Graeca.*
MPL—Migne, J., *Patrologia, Series Latina.*
N—Novellae Constitutiones.
R. J.—Regula Juris.
S. C. C.—Sacra Concilii Congregatio.
S. C. de Prop. Fide—Sacra Congregatio de Propaganda Fide.
S. C. S. Off.—Sacra Congregatio Sancti Officii.
S. R. C.—Sacrorum Rituum Congregatio.

INDEX OF CANONS

ALPHABETICAL INDEX

BIOGRAPHICAL NOTE

Cornelius Michael Power was born in Seattle, Washington, on December 18, 1913. He received his elementary education from the Sisters of the Holy Names of Jesus and Mary at St. Mary's School, Seattle. After one year at O'Dea High School, an Irish Christian Brother institution, he entered St. Joseph's Preparatory Seminary, Mountain View, California, in September, 1928. His studies in philosophy were made at St. Patrick's Seminary, Menlo Park, California, during the years 1933 to 1935. In September, 1935, he entered St. Edward's Seminary, Seattle, Washington, from which he was ordained priest, June 3, 1939. After one year of parochial work in the Diocese of Seattle, he enrolled, in September, 1940, in the School of Canon Law at the Catholic University of America and received the degree of the Baccalaureate in Canon Law in June, 1941, and the degree of the Licentiate in Canon Law in May, 1942.

CANON LAW STUDIES *

1. FRERIKS, REV. CELESTINE A., C.PP.S., J.C.D., Religious Congregations in Their External Relations, 121 pp., 1916.
2. GALLIHER, REV. DANIEL M., O.P., J.C.D., Canonical Elections, 117 pp., 1917.
3. BORKOWSKI, REV. AURELIUS L., O.F.M., J.C.D., De Confraternitatibus Ecclesiasticis, 136 pp., 1918.
4. CASTILLO, REV. CAYO, J.C.D., Disertacion Historico-Canonica sobre la Potestad del Cabildo en Sede Vacante o Impedida del Vicario Capitular, 99 pp., 1919 (1918).
5. KUBELBECK, REV. WILLIAM J., S.T.B., J.C.D., The Sacred Penitentiaria and Its Relation to Faculties of Ordinaries and Priests, 129 pp., 1918.
6. PETROVITS, REV. JOSEPH, J.C., S.T.D., J.C.D., The New Church Law on Matrimony, X-461 pp., 1919.
7. HICKEY, REV. JOHN J., S.T.B., J.C.D., Irregularities and Simple Impediments in the New Code of Canon Law, 100 pp., 1920.
8. KLEKOTKA, REV. PETER J., S.T.B., J.C.D., Diocesan Consultors, 179 pp., 1920.
9. WANENMACHER, REV. FRANCIS, J.C.D., The Evidence in Ecclesiastical Procedure Affecting the Marriage Bond, 1920 (Printed 1935).
10. GOLDEN, REV. HENRY FRANCIS, J.C.D., Parochial Benefices in the New Code, IV-119 pp., 1921 (Printed 1925).
11. KOUDELKA, REV. CHARLES J., J.C.D., Pastors, Their Rights and Duties According to the New Code of Canon Law, 211 pp., 1921.
12. MELO, REV. ANTONIUS, O.F.M., J.C.D., De Exemptione Regularium, X-188 pp., 1921.
13 SCHAAF, REV. VALENTINE THEODORE, O.F.M., S.T.B., J.C.D., The Cloister, X-180 pp., 1921.
14. BURKE, REV. THOMAS JOSEPH, S.T.D., J.C.D., Competence in Ecclesiastical Tribunals, IV-117 pp., 1922.
15. LEECH, REV. GEORGE LEO, J.C.D., A Comparative Study of the Constitution "Apostolicae Sedis" and the "Codex Juris Canonici," 179 pp., 1922.
16. MOTRY, REV. HUBERT LOUIS, S.T.D., J.C.D., Diocesan Faculties According to the Code of Canon Law, II-167 pp., 1922.
17. MURPHY, REV. GEORGE LAWRENCE, J.C.D., Delinquencies and Penalties in the Administration and the Reception of the Sacraments, IV-121 pp., 1923.
18. O'REILLY, REV. JOHN ANTHONY, S.T.B., J.C.D., Ecclesiastical Sepulture in the New Code of Canon Law, II-129 pp., 1923.

* Below n. 100 only the following numbers are still available: Nn. 3, 4, 9, 25, 34, 57 and 75. Beginning with n. 100 only the following are unavailable: Nn. 100, 101, 102, 104, 105, 107, 108, 109, 111 and 113.

19. Michalicka, Rev. Wenceslas Cyrill, O.S.B., J.C.D., Judicial Procedure in Dismissal of Clerical Exempt Religious, 107 pp., 1923.
20. Dargin, Rev. Edward Vincent, S.T.B., J.C.D., Reserved Cases According to the Code of Canon Law, IV-103 pp., 1924.
21. Godfrey, Rev. John A., S.T.B., J.C.D., The Right of Patronage According to the Code of Canon Law, 153 pp., 1924.
22. Hagedorn, Rev. Francis Edward, J.C.D., General Legislation on Indulgences, II-154 pp., 1924.
23. King, Rev. James Ignatius, J.C.D., The Administration of the Sacraments to Dying Non-Catholics, V-141 pp., 1924.
24. Winslow, Rev. Francis Joseph, O.F.M., J.C.D., Vicars and Prefects Apostolic, IV-149 pp., 1924.
25. Correa, Rev. Jose Servelion, S.T.L., J.C.D., La Potestad Legislativa de la Iglesia Catolica, IV-127 pp., 1925.
26. Dugan, Rev. Henry Francis, A.M., J.C.D., The Judiciary Department of the Diocesan Curia, 87 pp., 1925.
27. Keller, Rev. Charles Frederick, S.T.B., J.C.D., Mass Stipends, 167 pp., 1925.
28. Paschang, Rev. John Linus, J.C.D., The Sacramentals According to the Code of Canon Law, 129 pp., 1925.
29. Piontek, Rev. Cyrillus, O.F.M., S.T.B., J.C.D., De Indulto Exclaustrationis necnon Saecularizationis, XIII-289 pp., 1925.
30. Kearney, Rev. Richard Joseph, S.T.B., J.C.D., Sponsors at Baptism According to the Code of Canon Law, IV-127 pp., 1925.
31. Bartlett, Rev. Chester Joseph, A.M., LL.B., J.C.D., The Tenure of Parochial Property in the United States of America, V-108 pp., 1926.
32. Kilker, Rev. Adrian Jerome, J.C.D., Extreme Unction, V-425 pp., 1926.
33. McCormick, Rev. Robert Emmett, J.C.D., Confessors of Religious, VIII-266 pp., 1926.
34. Miller, Rev. Newton Thomas, J.C.D., Founded Masses According to the Code of Canon Law, VII-93 pp., 1926.
35. Roelker, Rev. Edward G., S.T.D., J.C.D., Principles of Privilege According to the Code of Canon Law, XI-166 pp., 1926.
36. Bakalarczyk, Rev. Richardus, M.I.C., J.U.D., De Novitiatu, VIII-208 pp., 1927.
37. Pizzuti, Rev. Lawrence, O.F.M., J.U.L., De Parochis Religiosis, 1927. (Not Printed.)
38. Bliley, Rev. Nicholas Martin, O.S.B., J.C.D., Altars According to the Code of Canon Law, XIX-132 pp., 1927.
39. Brown, Mr. Brendan Francis, A.B., LL.M., J.U.D., The Canonical Juristic Personality with Special Reference to its Status in the United States of America, V-212 pp., 1927.
40. Cavanaugh, Rev. William Thomas, C.P., J.U.D., The Reservation of the Blessed Sacrament, VIII-101 pp., 1927.

41. Doheny, Rev. William J., C.S.C., A.B., J.U.D., Church Property: Modes of Acquisition, X-118 pp., 1927.
42. Feldhaus, Rev. Aloysius H., C.PP.S., J.C.D., Oratories, IX-141 pp., 1927.
43. Kelly, Rev. James Patrick, A.B., J.C.D., The Jurisdiction of the Simple Confessor, X-208 pp., 1927.
44. Neuberger, Rev. Nicholas J., J.C.D., Canon 6 or the Relation of the Codex Juris Canonici to the Preceding Legislation, V-95 pp., 1927.
45. O'Keefe, Rev. Gerald Michael, J.C.D., Matrimonial Dispensations, Powers of Bishops, Priests, and Confessors, VIII-232 pp., 1927.
46. Quigley, Rev. Joseph A. M., A.B., J.C.D., Condemned Societies, 139 pp., 1927.
47. Zaplotnik, Rev. Johannes Leo, J.C.D., De Vicariis Foraneis, X-142 pp., 1927.
48. Duskie, Rev. John Aloysius, A.B., J.C.D., The Canonical Status of the Orientals in the United States, VIII-196 pp., 1928.
49. Hyland, Rev. Francis Edward, J.C.D., Excommunication, Its Nature, Historical Development and Effects, VIII-181 pp., 1928.
50. Reinmann, Rev. Gerald Joseph, O.M.C., J.C.D., The Third Order Secular of Saint Francis, 201 pp., 1928.
51. Schenk, Rev. Francis J., J.C.D., The Matrimonial Impediments of Mixed Religion and Disparity of Cult, XVI-318 pp., 1929.
52. Coady, Rev. John Joseph, S.T.D., J.U.D., A.M., The Appointment of Pastors, VIII-150 pp., 1929.
53. Kay, Rev. Thomas Henry, J.C.D., Competence in Matrimonial Procedure, VIII-164 pp., 1929.
54. Turner, Rev. Sidney Joseph, C.P., J.U.D., The Vow of Poverty, XLIX-217 pp., 1929.
55. Kearney, Rev. Raymond A., A.B., S.T.D., J.C.D., The Principles of Delegation, VII-149 pp., 1929.
56. Conran, Rev. Edward James, A.B., J.C.D., The Interdict,, V-163 pp., 1930.
57. O'Neill, Rev. William H., J.C.D., Papal Rescripts of Favor, VII-218 pp., 1930.
58. Bastnagel, Rev. Clement Vincent, J.U.D., The Appointment of Parochial Adjutants and Assistants, XV-257 pp., 1930.
59. Ferry, Rev. William A., A.B., J.C.D., Stole Fees, V-136 pp., 1930.
60. Costello, Rev. John Michael, A.B., J.C.D., Domicile and Quasi-Domicile, VII-201 pp., 1930.
61. Kremer, Rev. Michael Nicholas, A.B., S.T.B., J.C.D., Church Support in the United States, VI-136 pp., 1930.
62. Angulo, Rev. Luis, C.M., J.C.D., Legislation de la Iglesia sobre la intencion en la application de la Santa Misa, VII-104 pp., 1931.
63. Frey, Rev. Wolfgang Norbert, O.S.B., A.B., J.C.D., The Act of Religious Profession, VIII-174 pp., 1931.

64. Roberts, Rev. James Brendan, A.B., J.C.D., The Banns of Marriage, XIV-140 pp., 1931.
65. Ryder, Rev. Raymond Aloysius, A.B., J.C.D., Simony, IX-151 pp., 1931.
66. Campagna, Rev. Angelo, Ph.D., J.U.D., Il Vicario Generale del Vescovo, VII-205 pp., 1931.
67. Cox, Rev. Joseph Godfrey, A.B., J.C.D., The Administration of Seminaries, VI-124 pp., 1931.
68. Gregory, Rev. Donald J., J.U.D., The Pauline Privilege, XV-165 pp., 1931.
69. Donohue, Rev. John F., J.C.D., The Impediment of Crime, VII-110 pp., 1931.
70. Dooley, Rev. Eugene A., O.M.I., J.C.D., Church Law on Sacred Relics, IX-143 pp., 1931.
71. Orth, Rev. Clement Raymond, O.M.C., J.C.D., The Approbation of Religious Institutes, 171 pp., 1931.
72. Pernicone, Rev. Joseph M., A.B., J.C.D., The Ecclesiastical Prohibition of Books, XII-267 pp., 1932.
73. Clinton, Rev. Connell, A.B., J.C.D., The Paschal Precept, IX-108 pp., 1932.
74. Donnelly, Rev. Francis B., A.M., S.T.L., J.C.D., The Diocesan Synod, VIII-125 pp., 1932.
75. Torrente, Rev. Camilo, C.M.F., J.C.D., Las Procesiones Sagradas, V-145 pp., 1932.
76. Murphy, Rev. Edwin J., C.PP.S., J.C.D., Suspension Ex Informata Conscientia, XI-122 pp., 1932.
77. MacKenzie, Rev. Eric F., A.M., S.T.L., J.C.D., The Delict of Heresy in its Commission, Penalization, Absolution, VII-124 pp., 1932.
78. Lyons, Rev. Avitus E., S.T.B., J.C.D., The Collegiate Tribunal of First Instance, XI-147 pp., 1932.
79. Connolly, Rev. Thomas A., J.C.D., Appeals, XI-195 pp., 1932.
80. Sangmeister, Rev. Joseph V., A.B., J.C.D., Force and Fear as Precluding Matrimonial Consent, V-211 pp., 1932.
81. Jaeger, Rev. Leo A., A.B., J.C.D., The Administration of Vacant and Quasi-Vacant Episcopal Sees in the United States, IX-229 pp., 1932.
82. Rimlinger, Rev. Herbert T., J.C.D., Error Invalidating Matrimonial Consent, VII-79 pp., 1932.
83. Barrett, Rev. John D. M., S.S., J.C.D., A Comparative Study of the Third Plenary Council of Baltimore and the Code, IX-221 pp., 1932.
84. Carberry, Rev. John J., Ph.D., S.T.D., J.C.D., The Juridical Form of Marriage, X-177 pp., 1934.
85. Dolan, Rev. John L., A.B., J.C.D., The Defensor Vinculi, XII-157 pp., 1934.
86. Hannan, Rev. Jerome D., A.M., S.T.D., LL.B., J.C.D., The Canon Law of Wills, IX-517 pp., 1934.

87. LEMIEUX, REV. DELISE A., A.M., J.C.D., The Sentence in Ecclesiastical Procedure, IX-131 pp., 1934.
88. O'ROURKE, REV. JAMES J., A.B., J.C.D., Parish Registers, VII-109 pp., 1934.
89. TIMLIN, REV. BARTHOLOMEW, O.F.M., A.M., J.C.D., Conditional Matrimonial Consent, X-381 pp., 1934.
90. WAHL, REV. FRANCIS X., A.B., J.C.D., The Matrimonial Impediments of Consanguinity and Affinity, VI-125 pp., 1934.
91. WHITE, REV. ROBERT J., A.B., LL.B., S.T.B., J.C.D., Canonical Ante-Nuptial Promises and the Civil Law, VI-152 pp., 1934.
92. HERRERA, REV. ANTONIO PARRA, O.C.D., J.C.D., Legislacion Ecclesiastica sobra el Ayuno y la Abstinencia, XI-191 pp., 1935.
93. KENNEDY, REV. EDWIN J., J.C.D., The Special Matrimonial Process in Cases of Evident Nullity, X-165 pp., 1935.
94. MANNING, REV. JOHN J., A.B., J.C.D., Presumption of Law in Matri monial Procedure, XI-111 pp., 1935.
95. MOEDER, REV. JOHN M., J.C.D., The Proper Bishop for Ordination and Dimissorial Letters, VII-135 pp., 1935.
96. O'MARA, REV. WILLIAM A., A.B., J.C.D., Canonical Causes for Matrimonial Dispensations, IX-155 pp., 1935.
97. REILLY, REV. PETER, J.C.D., Residence of Pastors, IX-81 pp., 1935.
98. SMITH, REV. MARINER T., O.P., S.T.Lr., J.C.D., The Penal Law for Religious, VIII-169 pp., 1935.
99. WHALEN, REV. DONALD W., A.M., J.C.D., The Value of Testimonial Evidence in Matrimonial Procedure, XIII-297 pp., 1935.
100. CLEARY, REV. JOSEPH F., J.C.D., Canonical Limitations on the Alienation of Church Property, VIII-141 pp., 1936.
101. GLYNN, REV. JOHN C., J.C.D., The Promoter of Justice, XX-337 pp., 1936.
102. BRENNAN, REV. JAMES H., S.S., M.A., S.T.B., J.C.D., The Simple Convalidation of Marriage, VI-135 pp., 1937.
103. BRUNINI, REV. JOSEPH BERNARD, J.C.D., The Clerical Obligations of Canons 139 and 142, X-121 pp., 137.
104. CONNOR, REV. MAURICE, A.B., J.C.D., The Administrative Removal of Pastors, VIII-159 pp., 1937.
105. GUILFOYLE, REV. MERLIN JOSEPH, J.C.D., Custom, XI-144 pp., 1937.
106. HUGHES, REV. JAMES AUSTIN, A.B., A.M., J.C.D., Witnesses in Criminal Trials of Clerics, IX-140 pp., 1937.
107. JANSEN, REV. RAYMOND J., A.B., S.T.L., J.C.D., Canonical Provisions for Catechetical Instruction, VII-153 pp., 1937.
108. KEALY, REV. JOHN JAMES, A.B., J.C.D., The Introductory Libellus in Church Court Procedure, XI-121 pp., 1937.
109. MCMANUS, REV. JAMES EDWARD, C.SS.R., J.C.D., The Administration of Temporal Goods in Religious Institutes, XVI-196 pp., 1937.

110. MORIARTY, REV. EUGENE JAMES, J.C.D., Oaths in Ecclesiastical Courts, X-115 pp., 1937.

111. RAINIER, REV. ELIGIUS GEORGE, C.SS.R., J.C.D., Suspension of Clerics, XVII-249 pp., 1937.

112. REILLY, REV. THOMAS F., C.SS.R., J.C.D., Visitation of Religious, VI-195 pp., 1938.

113. MORIARTY, REV. FRANCIS E., C.SS.R., J.C.D., The Extraordinary Absolution from Censures, XV-334 pp., 1938.

114. CONNOLLY, REV. NICHOLAS P., J.C.D., The Canonical Erection of Parishes, X-132 pp., 1938.

115. DONOVAN, REV. JAMES JOSEPH, J.C.D., The Pastor's Obligation in Prenuptial Investigation, XII-322 pp., 1938.

116. HARRIGAN, REV. ROBERT J., M.A., S.T.B., J.C.D., The Radical Sanation of Invalid Marriages, VIII-208 pp., 1938.

117. BOFFA, REV. CONRAD HUMBERT, J.C.D., Canonical Provisions for Catholic Schools, VII-211 pp., 1939.

118. PARSONS, REV. ANSCAR JOHN, O.M.Cap., J.C.D., Canonical Elections, XII-236 pp., 1939.

119. REILLY, REV. EDWARD MICHAEL, A.B., J.C.D., The General Norms of Dispensation, XII-156 pp., 1939.

120. RYAN, REV. GERALD ALOYSIUS, A.B., J.C.D., Principles of Episcopal Jurisdiction, XII-172 pp., 1939.

121. BURTON, REV. FRANCIS JAMES, C.S.C., A.B., J.C.D., A Commentary on Canon 1125, X-222 pp., 1940.

122. MIASKIEWICZ, REV. FRANCIS SIGISMUND, J.C.D., Supplied Jurisdiction According to Canon 209, XII-340 pp., 1940.

123. RICE, REV. PATRICK WILLIAM, A.B., J.C.D., Proof of Death in Prenuptial Investigation, VIII-156 pp., 1940.

124. ANGLIN, REV. THOMAS FRANCIS, M.S., J.C.D., The Eucharistic Fast, VIII-183 pp., 1941.

125. COLEMAN, REV. JOHN JEROME, J.C.D., The Minister of Confirmation, VI-153 pp., 1941.

126. DOWNS, REV. JOSEPH EMMANUEL, A.B., J.C.D., The Concept of Clerical Immunity, XI-163 pp., 1941.

127. ESSWEIN, REV. ANTHONY ALBERT, J.C.D., Extrajudicial Penal Powers of Ecclesiastical Superiors, X-144 pp., 1941.

128. FARRELL, REV. BENJAMIN FRANCIS, M.A., S.T.L., J.C.D., The Rights and Duties of the Local Ordinary Regarding Congregations of Women Religious of Pontifical Approval, V-195 pp., 1941.

129. FEENEY, REV. THOMAS JOHN, A.B., S.T.L., J.C.D., Restitutio in Integrum, VI-169 pp., 1941.

130. FINDLAY, REV. STEPHEN WILLIAM, O.S.B., A.B., J.C.D., Canonical Norms Governing the Deposition and Degradation of Clerics, XVII-279 pp., 1941.

131. GOODWINE, REV. JOHN, A.B., S.T.L., J.C.D., The Right of the Church to Acquire Property, VIII-119 pp., 1941.
132. HESTON, REV. EDWARD LOUIS, C.S.C., Ph.D., S.T.D., J.C.D., The Alienation of Church Property in the United States, XII-222 pp., 1941.
133. HOGAN, REV. JAMES JOHN, A.B., S.T.L., J.C.D., Judicial Advocates and Procurators, XIII-200 pp., 1941.
134. KEALY, REV. THOMAS M., A.B., Litt.B., J.C.D., Dowry of Women Religious, IX-152 pp., 1941.
135. KEENE, REV. MICHAEL JAMES, O.S.B., J.C.D., Religious Ordinaries and Canon 198, V-164 pp., 1942.
136. KERIN, REV. CHARLES A., S.S., M.A., S.T.B., J.C.D., The Privation of Christian Burial, XVI-279 pp., 1941.
137. LOUIS, REV. WILLIAM FRANCIS, M.A., J.C.D., Diocesan Archives, X-101 pp., 1941.
138. MCDEVITT, REV. GILBERT JOSEPH, A.B., J.C.D., Legitimacy and Legitimation, X-247 pp., 1941.
139. MCDONOUGH, REV. THOMAS JOSEPH, A.B., J.C.D., Apostolic Administrators, X-217 pp., 1941.
140. MEIER, REV. CARL ANTHONY, A.B., J.C.D., Penal Administrative Procedure Against Negligent Pastors, XI-240 pp., 1941.
141. SCHMIDT, REV. JOHN ROGG, A.B., J.C.D., The Principles of Authentic Interpretation in Canon 17 of the Code of Canon Law, XII-331 pp., 1941.
142. SLAFKOSKY, REV. ANDREW LEONARD, A.B., J.C.D., The Canonical Episcopal Visitation of the Diocese, X-197 pp., 1941.
143. SWOBODA, REV. INNOCENT ROBERT, O.F.M., J.C.D., Ignorance in Relation to the Imputability of Delicts, IX-271 pp., 1941.
144. DUBÉ, REV. ARTHUR JOSEPH, A.B., J.C.D., The General Principles for the Reckoning of Time in Canon Law, VIII-299 pp., 1941.
145. MCBRIDE, REV. JAMES T., A.B., J.C.D., Incardination and Excardination of Seculars, XX-585 pp., 1941.
146. KRÓL, REV. JOHN T., J.C.D., The Defendant in Ecclesiastical Trials, XII-207 pp., 1942.
147. COMYNS, REV. JOSEPH J., C.SS.R., A.B., J.C.D., Papal and Episcopal Administration of Church Property, XIV-155 pp., 1942.
148. BARRY, REV. GARRETT FRANCIS, O.M.I., J.C.D., Violation of the Cloister, XII-260 pp., 1942.
149. BOLDUC, REV. GATIEN, C.S.V., A.B., S.T.L., J.C.D., Les Études dans les Religions Cléricales, VIII-155 pp., 1942.
150. BOYLE, REV. DAVID JOHN, M.A., J.C.D., The Juridic Effects of Moral Certitude on Pre-Nuptial Guarantees, XII-188 pp., 1942.
151. CANAVAN, REV. WALTER JOSEPH, M.A., LITT.D., J.C.D., The Profession of Faith, XII-143 pp., 1942.
152. DESROCHERS, REV. BRUNO, A.B., PH.L., S.T.B., J.C.D., Le Premier Concile Plénier de Québec et le Code de Droit Canonique, XIV-186 pp., 1942.

153. Dillon, Rev. Robert Edward, A.B., J.C.D., Common Law Marriage, X-148 pp., 1942.
154. Dodwell, Rev. Edward John, Ph.D., S.T.B., J.C.D., The Time and Place for the Celebration of Marriage, X-156 pp., 1942.
155. Donnellan, Rev. Thomas Andrew, A.B., J.C.D., The Obligation of the Missa pro Populo, VII-131 pp., 1942.
156. Eltz, Rev. Louis Anthony, A.B., J.C.L., Cooperation in Crime.
157. Gass, Rev. Sylvester Francis, M.A., J.C.D., Ecclesiastical Pensions, XI-206 pp., 1942.
158. Guiniven, Rev. John Joseph, C.SS.R., J.C.D., The Precept of Hearing Mass, XIV-188 pp., 1942.
159. Gulczynski, Rev. John Theophilus, J.C.D., The Desecration and Violation of Churches, X-126 pp., 1942.
160. Hammill, Rev. John Leo, M.A., J.C.D., The Obligations of the Traveler According to Canon 14, VIII-204 pp., 1942.
161. Haydt, Rev. John Joseph, A.B., J.C.D., Reserved Benefices, XI-148 pp., 1942.
162. Huser, Rev. Roger John, O.F.M., A.B., J.C.D., The Crime of Abortion in Canon Law, XII-187 pp., 1942.
163. Kearney, Rev. Francis Patrick, A.B., S.T.L., J.C.L., The Principles of Canon 1127.
164. Linahen, Rev. Leo James, S.T.L., J.C.D., De Absolutione Complicis In Peccato Turpi, 114 pp., 1942.
165. McCloskey, Rev. Joseph Aloysius, A.B., J.C.D., The Subject of Ecclesiastical Law According to Canon 12, XVII-246 pp., 1942.
166. O'Neill, Rev. Francis Joseph, C.SS.R., J.C.D., The Dismissal of Religious in Temporary Vows, XIII-220 pp., 1942.
167. Prince, Rev. John Edward, A.B., S.T.B., J.C.D., The Diocesan Chancellor, X-136 pp., 1942.
168. Riesner, Rev. Albert Joseph, C.SS.R., J.C.D., Apostates and Fugitives from Religious Institutes, IX-168 pp., 1942.
169. Stenger, Rev. Joseph Bernard, J.C.D., The Mortgaging of Church Property, 186 pp., 1942.
170. Waldron, Rev. Joseph Francis, A.B., J.C.D., The Minister of Baptism, XII-197 pp., 1942.
171. Willett, Rev. Robert Albert, J.C.D., The Probative Value of Documents in Ecclesiastical Trials, X-124 pp., 1942.
172. Woeber, Rev. Edward Martin, M.A., J.C.D., The Interpellations, XII-161 pp., 1942.
173. Benko, Rev. Matthew Aloysius, O.S.B.. M.A., J.C.L., The Abbot *Nullius*.
174. Christ, Rev. Joseph James, M.A., S.T.L., J.C.L., Dispensation from Vindicative Penalties.
175. Clancy, Rev. Patricn M. J., O.P., A.B., S.T.Lr., J.C.D., The Local Religious Superior, X-229 pp., 1943.

176. Clarke, Rev. Thomas James, J.C.D., Parish Societies, XII-147 pp., 1943.
177. Connolly, Rev. John Patrick, S.T.L., J.C.L., Synodal Examiners and Parish Priest Consultors.
178. Drumm, Rev. William Martin, A.B., J.C.L., Hospital Chaplains.
179. Flanagan, Rev. Bernard Joseph, A.B., S.T.L., J.C.L., The Canonical Erection of Religious Houses, X-147 pp., 1943.
180. Kelleher, Rev. Stephen Joseph, A.B., S.T.B., J.C.L., Discussions with Non-Catholics: Canonical Legislation, X-93 pp., 1943.
181. Lewis, Rev. Gordian, C.P., J.C.L., Chapters in Religious Institutes, XII-169 pp., 1943.
182. Marx, Rev. Adolph, J.C.L., The Declaration of Nullity of Marriages Contracted Outside the Church, X-151 pp., 1943.
183. Matulenas, Rev. Raymond Anthony, O.S.B., A.B., J.C.L., Communication, a Source of Privileges.
184. O'Leary, Rev. Charles Gerard, C.SS.R., J.C.L., Religious Dismissed After Perpetual Profession.
185. Power, Rev. Cornelius Michael, J.C.L., The Blessing of Cemeteries.
186. Shuhler, Rev. Ralph Vincent, O.S.A., J.C.L., Privileges of Religious to Absolve and Dispense, XII-195 pp., 1943.
187. Ziolkowski, Rev. Thaddeus Stanislaus, A.B., J.C.L., The Consecration and Blessing of Churches, XII-151 pp., 1943.
188. Heneghan, Rev. John Joseph, S.T.D., J.C.L., The Marriages of Unworthy Catholics.

www.ingramcontent.com/pod-product-compliance
Lightning Source LLC
LaVergne TN
LVHW050249080826
844660LV00012B/613

* 9 7 8 0 8 1 3 2 2 3 7 4 2 *